# ADVENT, CHRISTMAS, and EPIPHANY

D0470542

Dear Eva —
May God always be
a great & shining advent-
ure for you. with blessings
love, meg

# ADVENT, CHRISTMAS, and EPIPHANY

*Stories and Reflections
on the Sunday Readings*

— ✠ —

## Megan McKenna

ORBIS BOOKS

Maryknoll, New York 10545

The Catholic Foreign Mission Society of America (Maryknoll) recruits and trains people for overseas missionary service. Through Orbis Books, Maryknoll aims to foster the international dialogue that is essential to mission. The books published, however, reflect the opinions of their authors and are not meant to represent the official position of the society.

Published by Orbis Books, Maryknoll, NY 10545-0308

Manufactured in the United States of America

**Library of Congress Cataloging-in-Publication Data**
McKenna, Megan.
    Advent, Christmas, and Epiphany : stories and reflections on the Sunday readings / Megan McKenna.
      p. cm.
    Includes bibliographical references.
    ISBN 1-57075-218-4 (pbk.)
     1. Advent – Prayer-books and devotions – English. 2. Christmas – Prayer-books and devotions – English. 3. Epiphany season – Prayer-books and devotions – English. 4. Catholic Church – Prayer-books and devotions – English.  I. Title.
BV40.M33  1998
242′.33 – DC21                           98-7761

*Dedicated lovingly to my friend Jim Smith,*
*who meets me coming and going.*
*You taught me the meaning of visitation.*
*Incarnation comes home to us in our friends,*
*and Epiphany hides in fleeting moments.*
*Such good company makes*
*for a grand Advent in any season.*

# Contents

# Introduction

The ancient greeting of the Kalahari Bushmen: "I saw you looming up afar, and I am dying of hunger. Now that you have come, my hunger is gone."

The response: "Good day! I have been dead, but now that you are come, I live again!"

An East African story begins: "Once upon a time there was a man who couldn't find God." And the story continues:

✤ All the people lived on the plains and they were like people everywhere, some bad and some good. A man named John Shayo lived in the valley. He was a faithful Christian and participated in his small Armani Christian community, helping the poor and needy, especially the lepers that lived on the slope. But in the valley itself there was discord, thieves and tricksters walked about openly. There was fighting, witchcraft, and lying. Finally John decided to move, saying to himself, "God isn't here. God is the Unsurpassed Great Spirit who doesn't like fighting and discord. He wants peace and harmonious relationships in his human family."

John saw a mountain in the distance and thought, "Ah, God our Great Ancestor must live up there in the quiet and peace. I will go and find God."

It took a long time, days and days, until he reached the mountain, and then he undertook the arduous climb in the burning equatorial sun. Late one day he rested by the side of the footpath. He was startled to see a bearded stranger with a staff making his way *down* the mountain! "Jambo!" they greeted each other. "What is the news?"

John told him he was on his way up the mountain to see God the Creator and Source. The traveler said he was on his way down the mountain to live with all the people below. They talked as was the custom and parted with the greeting, "Goodbye until we meet again."

As he continued his climb, John thought of the man and admired him. He spoke well. John wondered why he was going down to the valley.

As John climbed the air thinned and John moved more slowly. It was quiet and still, with the only noise coming from the birds. He thought, "Ah, now I will find God here." He looked around, but there was no one there. Then he cried out, "Is God home? Where is God?"

Suddenly a gaunt old man appeared and greeted John, "Welcome. Rest after your journey and climb."

John told him of the journey and how he sought the All Peaceful One. The old man listened and then answered, "I'm sorry, but God doesn't live here. I live alone. But, surely, you met God on the path. He was going *down* to live with the people there."

John was astonished. "Are you sure? I thought he'd be up here. Why would he want to live down there among the fighting, jealousies, and anger of people?"

The old one answered, "God knows the weaknesses of his people. There is an African fable about an African hunter who was angry with God. He shot an arrow into the clouds. So God withdrew into the high heavens to get away from the angry human beings. But God the Great Elder loved his human family and wanted to give them tender care. So God our Great Ancestor sent his Son to pitch his tent among us, to live with us, to share our joys and sorrows, successes and failures in order to save us. This is Christmas."

John was moved and listened as the old man (the *mzee*, the wise one) spoke. "This Jesus, Emmanuel, is a mystery who prefers the company of the poor, the lowly, the simple, and the needy."

John knew he had learned the wisdom of the mountain top but now it was time to go *down* to the valley where God was. He told the old one, "I need to live with the people as God lives."

The old one reached out and touched John's head. John turned slowly and the valley stretched out before him. He began his climb down. Now he knew where to find God. (Adapted from "The Man Who Couldn't Find God," in *What Language Does God Speak? African Stories about Christmas and Easter,* ed. Joseph G. Healey, M.M. [Nairobi: St. Paul Publications], 17)

God came down. This is core of the seasons of Advent, Christmas, and Epiphany. God prefers to live with us in spite of our anger, our violence, and our lack of love for one another. We find God here on earth.

One of the Hebrew liturgical psalms sings out: "Gates, lift up your heads! Stand erect, ancient doors, and let in the King of glory." This announcement invites us into the season of Advent, the season of comings. There are so many comings: of Christ in glory at the end of time, of God as human in the birth of Jesus-Emmanuel, of the Word made flesh entering our hearts, and of peace with justice on earth. Along with the season of Christmas, the celebration of the coming of God among us as a human being in the mystery of the incarnation, Advent reminds us of the coming of God as King of glory and Judge of the universe.

The readings for these seasons are rich and layered. They compress past, present, and future into the single moment of now! Now decides what comes. The first Advent was incarnation, Christmas, and Epiphany; the second Advent will be the coming of Christ in glory to fulfill the kingdom brought to earth in the person of Jesus. This second Advent is "simply the longing and waiting of the church for the return of the Lord Jesus, the King of glory."

The person who singularly echoes and reveals the depth of both advents is Mary. Her feasts of Immaculate Conception, Guadalupe, and the fourth Sunday of Advent are important milestones on the journey to Christmas. She is always present, if only as a figure in the background, as in Luke's mention of "the child with his mother." Then, she is celebrated again on January 1, then along with Joseph and Jesus on the feast of the Holy Family, and she is also present at the coming of the magi. And she "ponders all these things in her heart," the image of the Christian before the face of God. As Mary ponders the human and divine, she seeks to live a mystery that comes to us all as the beloved children of God.

*Our Lady of the New Advent,* the icon that appears on the cover of this book, has an interesting history. In 1991, William Hart Mc-Nichols, S.J., was commissioned by Archbishop Francis Stafford of Denver to create an icon capturing the theme of the New Advent as a source of prayer for the archdiocese of Denver. In a booklet, *Advent Novena with Our Lady of the New Advent,* Father McNichols writes that Pope John Paul II has spoken of a "New Advent" throughout his papacy in both his encyclicals and his apostolic letters, beginning in 1979 with *Redemptor Hominis* and culminating in the recent *Tertio Millennio Adveniente.* According to McNichols, "John Paul II has designated the years preceding the turn of the century as a time of intense preparation and prayer for the coming of the Third Millennium of Christianity. This leads to the 'Great Jubilee' to be celebrated throughout the world in the year 2000."

Also in 1991, Archbishop Stafford petitioned the Vatican for a feast day for Our Lady of the New Advent for the archdiocese of Denver and, in answer, received the date December 16. Father Mc-Nichols notes that this is the day before the mystical and utterly beautiful "O Antiphons" begin, culminating on the eve of Christmas. In 1993, a second icon of Our Lady of the New Advent was commissioned and was then created by McNichols as a gift for the Holy Father during the celebration of World Youth Day in Denver in August 1993.

Bill McNichols explains his icons:

Both icons are renditions of the highly venerated, healing images of Our Lady of the Sign. In Byzantine icons Our Lady of the Sign is often seen at the top of Jacob's ladder, and in the midst of the burning bush before Moses. In these icons, the Mother of God is shown in the *orans* (prayer) posture, with uplifted hands. The Holy Child, or Christ Emmanuel, shines forth from an almond-shaped mandorla, or circular mandala, of her womb — or He nestles as the Child King in the arc and fold of her garments. The letters near the Virgin Mother, *MR OY,* are Greek abbreviations for Mother of God. The letters near the Child, *IC XC,* signify Jesus Christ. Sometimes there are jewels in the Child's halo or the letters *WON,* which signify the Child's divinity. . . . "I am who I am."

The symbolism of the figures in the 1991 icon is rich in meaning. The child has an old face. He is Son of God and son of Mary, divine and human, ancient and newly born. The three bars in the halo echo the Trinity, and the child wears red, for he is both victim and priest, offered as sacrifice and offering himself and the world to the Father. The flowers that the child holds in his hand are columbines (the state flower of Colorado), from the Latin *columbinus,* meaning five doves, an ancient symbol of the Holy Spirit.

In the icon Mary is dressed in the purple of royalty, the traditional color of Advent. She is the queen in heaven leading earth to the second Advent. Her halo is symbolic of her holiness, her obedience, and her surrender to God. The stars on her forehead and shoulders declare that she is ever virgin, ever belonging to God first and foremost, and totally dedicated to the coming of her child's kingdom. The gold cuffs with jewels on the sleeves were often worn by queens, a sign of intercession on behalf of the people, and her hands are raised in supplication, as a priest prays in the name of the people.

This is the woman of the Magnificat, the woman-prophet, the singer and defender of the honor of God and the coming of justice to the poor ones of the earth. This is the woman who prays with her people, for her people, and as one of the people. Dietrich Bonhoeffer wrote from prison in 1943 about a painting by a German artist, Albrecht Altdorfer (1480–1538). The painting is a rendition of Christmas and the Holy Family at a manger amid the ruins of a dilapidated house. For Bonhoeffer, the cross and the manger were one symbol bound together. It was only a matter of time before the wood of the manger became the wood of the cross. Ten years earlier, Bonhoeffer had preached on the Magnificat and on the woman Mary. In a portion of a sermon entitled "A Woman's Passionate Song," he wrote:

> This song of Mary is the oldest Advent hymn. It is at once the most passionate, the wildest, and one might even say, the most revolutionary Advent hymn ever sung. This is not the gentle, tender, dreamy Mary whom we sometimes see in paintings; this is the passionate, surrendered, proud, enthusiastic Mary who speaks out here. This song has none of the sweet, nostalgic, or even playful tones of some of our Christmas carols. It is, instead, a hard, strong inexorable song about collapsing thrones and humbled lords of this world, about the power of God and the powerlessness of humankind. These are the tones of the women prophets of the Old Testament that now come to life in Mary's mouth. (In *The Mystery of Holy Night* [New York: Crossroad, 1997], 6)

This is the woman Mary, the queen of the poor and of the remnant that waits for the glory of God to be let loose in the world. And her son is the God of Advent, the child-king who will rule from the manger and the cross, calling us all to come home to our own humanity in the incarnation and to God in the Trinity. William Stringfellow writes: "In the First Advent, Christ comes as Lord; in the next Advent, Christ comes as judge of the world and the world's principalities and thrones, in vindication of his reign and of the sovereignty of the Word of God in history. This is the wisdom, which the world deems folly, which biblical people bear and by which they live as the church in the world for the time being" (*The Second Advent of the Lord* [1977]).

At every liturgy we proclaim, "Christ will come again!" For Christians, this is as sure as the first coming in the incarnation, and its completeness is already set in motion by the coming of Christ in our hearts in the Word of the Lord and in hope born of the cross and resurrection. We live between the two Advents. They are our meaning and source, our horizon and shadow. The first Advent turns our eyes and hearts toward the mystery of God's presence among us. As the story above reminds us, the first Advent turns us toward the valley, the vale of tears where people dwell in joy and tears, in mildness and violence, in justice and injustice. This is where we find God.

The second Advent commands us to turn our eyes and hearts toward the Word of God that reveals the mystery of God's plan for the world, its freedom and liberation, its transformation, and its holiness, as it was meant to be in the beginning.

Advent, Christmas, and Epiphany are about God being here, God who has come and will return. God does return as we let God in — into our political and economic systems, our relationships, and all the places that are in sore need of redemption. The child-king rules within Mary's womb, and the child and the woman are both in the womb of God's world, the universe that was created to be a blessing and a dwelling place secure for all men and women. This is God in lowliness. Then, it will be God in glory.

We wait, as the remnant of Israel waited, as the prophets and people in exile waited, as Mary and Joseph waited, as all those who are poor, imprisoned, oppressed, and in darkness wait for the light to dawn and God to save. Once upon a time, when God came, a seed was planted in the world, and now all creation groans until it springs forth and life blooms for all again. Then when God comes, the blossom will declare a new springtime, an everlasting spring of everlasting life. In the meantime, we wait, we sing, we decide aright for the land's afflicted, and we go where God first came — among the people. And we take the light of incarnation, of the Word made flesh, of God-with-us always and forever, out into the ends of the earth and tell the good news that God is in our land. And we can pray Father McNichols's "Prayer to Our Lady of the New Advent":

O Lady and Mother
of the One who was and is and is to come,
dawn of the New Jerusalem,
we earnestly beseech you,
bring us by your prayers
so to live in love
that the Church, the Body of Christ,
may stand in this world's dark
as fiery icon of the New Jerusalem.
We ask you to obtain for us this mercy
through Jesus Christ, your Son and Lord,
who lives and reigns
with the Father in the Holy Spirit
one God forever and ever.
Amen.

•

I wrote this and the accompanying volume in response to many requests that followed the publication of the two volumes *Lent: The Daily Readings: Reflections and Stories* and *Lent: The Sunday Readings: Reflections and Stories*. These reflections are offered in the hope that this three-part season of Advent, Christmas, and Epiphany will live and sing in our souls and transform our lives so that it is clear that God is with us still and that we believe that God became flesh so that our flesh could bear witness to the love incarnate now in all human beings. This is the time of God coming to us, and it is the time for us to come home to one another and to God together. Come! Come! Come, Lord Jesus!

For specific references and background for saints commemorated during the Advent, Christmas, and Epiphany seasons, and for aid in further contemporizing and giving pastoral insight to the readings, I suggest Robert Ellsberg's book *All Saints: Daily Reflections on Saints, Prophets, and Witnesses for Our Time* (New York: Crossroad, 1997). And I am indebted to Bill McNichols for his rich insights into the overarching symbol of the New Advent and his vision of the woman Mary and the child-king coming, ever coming.

# CYCLE A

✠

# First Sunday of Advent

*Isaiah 2:1–5*
*Psalm 122:1–9*
*Romans 13:11–14*
*Matthew 24:37–44*

"O house of Jacob, come, let us walk in the light of the Lord." The ancient prophet Isaiah sounds the trumpet blast and summons all the world to a new vision of life so full of hope and peace that it could only be dreamed of by God, who will make it come true. It is Advent. It is homecoming, both ours and God's, being welcomed back after long absence. It is the memory of the coming of the child that was the Peace of God so long ago in history and the return of the child into our world in our hearts this year. And it reminds us of the final reunion, when God will come again to reclaim all the world. So we begin this season with three homecomings: those of our past, our present, and our end — all that was meant to come true since the beginning.

It begins with righting great wrongs: the wrongs of war, of peoples divided and separated calling one another enemy instead of friend, and the toll this hate takes on all peoples and the earth itself. We begin with the first lesson: the need "to beat our swords into plowshares and our spears into pruning hooks. How not to raise our swords against others; and how to stop training for war ever again." It is a lesson in raising food instead of hate as the substance that is core to all human living. It is a lesson that repairs broken covenants and restores the possibility of life truly lived in freedom and hope for all peoples.

This homecoming is a repeat performance. God tried it before in Noah's time, though others didn't heed the warnings. Will it be the same this year for us? Or have we learned some things from the past? God is coming! The Son of Man is coming! The reign of peace is coming! The moment it arrives is going to be quick, definitive, and decisive, and it will come for everyone. So what are we to do?

Stay awake! This is the moment when it begins, when the world begins to turn toward home and everything we know changes. God is coming and he's creeping up on us like a thief breaking into our house and into our world. Advent is a guard dog barking loudly and rousing us from a sound sleep. There is an intruder in the house, in the world. Are we awake? Today we are warned: throw open the door! Rouse everyone in the house! Roll out the red carpet. Get busy with preparations. Sweep the house and be on your toes. God is so close!

Isaiah's vision is centered on the Lord's mountain, Jerusalem, but this involves more than a geographical location: it is a place of light and truth, of justice and judgment where God's supreme power and authority are honored and enacted. It is a vision place, a place of no more war. Isaiah's words have over the centuries been used by poets, musicians, preachers, and common folk alike to dream aloud of what is possible for human beings here on earth. But they are words of prophets too: words of warning of the dire consequences that will follow upon those who refuse to heed the words that outlaw war, violence, and the destruction of the earth and its kind. To stop training for war and to unlearn violence and these things abhorrent to the Holy One are the beginning of instruction in the Lord's ways. We begin way back at the beginning — at the first lesson — and turn again into the path of God.

Welcome to Advent! This is our wake-up call. Time to shake off sleep, lethargy, and old ways and habits. It is meant to be a rude awakening, like a trumpet blast that signals hope, glory, and worldwide judgment. What are we concerned about? Do our day-to-day lives reveal that we have "put on the Lord Jesus Christ"? The event itself will be momentous. Do we wear the livery of the Son of Man? Do we live proclaiming that we belong to the light? Or do we carouse in drunkenness, in greed, in piling up material possessions? Do we live excessively, emotionally, sexually, with revenge and quarrels, dissension and jealousy? Do we participate in war, train for war, and live off the spoils of war, or do we dismantle weapons and till the earth for food and a harvest of justice?

This first Sunday of the season looks at universal issues — time and eternity, our lives against that backdrop, war and peace, salvation and death. It is about the connections between the poor and the push to kill through weapons of mass misery, arms sales, land mines, and the manufacture of ever-new forms of destruction. It is about hard questions like this one asked by Korean theologian Chung Hyun Kyung: "Your economy is based on inflicting pain in other persons' lives. So, I ask, where is God in your country?" (from Maryknoll's film *Arms for the Poor*).

The voices of the prophets and the poor stir our consciences, awaken and nudge our hearts, oppose our politics and our prayers. We, here in the United States, are the leaders by a wide margin in arms sales around the world: $11.3 billion in 1996 alone (with England and Russia far behind us). The warning of President Eisenhower in 1953 still rings true today: "Every gun that is made, every warship launched, every rocket fired signifies, in the final sense, a theft from those who hunger and are not fed, those who are cold and are not clothed." Advent begins with the lesson that if we are followers of the child who was threatened by Herod's sword, then we must convert the weapons of mass destruction into technology and resources for food and the future of the children of earth. A prayer text from the inside of a contemporary Christmas card says it well: "Above the clamor of our violence your word of truth resounds, O God of majesty and power. Over nations enshrouded in despair your justice dawns. Grant your household a discerning spirit and a watchful eye to perceive the hour in which we live. Hasten the advent of that day when the weapons of war shall be banished and all your scattered children gathered into one."

The imagery of this Sunday often disconcerts people, even disorients: that of thieves and God as a thief in the night, breaking into our house. But it is a familiar image, for one of the readings for the previous Sunday (the last Sunday of the church year's readings) concerns the thieves on either side of Jesus at the crucifixion. One thief acknowledges Jesus, even in pain, and is taken into paradise. The other cannot see, curses, and joins those who mock and scorn and is lost to hope. Now the image overlaps and continues in this reading of the first Sunday of the church year. Our text from Matthew's gospel refers first to Noah, who beckoned to others to join him, but they refused, and the flood came and destroyed them even while they were "eating and drinking and marrying." The text says it will be the same when the Son of Man comes: "Two men will be out in the field; one will be taken and one will be left. Two women will be grinding meal; one will be taken and one will be left." So, stay awake! Live like you expect to be broken into! visited by a thief! robbed while you sleep! What provisions are you making, taking? For the Son of Man is coming when we least expect him to appear. But this coming is not so much about our individual deaths or end of our lives. It is more plural, communal. This is about universal judgment.

Matthew's call is to look, to see. It is connected to Isaiah's vision, and it is focused in a single point: the presence and overwhelming image of the Son of Man. This image of God is not one that we often look to, contemplate, or pray to, for it's frightening, often confusing. The best description of the Son of Man comes in the visions of Daniel the prophet. They are terrifying, involving the judging of nations, yet they bring hope to those oppressed and long burdened with others' rage and hate. Daniel writes:

> As the visions during the night continued, I saw One like a son of man coming, on the clouds of heaven; when he reached the Ancient One and was presented before him, he received dominion, glory, and kingship; nations and peoples of every language serve him. His dominion is an everlasting dominion that shall not be taken away, his kingship shall not be destroyed. (Daniel 7:13–14)

This person is dazzling, coming on the clouds of heaven, accompanied by angels, coming to judge the nations with justice. He is human, yet full of power, glory, and light. It is an odd mixture of a king robed in majesty and holiness, splendor and strength (Psalm 93:1–2, 5), and the Lamb of God from the book of Revelation and from ancient descriptions of the paschal lamb of sacrifice, slaughtered so that the people might escape from death. This one is innocent, going freely to death to save others, a ransom for the many and the only one worthy to open the scrolls of revelation and judge the living and the dead, all the nations with justice, because he himself has suffered unjustly at the hands of all the peoples.

This Son of Man is described in Revelation as

> Jesus Christ the faithful witness, the firstborn from the dead and ruler of the kings of earth. To him who loves us and freed us from our sins by his own blood, who has made us a royal nation of priests in the service of his God and Father — to him be glory and power forever and ever! Amen.

See, he comes amid the clouds! Every eye shall see him. All the peoples of the earth shall lament him bitterly. So it is to be! Amen! The Lord God says, "I am the Alpha and the Omega, the One who is and who was and who is to come, the Almighty!" (Revelation 1:5–8)

This Son of Man is Christ the King, crucified on the cross, standing with all those who die unjustly, innocently before their time, unnecessarily, followers of the lamb who are slaughtered in war or for profit. To stand before this one is to stand before the God of peace, justice, mercy, and hope for the lost and downtrodden of the earth. It is to know that this is a day of vindication by our God. It is like standing before a towering icon of the Christ, first born of the dead, the presence of life torn to death and now bursting out of all bounds.

And we are told to stand there together, prepared, awake, living out the vision in today's world that Isaiah promised in hope to all the people mourning and waiting on God. We have been instructed in the Lord's ways; now it is time to walk in them and take the Word of the Lord forth into the world, to impose terms on people: the terms of care for the poor; the terms of peace; the terms of unity and enduring justice for all, especially those most in need of restitution and hope.

The image is of God as a thief. Have you ever been robbed? Has your home been broken into? How does the image of God as a thief strike you? Do you have a lot to steal? Would he find you vigilant? ready for him? waiting?

There is an old story from the Hasidic tradition called "The Seer of Lublin's Shirt" that perhaps can put some of this in a new light, a perspective of hope. It is a story within a story within a story, much like the readings today and the season of Advent itself. I first heard the story told by Rabbi Shlomo Carlebach, when he told it to his congregation on Yom Kippur, September 1982. Here it is:

✣ Once upon a time there was a poor man named Moshe. He went to the synagogue on the Sabbath as everyone else did to hear the Seer of Lublin preach and to pray. The Seer of Lublin looked at him, among all the members of his congregation, and sighed. Moshe looked terrible, ragged and dirty, his shirt torn and soiled, and here he was on the Sabbath. How could he? The Seer grabbed hold of Moshe's arm and scolded him on his apparel, but Moshe protested, "This is my only shirt. If I had another I would have worn it." The Seer of Lublin was cut to the heart. "Wait here," he commanded Moshe.

He returned momentarily with one of his own shirts. It was linen, elegant, and the color of sky. Moshe's eyes grew big. "For me?"

"Yes," said the rabbi, "for you." And immediately Moshe ripped off his old shirt and put on the rabbi's gift. The Seer of Lublin watched him dance down the street in his new shirt and was pleased with the gift he gave.

Moshe walked along, and outside of town he met one of his friends, a drunk, weaving down the road. But then the drunk saw Moshe and his new shirt. "Oh, Moshe, where did you get it? It's beautiful. I've never seen such a shirt!" And happily Moshe told him that it was a gift — from the Seer of Lublin himself! "What a shirt! What good fortune!" cried the drunk. He pawed the shirt and began to weep. "No one ever gave me such a gift, such a shirt." In a moment of rash generosity, Moshe took the shirt off and gave it to his friend, the drunk. The man was delighted, utterly wild, and went dancing away, and Moshe was pleased that he'd given the Seer's gift to someone who appreciated it so much.

The drunk found his way to the tavern in town and proceeded to put the Seer's shirt up for sale to the highest bidder. What was such a shirt worth? After all, it was, said the drunk, the shirt of the Seer. To a businessman, it could bring prosperity! To a barren wife, sons! Lord knows what else. Bids flew back and forth, but it was the tavern owner who knew the drunk best and offered him drinks on the house for the day. Sold. Next morning the tavern owner went early to the market to sell the Seer's shirt. He hawked it in the streets, yelling, "The Seer of Lublin's shirt! What do you offer me for it? Balm for the sick and weary, good luck for business and good fortune, children for your old age, for everyone knows that the shirt of a holy man can bring you your dreams!" It sold for a huge sum of money. And who should be in the marketplace that morning to see it sold but the Seer of Lublin himself. He was livid with anger and went looking for Moshe. When he found him, he berated him, insulted him, shamed him: How could he sell his gift? And he left, leaving poor Moshe feeling terrible, with no chance to tell the Seer that he had also given it as a gift.

Moshe was distressed. He walked outside town to his place in the cemetery and sat on a grave, feeling miserable. Another friend came down the road. "Moshe, you look terrible! Did your wife die?"

"No, worse than that."

"Did your children die?"

"No, worse still." And he told of his humiliation in front of the rabbi and what the rabbi now thought of him.

His friend sat beside him on the grave and began, "Listen, Moshe. I'll tell you a story. It will help.

"Once upon a time there was a thief. He was good. The best. He stole from everyone in town, his wife's own family, the rabbi and synagogue, his fellow thieves. He was good. But every Sabbath he saw the wealthy businessmen and merchants and their families going to the synagogue and sitting up there in the front pews, and he wanted that for his family. After all he worked hard too; they were as much thieves in their way as he was in his. And so he bought a pew in the synagogue, in the front row. The next Sabbath, he was there with his family, proud, and eyeing the others in their front seats. Everyone was scandalized, but the rabbi wasn't picky — money was money and it was needed. Sabbath after Sabbath the thief was there with his family.

"And then something terrible happened. Unexpectedly. He heard the Scriptures and they touched his heart. He believed. He knew instantaneously that he had to stop being a thief. But what else could he do? But he stopped right then and there. He began to lose everything: his goods, his coach and horses, his finery and house. Then his wife left him, taking the children. He tried to get a job, but no one trusted him. He was a thief. Soon he was reduced to begging, sitting on the steps of the synagogue, on Sabbaths and all days. His life was miserable, but he knew he could not return to his old way of life, though his friends pushed him and baited him to come back and steal again.

"One day a rich man saw him on the steps and felt sorry for him. He thought to himself, 'How terrible. It's hard enough to be poor all your life and have to beg, but to have once had it all, to be rich, and then lose it all and be shamed and have to beg just to survive miserably! What would I ever do if that happened to me?' And so the rich man arranged every Sabbath eve for his servant to bring the beggar-thief a bit of fresh bread, a fish, some oil and a candle, providing him with some dignity to celebrate the Sabbath. And so it continued for years. Then the rich man and the thief both died on the same day. Two funerals in different parts of town. Everyone came to the rich man's funeral, lamenting his passing, praising his generosity, mourning his absence. Hardly anyone showed up for the thief's funeral: only a few of his old thieving buddies who lamented how good he was, until he got religion and retired. Such a waste, such a loss.

"But up in heaven it was another story altogether. The thief was welcomed into the kingdom like royalty, embraced by the Holy One. But when the rich man came to the gate it was slammed in his face. He was shocked. God, blessed be his Name, was on the other side of the gate with the thief, and was staring at him harshly and shaking his head: 'No, you cannot come in.' The rich man pleaded and wept, saying, 'I was generous and kind. I gave to the poor.' But God spurned his words, saying, 'No, you were not. You gave but you cared only for show, for people's good opinion of you, the praise and adulation.' The man was desperate, crying, 'But the thief — that man there — he never knew it was me that sent him alms on the Sabbath eve so that he could have some dignity.' 'No,' God answered, 'you only did that because of self-pity. You didn't ever want that to happen to you. No!' God was adamant and turned away from the man.

"But then something surprising happened. The rich man started to rise, and soon he was floating up high over the gate and he dropped right in front of God inside the kingdom of heaven! God was startled and reacted, 'What in the world is going on here?' An angel appeared in the wings and whispered in God's ear. And God laughed and laughed heartily. The rich man was stunned: 'What am I doing here?' God smiled at him and said, 'Don't question it, you're here! You're in!' 'But I don't understand,' the rich man said. God smiled and pointed to the thief: 'It's him,' he said, 'that man, the thief stole your sins! Welcome home to heaven!'"

The thief stole the rich man's sins, returning the favor of the Sabbath gifts. God is a thief, intent on stealing our sins, our evil and vengeance, our violence, and all that clutters and stands in the way of hope, of salvation, and unity among us all. Our God is a thief, and Advent is the beginning of the adventure, the time when God breaks into our house, our world, and steals us blind, shifting all of history and saving the lost. It is a story worth telling over and over, a story within a story, within a story, within a story! It is God's story, the earth's story, and our story today, singularly and as a nation. Advent is about dreams and visions, old ones from the prophets (primarily, in this cycle of readings, from Isaiah), and how the dreams come true in flesh and blood, in a child born to us, Jesus, human and Son of Man, Son of Justice, Sun of God, son of Mary and Joseph.

It is a time of patient endurance and waiting, hoping outrageously for peace now, for passionate repentance, for justice to come among us. It is a time for clothing ourselves again in the garments of light we were given in our baptisms, of putting on glory, of putting on the Lord Jesus, of wearing those garments publicly, proudly, boldly, as once Noah built an ark. And if we do that, people will stream toward the Word of the Lord heard in our midst once again, seen in our lives this year of the Lord. Advent is about judgment and standing in the presence of the thief, the Son of Man, not flinching, looking God straight in the eye, and rejoicing that our God is on the side of the poor, the immigrant, the family struggling in the system and falling through the cracks and being blamed for that and a host of other social ills. God is against the arms buildup, the war machine, the threats and hard lines, the uncapped spending on military endeavors, and anything that does not make for peace for all and the restoration of human dignity and life on earth for those to come after us. It is a time of hope, fiery change, and light, a time for seekers of vision and hope-bringers. The kingdom is come and dwells among us — Where? The Holy One is coming to visit and is intent on stealing us away from all we are attached to and binding us to one another in peace. The Son of Man is coming at the time we least expect!

Our response to this pronouncement is that of the Psalmist: "I rejoiced when I heard them say: 'Let us go to the house of the Lord.'...I will say: 'Peace be within you! Because of the house of the Lord, our God, I will pray for your good'" (Psalm 122:1–9).

## Some Prayers

Come, Lord, and work. Arouse us and incite. Kindle us, sweep
us onwards. Be fragrant as flowers, sweet as honey. Teach us to
love and to run.                               — St. Augustine

O give me grace to see Thy face and be a constant mirror
eternity.                                    — Thomas Traherne

Grant us grace to rest from all sinful deeds and thoughts, to
surrender ourselves wholly unto Thee, and keep our souls still
before Thee like a still lake, so that the beams of Thy grace
may be mirrored therein, and may kindle in our hearts the
glow of faith and love and prayer.
                        — collect from the eighteenth century

A song that is filled with the images of this season and cycle of
readings, and that builds through the weeks, is "City of God" by
Dan Schutte. Each week you can add another verse and build toward
the fullness of the coming of God among us in a child born of
Mary, the child who is the new ark of the covenant and city of God.
Through him we build a place of peace and justice in the world,
shedding light and hope to all.

*Refrain*
Let us build the city of God!
May our tears be turned into dancing!
For the Lord, our light and our love,
has turned the night into day!

Awake from your slumber! Arise from your sleep!
A new day is dawning for all those who weep.
The people in darkness have seen a great light.
The Lord of our longing has conquered the night.
O city of gladness, now lift up your voice!
Proclaim the good tidings that all may rejoice!

# Second Sunday of Advent

*Isaiah 11:1–10*
*Psalm 72:1–2, 7–8, 12–13, 17*
*Romans 15:4–9*
*Matthew 3:1–12*

On this Sunday two prophets are shouting at us: Isaiah and John the Baptist. And the vision grows from a shoot into a branch and then into fruit, into a person who judges all the world with justice, especially the poor and the meek. And everything shifts toward the fruit of justice, which is peace. All adversaries and enemies become friends: the wolf and the lamb; the leopard and the kid; the calf and the lion cub; the cow and the bear; the cobra and the child. And there is no harm, no violence: only peace!

Transforming this vision into reality will take work, change, and repentance, a restoring of order and a healing of wounds. This is the work of John the Baptist, of the Holy Spirit and fire, and it begins with confession, and with acknowledgment of our sin, followed by a wholehearted turning into the way of the Lord who is coming. It is a straightening out of knots and mazes and dead ends in the world and in our hearts.

✤ An ancient story tells of the Buddha being threatened by a bandit as he traveled a remote mountain road. Buddha had no money to give him, and the bandit informed him that he would then take his life. Buddha bowed and requested at least that his dying wish be granted. The thief said he would grant it if he could. "Please," Buddha pleaded, "cut off the branch of that tree," pointing to a great pine. The bandit laughed and said, "Easily done," and he slashed away. "Now," the Buddha continued, "put it back together again." The bandit laughed again, and then when he saw that the Buddha was serious, he mocked him and said he was insane, stupid, and ignorant because that was impossible.

But the Buddha looked at him and said that he, the thief, was the one who was stupid and insane because it is easy and stupid to destroy mindlessly, to kill and cut off and stop growth. What is truly hard — work that needs imagination, skill, and grace — is to heal, to create, and to restore to life. The thief was stopped in his tracks, fell to his knees, and asked to become a disciple, to learn this kind of skill and power. His long and creative apprenticeship began.

This is the task this week, as we work alongside Isaiah and John the Baptist. We are to shout in the desert, to prepare a way for the Lord, to make friends of old enemies, to sit side by side sharing food and life, and to make peace on earth. It is time to get serious about our intent and work of converting the world through justice, so that peace will find a dwelling place among us.

Isaiah's vision of hope continues to expand. It is a sprout, a shoot from a stump, from inauspicious beginnings, unnoticed yet strong and sure, powerful and transformative. This vision begins to take shape and form in a person who is described as filled with the gifts of the Spirit. These gifts are given so that the one who receives them may judge, not by appearances or hearsay, but judge the land's poor and afflicted and protect them from the ruthless, the powerful, and the wicked.

The vision grows further, and in baptism and confirmation, we receive these gifts. The gifts are these: wisdom, understanding, counsel, fortitude (courage), knowledge, piety, fear of the Lord, and delight (awe). Specifically, wisdom is the gift of seeing the world, its history and events, its powers and personalities as God sees, from the long-range view of eternity and from the vantage point of the cross. Understanding is the gift of humility, of standing in others' shoes and viewing life from their place, being one with them in solidarity. Counsel is the gift of knowing how to use wisdom in particular cases for other people's growth in holiness, in their struggle with sin and for the kingdom. It is practical wisdom used on immediate issues of economics, politics, nationalism, and matters that must lead us to conversion.

Then there is fortitude or courage. This is the gift of doing what is wise, good, and necessary in the face of opposition, rejection, and sin, day in and day out, in spite of losing ground or stature. This is connected to the gift of knowledge: a depth of information in areas of faith, justice, tradition, truth, and prayer. It involves using all information to hasten the coming of God's justice into the world, to care for the poor, to transform all areas of life, and to employ technology and resources so as to honor God and all God's creation.

Traditionally the last two gifts are fear of the Lord and piety, or awe and delight in God. These are gifts of obedience and the practice of true religion that reverences and worships God, living under God's authority, in the right awareness of who God is and who we are and are not, seeing God's presence in all things. We are given these gifts so that we might truth-tell those in power, to take up the cause of those with no voice. All these gifts serve to make us faithful, attentive to God's reign in the world. On this second Sunday of Advent we might ask ourselves if we need one of these gifts for Christmas and pray the Spirit of God to come and rest upon us so that we can bring peace to earth in our portion of paradise. For this is the signal for the nations that God's coming and this dwelling of God among us will be glorious to behold — in us.

This vision is about justice, and the result will be extended even to the animal kingdom where harmony, communion, and peace will reign! All the earth will be at home together with a child to guide us. The earth will be a marvelous place, a peaceable kingdom. The vision will seep down into every crevice and corner to touch all living creatures and the earth itself. The description of the animals binds together traditional enemies in the animal kingdom: wolf and lamb; leopard and kid; calf and lion; cow and bear; lion and ox, baby and cobra. But it is also about human beings and traditional enemies: the English and the Irish; Arabs and Israelis; white and black South Africans; Muslims and Hindus; North Americans of European descent and Native Americans; Japanese and Koreans; Americans and Iraqis; Bosnian Serbs and Croatians; Muslims and Christians; even men and women. These are only some pairings, some sets of enemies today, and we could easily insert these groups wherever the animals are mentioned in Isaiah to catch a glimpse of the depth of change, the altering of reality, that is part of the vision of Isaiah and the call of John the Baptist:

> Then the Arab will be the guest of the Israeli,
>     and the white South African will lie down with the black.
> The English and the Irish will stroll together,
>     with a little child to guide them.
> The Bosnian Serb and the Croatian will be neighbors;
>     their young will rest together.
> The Muslim and the Christian will break bread together.
> The baby will play by the cobra's den,
>     and the child lay his hand on the adder's lair.

There shall be no harm or ruin on all God's holy mountain;
for the earth shall be filled with knowledge of the Lord,
as water covers the sea. (Paraphrase of Isaiah 11)

On that day there will be peace on earth! But what in the world
needs to happen if this is to come to pass?
Enter John the Baptist! This is the second prophet of Advent and
vision-bringer, a preacher, a herald's voice in the desert, an ascetic, a
truth-teller who attracts all sorts of people from everywhere. They
stream toward him (as in the vision) and toward Jerusalem, which
is the center of religious activity and organized religion and power.
They confess their sins and take responsibility for their actions. They
are baptized in water.

But John is the prophet who is turned toward and tuned into
what is coming, who is coming. He is here to straighten out the
paths and way of the Lord, to straighten us out, and he sees, really
sees, through all who are coming to be baptized. And he lashes out
at some of them: calling them "a brood of vipers" and warning
them of the judgment to come and the justice that accompanies it.
They won't be able to escape with superficial outward pieties. They
need to show some serious sign that they intend to reform. For the
coming of judgment will go straight to the root, to the heart of
each of us, all of us, laying us bare. We won't be able to fall back on
our past, our perceived relationship to God, or our prayer. "Every
tree that is not fruitful will be cut down and thrown into the fire."
We will be judged according to our actions, our choices, and our
relationships to one another.

The verses of the responsorial psalm catalog what we are supposed to do in imitation of God: "Justice is to flourish in our time
and fullness of peace forever." How does that come about? We (and
our governments) are to be just, to look out for the afflicted first, en-
suring equal distribution of goods and basic necessities of life (food,
shelter, health care, education, work, clothing, dignity...).

This is the kind of justice that will flower in the days of the One
upon whom the Spirit of the Lord rests. He is where profound
peace begins. We prepare for this One. We make straight his paths.
John is his herald and his forerunner, his cousin and the trumpet
blast that goes before him.

And yet John has something startling to say about him. John baptizes in water for the sake of reform, but the one who will follow
after him will be more powerful. John, the great prophet, is not

even fit to carry his sandals, to be his slave. This one will baptize us in the Holy Spirit and fire. This one is born of the Spirit and fire and judges with his winnowing fan in hand, clearing out the threshing floor and gathering, burning and separating. This is another powerful image of the Son of Man. The readings are packed with passion, hope, warnings, longings for justice and life, especially for those oppressed and heavy burdened by others through injustice, war, and sin. These readings are about sin and evil, about the necessity of facing them in our lives before we can see or recognize the Son of Man, or even want to see him.

This second Sunday turns the eye of John the Baptist upon us. It is not the eye of the Son of Man, but it burns and exposes us surely. It is time to give some evidence that we mean to reform. We, us, not any other. It starts here, in our families, jobs, politics, economics, generosity or lack thereof, truthfulness and lies.

There is a story to tell, another thief story, this one called "The Pomegranate Seed." It is found in many collections of morality tales, Jewish stories, and folktales of all traditions.

✤ Once upon a time there was a thief. He wasn't really good at it. Not a professional at all. He was just a poor man, with hungry children and a wife who labored hard. He worked sometimes, but more often than not there was no job to be had and so no food either for hungry mouths. It pained him to see his wife and children suffer so and angered him that there was no pity in the kingdom, no kindness or generosity in his neighbors. He took a chance, a big chance, and stole some food. The king's law was death by hanging if a thief was caught. He got away with it often. He took bread, apples, and flour when he could and sometimes a ribbon or two for the one he loved so.

But he wasn't good at it. He was just poor and hungry and desperate, and finally he got caught, with the bread in hand. He was jailed and sentenced to be hanged until dead, in public for all to see, as a warning to others. He was desperate, for life, for his family, and for their future. In jail the night before the execution he told one of the guards in confidence that it was a shame that he would die tomorrow, for a secret, a great secret, and a skill would die with him. Too bad he couldn't tell the secret to someone who could use it wisely or get it to the king, who certainly would be interested in it.

The jailer said that he'd be happy to take the secret of the dying man. And so the man told him: "I can take a pomegranate seed, plant it in the ground, water it, and make it grow so that it will bear fruit overnight. My father taught it to me, as his father taught him, for generations. But tomorrow it dies with me."

The jailer could hardly believe his ears and immediately brought word to the king. The next day, before the execution, the king arrived and had the poor man brought forward. "Let me see you do this marvelous thing," the king commanded. And so the man asked for a spade, dug a hole, asked for a pomegranate seed, and then turned to the king and spoke: "This seed can only be planted by someone who has never stolen anything in his life or someone who has never taken anything that did not belong to him by right. Of course, I am a thief, caught stealing bread for my children and wife, so I can't plant it. You'll have to have someone else do it."

The king turned to his counselor and commanded him to plant it. The man froze and stuttered: "Your majesty, I can't."

"What do you mean you can't?" the king uttered.

The counselor explained, "Once, when I was young, before I was in your employ, I took something from a house where I was staying. I returned it, of course, but I can't plant it."

The king was annoyed and turned to his treasurer and commanded him to plant it. The man went chalk white and shook. "I can't, your majesty," he confessed.

"What, you, too? What have you done? Have you stolen from me?"

"No, no, my king," he protested, "but I work with figures, calculating all the time, and it's easy to make mistakes, and I am forever trying to balance accounts, taking from here to put there. With huge sums of money, land deeds, contracts, and so on it's easy to overlook something. Besides I often have to make deals with people so that better deals can be made later. It's business, sire."

The king turned to another, and instinctively the next man shrunk away from him. It was the poor man who spoke next. "Your majesty, perhaps you could plant it yourself." This time it was the king who hesitated. So many things went through his mind. He remembered stealing from his father in anger, impatient to be king himself and wanting that power and freedom, that access to wealth. The poor man spoke boldly, "Your majesty, even you cannot plant the seed, you who are mighty, with power over life and death; you who have wealth and much more than you need to live on; you who make laws that destroy even the poor who are desperately hungry and caught in the web of others' greed and insensitivity. You can't plant the seed. You are a thief. Why are you so hard on me, a poor man who stole bread to feed his family? You are going to hang me, leaving others in need with no recourse."

The king stopped. He heard, thank heaven, and repented of his harshness and injustice, his callousness and disdain for others. He pardoned the man who reminded him to first change the laws and then to work at making life worth living for so many in his kingdom. The king was impressed with the poor man's wisdom, cleverness, and understanding and took him into his employ. Things began to change, or so the story goes. Would that it were true for all those who hear this tale told this day.

Ah, would that it were true for all of *us* who hear the story. It seems too good to be true, too easy. And indeed John the Baptist tips us off that changing reality — shifting the basis of laws and giving hope to the poor who are the victims of the unjust systems and laws perpetuated by those with more food, more wealth, and more violence — is far from easy. This making of peace is a daunting task. If he cannot stoop before the one who is coming and carry his sandals, walking behind him, how are we to have the audacity to change political and economic structures? We find a source, a root, of that audacity in Paul's letter to the Romans. We are told to first look to the Scriptures, that they were written for our instruction. We are told "that we might derive hope from the lessons of patience and the words of encouragement found in the Scriptures." And we are prayed over:

> May God, the source of all patience and encouragement, en-able you to live in perfect harmony with one another according to the spirit of Christ Jesus, so that with one heart and voice you may glorify God, the Father of our Lord Jesus Christ.

We can't do this by ourselves. It is God who makes the vision come true, in us, on earth, by his grace and mercy. It is God who gives us the courage and strength to change, to alter course, to straighten out, to reform our lives, our political and economic systems, even our religious practices. The waters of our baptisms are

for encouraging justice to flourish among us. The fire of our con-
firmations and the gifts of the Spirit are for stopping the harm
and hurt on the holy mountain of God, in our communities and
churches, our nations and world.

This transformation begins, we are told in Romans, by "accepting
one another, as Christ accepted you, for the glory of God." Jesus
became a servant, faithfully fulfilled God's promises to his chosen
people, and extended that mercy to the Gentiles, to us. We are to
become servants of God, "with justice the band around our waists
and faithfulness a belt upon our hips." This is the glory of God
manifest in our midst. This is the way we sing the praises of the
name of our God, the child who will guide us.

In this second week of Advent we can sing another verse of the
"City of God" by Dan Schutte (see above, p. 10):

> We are sons of the morning, we are daughters of day.
> The one who has loved us has brightened our way.
> The Lord of all kindness has called us to be
> a light for his people, to set their hearts free.

Most of us don't do well with a John the Baptist yelling at us,
"You brood of vipers!" but we are called this Sunday to encourage
and remind one another that we need to reform and show it. In
my parish, when we want to remind one another that each of us
needs to reform and repent, we sing together an alternative version
of "You'd Better Watch Out" by our pastor. It goes like this:

> Oh, you better watch out, you better not lie;
> you better help out I'm telling you why:
> the Messiah's coming to town.

> He knows when you are cheating.
> He knows when you're a fake.
> He knows when you've been just or not.
> So be just for justice' sake.

> He's making a list of virtue and vice,
> gonna find out who's foolish or wise:
> the Messiah's coming to town.

> He asks us to be ready.
> He warns us, "Stay awake."
> He'll gather all who've done his will,
> and the others will all shake!

He's coming anew,
coming in might,
coming in power and glory, what fright!
To judge all the people in town.

Usually everyone is laughing long before we get to the end of the song, but the point is made. It is Advent, and it's hard for us to live in a perpetual state of awareness and expectation. We are distracted easily, especially in the face of our culture's intent to derail us into coarse materialism and a superficial experience of the preparation for Christmas. It is the Spirit of God that keeps us expectant and turns us again and again toward light and hope, toward God coming toward us. It is a time to be silent and pray for one another, to be with our God, to deepen our expectations, and to ask for the gifts that our families and communities really need. Here are some old prayers to turn us again toward the light:

Give me, O Lord, a steadfast heart, which no unworthy affection may drag downwards; give me an unconquered heart, which no tribulation can wear out; give me an upright heart, which no unworthy purpose may tempt aside.

Bestow upon me also, O Lord my God, understanding to know you, diligence to seek you, wisdom to find you, and a faithfulness that may finally embrace you. — Thomas Aquinas

Do Thou meet us while we walk in the Way and long to reach the Country; so that following your light we may keep the Way of righteousness and never wander away into the darkness of this world's night.          — from the Mozarabic liturgy

O Loving-Kindness so old and still so new, I have been too late in loving you. O Lord, enlarge the chambers of my heart so that I may find room for your love. Sustain me by your power, lest the fire of your love consume me.
— Brother Lawrence

This is the Sunday of stumps, dead trees, and new life. During a visit to Israel, I became mindful of the olive trees — great gnarled trees, ancient, hundreds, even thousands of years old; and from those great stumps were shoots, green and ripe and growing: new hope. It's easy to hack off a branch, stunt growth. It takes more creativity, sap, and life to renew, make straight the way, start from seed, plant hope, and give the old most treasured gifts of dignity, justice, truthfulness, and compassion to one another, especially to our traditional enemies. But the best gifts are portents for the future — as with Isaiah's vision, John's sight of who is coming, the signal to the nations of justice with peace, our staking our lives on the kingdom of God in seed form in our midst, but belief too in the blossoming for our children and others who come after us. Our God is best, it seems, at stumps, dead ends, visions growing dim, tired and weary hearts, lost hopes and twisted routes. In this desert we prepare the way of the Lord!

# Third Sunday of Advent

*Isaiah 35:1–6, 10*
*Psalm 146:6–10*
*James 5:7–10*
*Matthew 11:2–11*

Have courage. Do not fear. See, your God comes, demanding justice. God comes to save us! God is getting closer and the effects are beginning to show. And what effects! The blind see. The deaf hear. The lame leap up. The dumb shout and sing for joy. The lepers are clean and whole. The dead come to life, and the poor have the good news given to them! Can we believe that? The desert becomes a garden, and the way is now a highway of holiness, befitting our God.

Gifts are given: strength, comfort, healing, restoration, justice, revelation, forgiveness, and, best of all, the possibility that this new life will be the future for all peoples. John the Baptist is now in jail for telling the truth and saying that everything will change drastically, that God is about making something new, and that justice is coming. And he's asking the question we all ask: Are you the one or should we expect someone else? John is suffering unjustly, and the times are dark and cruel and he wonders....

The vision is a bit blurred and indistinct. Our world is marked by such cruelties and injustice that it's hard to see in the dark of hate, amid so much inequality and suffering. Are you the one? How can we tell? Easy, really — everywhere the world leans toward justice, toward compassion, toward freedom, toward hope, we know that our God is present, near and turning the hearts of people toward one another and toward home. This day is for rejoicing, for summoning our courage, and for singing out together because the earth is being remade and refashioned into a place of springs and flowing waters and a garden — again.

Marty Haugen has written a song whose refrain puts it powerfully: "Let justice roll like a river, and wash all oppression away; Come, O God and take us, move and shake us, Come now, and make us anew, that we might live justly like you" ("Let Justice Roll Like a River" [GIA Publications, 1991]). Come, sing together to the glory of the Lord — we are invited. Our God is close enough to hear us singing! This kind of music is a message for all the world to hear and take heart from. Sing out!

Traditionally this Sunday is called "Gaudate" — the Sunday of rose-colored vestments indicating the dawn, the closeness of the coming of the Sun of Justice into the world, and the audible shift into rejoicing, even bordering on exaltation. And the vision of Isaiah comes closer to home. First it was the nations and world of wars and desires for peace, a judgment on history. Then it moved in closer to encompass enemies becoming friends and justice in a person who would judge aright for the most afflicted and distressed. Now even the land will rejoice, and the lame and broken and dispirited of the earth will be taken up into the dance, the splendor of our God. The trees, the steppe, the land will flower and the mountains will break into song.

Thus the vision both expands (breaking boundaries, from Jerusalem and its people to universal peace and harmony, and now earth itself will have cause to know the presence of God) and becomes more and more specific in its effects and consequences (the eyes of the blind will be opened, the ears of the deaf cleared...). Everything will be touched and changed by the presence of our God among us.

Even the response of the psalm is direct: "Lord, come and save us." We become much more direct in our entreaties and begin to describe God to each other to keep our spirits up and our hearts on fire. But this is not just about God. This is a summons to obey, to make the vision our reality. This is the heart and soul of Advent. We pray for the reign of our God who saves. We sing: come and save us! It is another way of singing "O Come, O Come Emmanuel," the ancient song of longing, yearning, and hope that begins as a lament, a plaintive plainsong chant, and becomes a rallying cry for those who put their trust in the promises of God.

But now we find John the Baptist in prison, oppressed for telling the truth. John, the one who goes before the face of the Lord, the forerunner, the prophet of preparation, a voice crying in the wilderness. The gospels tell us much about this man. Even before he entered the world, he was dancing, kicking, and leaping for joy in his mother's womb. He is a preacher whom the Son of Man praised! He is a torch brandished by the hand of God and a voice cutting through hardened hearts. He is one of the old ones: a prophet of honey and rock, a hermit of the desert, and a song raging the Lord's remembrance to a people gone deaf. He had informed those who wondered if he was the long-awaited one that he is not; he is not even worthy to be his sandal-bearer. The one he precedes is mighty, a judge to be reckoned with, more fiery than he, one who will cleanse the people of their evil and rid them of their sin.

But John's prophecy seems to be off the mark. This Jesus who has come after him doesn't seem to be following the plan. This man oozes mercy, calmness, almost stillness, and has a predilection for the most miserable of the earth: those suffering from ailments, exile, rejection, physical deformity, the revulsion and disdain of others. He is gentle, meek, and humble, making miracles of well-being, wholeness, forgiveness, and hope. He is not exactly what John was expecting or preaching to those he baptized in the waters of the Jordan. John is in prison. Advent, incarnation, and this coming of justice are experienced in the face of injustice, violence, and inhumanity from the very beginning. And so John sends his messengers to Jesus to ask him the question: "Are you the one who is to come?" Jesus' reply quotes Isaiah's old promises of new creation, healing, and what is impossible becoming reality. The blind recover their sight, cripples walk, lepers are cured, the deaf hear, the dead are raised to life, and the poor have the good news preached to them. And Jesus has his own addition to the prophecy: "Blessed is the one who finds no stumbling block in me." He is speaking forcibly and immediately to John himself who finds this preacher more merciful than he expected. That is Jesus' answer to the one who went before him.

And then Jesus turns from the messengers and speaks of who John is and what people were expecting when they went out to hear him in the wasteland. And he has high praise for this imprisoned man. He questions the crowds. Were they expecting "a reed swaying in the wind" or "someone luxuriously dressed, like those in royal palaces," or perhaps "a prophet"? Yes, Jesus says, John was a prophet, but was also a messenger of God, preparing the people for his advent, his coming. And Jesus goes on to say: "I solemnly assure you history has not known a man born of woman greater than John the Baptizer. Yet the least born into the kingdom of God is greater than he." With these words the preparation is over. The presence of God is declared; new reality displaces the old way; and all that is to come is greater by far than anything dreamed of in the past.

All those least born into the kingdom of God — that's all of us! — are greater than John the Baptist, the last and best of the prophets of God. Of course, this proclamation of Jesus is true only when we do what the vision reveals. We are called to commit ourselves to transformation, repairing the world, doing the works of Jesus, and professing publicly our belief in the incarnation: that God is in our flesh and dwelling daily with us in the world in the oppressed, the hungry, the captives, the blind and lame, the deaf and dumb, the poor and the deadened.

This is Gaudate Sunday, and with this Sunday the focus of Advent shifts from judgment and power to a child grown to be a man of hope and courage, a man of peace and justice who is the presence of God hidden in humanity, in vulnerability, poverty, and the ordinary wonder of life. Like John we wonder in our prisons and suffering, being drawn closer to the mystery of God in love and tenderness. We are taught, with John, that our God is recognizable in every child, man, woman, creature, and piece of earth waiting for us to find him out, love him back, and give him dignity and hope.

This is a day of blessing: "Blessed is the one who finds no stumbling block in me!" John adjusts his expectations, shifts his position on how the future is to be fashioned, on how the threshing floor is to be cleared. He will die in his prison, free, believing that Jesus is the one he prepared the way for and that the future will be full of wholeness, rich in mercy and justice. All these impossible things are coming true. The ancient hopes are couched in images of barren and deserted wilderness being turned into oases and places teeming with life, even lush with beauty. The images sing:

> The desert and the parched land will exult;
> the steppe will rejoice and bloom.
> They will bloom with abundant flowers,
> and rejoice with joyful song.

The glory of Lebanon will be given to them,
    the splendor of Carmel and Sharon;
They will see the glory of the Lord,
    the splendor of our God. (Isaiah 35:1–2)

The images interchange what will happen to earth that is empty and useless and to people who are equally shunned, feared, and looked upon as cursed by God. The letter of James continues with these image transformations. It is an exhortation to be patient. We must be steady, enduring with grace and without grumbling. We are told to remember and to take the prophets as models, prophets like Isaiah, who gave hope and sustained the people even as he was persecuted and suffered horribly for denouncing injustice, and John the Baptizer, who, in jail, asked a word from Jesus and endured to the end and died violently on the whim of Herod, a weak man with power. Oh, for an Isaiah and a John the Baptist, a people singing the praises of God in every nation, every diocese, every city, and every parish!

The third verse of the song "City of God" reminds us of what we are to do:

God is light; in him there is no darkness.
Let us walk in his light, his children, one and all.
O comfort my people; make gentle your words.
Proclaim to my city, the day of her birth.

*Refrain*
Let us build the city of God!
May our tears be turned into dancing!
For the Lord, our light and our love,
has turned the night into day!
O city of gladness, now lift up your voice!
Proclaim the good tidings that all may rejoice!

There are stories to teach us and question us on our relationship to this merciful preacher, the one who unexpectedly comes among us, intent on making whole those who are broken, yet doing this in such a way that makes us wonder: Are you the one? Advent is a story in itself about prisons, death, and suffering and how God is aligned with those, like the prophets and victims of injustice, cursed and judged by the world, but not by God's standards. John is not released from prison, but he is set free, loosed from his doubts and given hope, wings to fly. He is blessed. John has done his part, his work. Now, on this third Sunday of Advent, we are summoned to do our work, our part in preparing for the Holy One of God, the gentle preacher and healer among us.

What follows is a story about freedom that questions us and makes us look at what we think hope and liberation are — hope and liberation are what Jesus, the one long-awaited, is all about. It is called "The Lion and the Concentration Camp." People tell me that Anthony DeMello told the story. I heard it at a base community meeting in a barrio in Nicaragua over a decade ago during Ordinary Time. The community was struggling with how to live under the tension, pressure, and oppression of an embargo, the threat of the Contras, and poverty that was destroying their children and weakening everyone. After a long and bloody revolution, not much seemed to have changed in spite of all their best efforts. So much was against them, including the United States, and economic sanctions denied them even medical supplies, food, and building materials. Their response to the story was as startling as the story itself and connected to this gospel passage about John in prison sending his own disciples to question Jesus' methods and tactics.

✢ Once upon a time there was a lion who was caught by hunters. Overnight he was caged and lost his freedom, his wide-ranging home, and his wild life apart from others. His power was gone. But to his surprise he wasn't killed or skinned or put into a zoo. Instead he found that he was thrown into a concentration camp, a prison for lions. Not only that, he was surprised to find so many other lions like himself in the camp and to find out that many had been there for years.

In fact, most had settled into the routine of camp life, accepting their confinement as fact and reacting to it in a number of ways. For a while he kept his distance from all the others and watched, listening to see what was going on. There were four groups, each distinctive in its reaction to being in prison. The first group was interested in the past, what it was like to be a lion in the jungle. They tried to keep that experience alive for those who were born in captivity and had no experience of what life was really like for lions. They ritualized events, dances, songs, and initiation rites, trying to help the others remember who they were.

The next group was basically the organizers. They had been there long enough to realize that possibilities of getting free were slim at best, so it was up to them to make the best of a bad situation. So they organized the camp into areas, making sure that everyone had what they needed, that extras were shared evenly, and that newcomers were taught the lay of the land.

The next group was the revolutionaries. They plotted and planned a way to escape, trained, and kept in shape. Periodically a group made a rush for freedom, attacking the fence or the guards or trying to slip alone into the dark. Some died; some were wounded; some were put in solitary. These lions kept to themselves, away from the others in the camp.

The last group seemed to be the largest of all. They were hard to peg or figure out. They lived as though this were all they had ever known and counseled each other, set up programs of education, socialization, exercise, entertainment, and just ignored the fence and the guards.

After watching the interaction of the camp for a few weeks, the young new lion was wondering what to do, which group to join. He noticed one lion who kept to himself, wasn't part of a group. This lion paced by the fence, back and forth, incessantly, never deviating from the routine. He just kept moving. The young lion decided to fall in with this lion and see what he could learn. He walked with him for a day or two and then tried to approach him. He was swatted and clawed and told to shut up. He picked himself up and wondered if he'd done anything wrong. He watched and noticed that the other lions treated this one with respect, keeping their distance. Even the guards were more nervous and edgy around him and stayed out of his way. He went back to walking, pacing with him, and after another couple of days asked again what he was doing. Again he was slapped and clawed. But the third time he asked, the older lion stopped and eyed him directly. Then he answered, "What do you think I'm doing? I'm a lion. All the others have forgotten the one essential thing. This is a prison camp. I'm studying the nature of the fence." And with that, the young lion fell in behind him. Now there are two lions who are treated with respect, and they keep at the one essential thing: freedom.

The discussion that followed was startling and instructive. Of course, initially everyone decided which group they were in and if that was how they lived their own lives. And then the issue of freedom was broached: we discussed the nature of freedom and named the fences in our lives, those visible and invisible, spoken about and ignored. In the reading, John the Baptist is free even while in jail, and Jesus is about the one essential thing: freedom and the nature of the fence (sin, evil, lack, and what confines us, breaks us, and numbs us to our realities). How many of us are really free? Do we find ourselves all too quickly in one of the groups, missing the essential core of our lives as human beings, as Christians and as disciples of Jesus? In reality, is Jesus a stumbling block for us, someone who disorients us and makes us take stock of our priorities, questioning us on what we hope and what we do?

To put it bluntly, do we spend our lives as Jesus does? Are we attentive to the blind in our communities, both those who are forced to rely on their other senses and those who see but refuse to acknowledge what is happening around them and to take responsibility for their own part in it? Helen Keller once said:

> I have often thought it would be a blessing if each human being were stricken blind and deaf for a few days at some time during his early adult life. Darkness would make him appreciative of sight; silence would teach him the joys of sound.
>
> Now and then I have tested my seeing friends to discover what they see. Recently I was visited by a very good friend who had just returned from a long walk in the woods, and I asked her what she had observed. "Nothing in particular," she replied. I might have been incredulous had I not been accustomed to such responses, for long ago I became convinced that the seeing see little. (*Three Days to See,* 1933)

Are we in sore need of the lens of faith and moral audacity to perceive what is going on in our world? For instance, in regard to jails, Fyodor Dostoyevsky said: "The degree of civilization in a society can be judged by entering its prisons." If this is true, we in the United States are less civilized than most other human beings. Or, in reference to another area of life, Michael Harrington said: "People who are much too sensitive to demand of cripples that they run races ask of the poor that they get up and act just like everyone else in society." Not only do we demand that they participate in society at levels we are accustomed to, but we as a nation now blame the poor for the problems in the economy, the unbalanced budget, the crime rate, and whatever else we refuse to face squarely. Are we dead long before our hearts stop beating and we are "laid to rest"?

As Rabindranath Tagore wrote:

I slept and dreamt that life was joy.
I awoke and saw that life was service.
I acted and behold, service was joy.

Can we truthfully begin to say with Jesse Jackson, "My constituency is the desperate, the damned, the disinherited, the disrespected, and the despised"? Whom are we aligned with? Or are the friends of Jesus stumbling blocks for us? Sobering questions in the midst of winter's darkest time. And yet the light draws ever closer.

John the Baptist had to stretch his understanding and reach beyond the prison of his life, his circumstances, and even his conception of the Word of the Lord to let God maneuver in the world. And we, in this season of opening outward to the presence of God coming among us, must be stretched too.

A Hasidic story of Rabbi Naftali from the town of Roptchitz illustrates how important it is to know what we are about.

✚ It was the rabbi's custom every evening after the sun went down to go walking through the town and then into the outskirts. It provided him with time to reflect and kept him up on anything that was happening, the comings and goings of his own neighbors. It was also the custom of the wealthy landowners to hire watchmen to watch the perimeters of their property at night, whether they were home or not, as a security measure. One evening after dark, the rabbi met one of these watchers and asked him whom he worked for and was given an answer. The name was familiar. And the watcher assumed that the rabbi too was working for someone and asked him who his employer was.

The rabbi stopped in his tracks, for the question hit him squarely in his heart. Whom did he work for? Was it obvious that he served the Master of the Universe, blessed be His Name and work? He wasn't sure, and so he didn't answer right away. Instead he walked along with the man as he watched and walked the grounds of the rich man's estate. Then the rabbi spoke: "I'm not sure that I really work for anyone, I'm sorry to say. I am a rabbi in this town." After a long, silent walk, the rabbi asked the watcher, "Will you come and work for me?"

"Of course, I'd be delighted to, Rabbi," the man responded. "What would my duties entail?"

"Oh, there would just be one thing you would always do," the rabbi answered. "Remind me whom I work for, whose employ I'm in, and why I'm here — that's all. Remind me!"

The third Sunday of Advent is about reminding us that we who are the least in the kingdom of God are meant to be greater even than John the Baptist in preparing the way of the Lord. Our God is at the gate. It is time to go out and unlatch it and let the Holy One into our world.

## Some Prayers

O great incomprehensible God. You fill up all. Be thou my heaven. Let my spirit be indeed the music and the joy of your spirit. Do thou make music in me and may I make harmony in the divine kingdom of your joy, in the great love of God, in the wonders of your glory and splendor, in the company of your holy angelic harmonies.    — Jacob Boehme

O Lord, I pray for all those whom thou hast given me, whom I love with a special love, and whom you have made one thing with me. For they are my consolation, and for your sake I desire to see them running in the sweet and narrow way dead to self and pure from all judgment and murmuring against their neighbor. May they all attain to you, O eternal Father, to you who art their final end.    — Catherine of Siena

Lord, we pray not for tranquillity, nor that our tribulations may cease; we pray for your Spirit and your love that you grant us strength and grace to overcome adversity.
    — Savonarola

This week also begins the ancient tradition of praying the "O Antiphons," a way of praising God and waiting with growing joy and expectation for our Savior's coming. We will look at them in the next chapter in some detail, for they speak of Mary's child in language ever ancient and refreshing.

# Fourth Sunday of Advent

*Isaiah 7:10–14*
*Psalm 24:1–6*
*Romans 1:1–7*
*Matthew 1:18–24*

Ah, here it is at last, the birth announcement. The child's name shall be Emmanuel, which means God-with-us, God dwelling with us, sojourning with us, coming home and staying with us, forever. In the midst of evil and in a land fraught with division and hypocrisy, among kings who do not want God interfering with their policies, one is coming who will interrupt and alter the outcome of all history. But it's not happening with fanfare, public accolades, and in the places of power.

No, it's coming in dreams, in words of vision, among the poor and those who can hardly believe the good news sprung upon them. A sign — a child who will choose good and refuse evil. A child, born in poverty, in secret, amid ponderings and anguish, who triggers hard decisions for those associated with him, but a child who dispels fears and is born of the Spirit of God and whose very presence brings holiness and hope to those who have been waiting so long for his coming.

Now we meet Joseph, a dreamer who stakes his life on what he is told by a messenger of God, and Mary, who is entrusted to Joseph by the Spirit. And he is told a name for his child, Jesus, which means the one who will save his people from their sins. Because Joseph, a just man, has been living on dreams and the visions of the prophets all his life, this dream is the culmination of the pattern. He awakes and obeys the angel's words and takes into his heart and his home both Mary as his wife and the child to be born, Jesus Christ the Lord.

The time is so close. Now is the time for hard decisions, life-giving and life-sustaining decisions in the face of death and darkness, even despair. What are we waiting for? What are we living for?

✤ Once upon a time there was a young woman who was stricken with pneumonia and slowly dying. She would look out the window at a great tree whose leaves were torn by the wind and the cold. She was resigned to dying and told her friends that with the last leaf that fell from the tree, she would depart as well. But that last leaf refused to fall. It held on for dear life. It clung to that branch. And the woman lived. It was only then that she learned that that last leaf had been painted on the window by a friend as she slept.

Our story is even better than that one. God has made, is making, the dreams and the visions come true. Justice, peace, and hope are now a person, a child to be born in our midst. God will be made flesh among us and in our hearts and history again, by belief and obedience, as once it happened through Joseph and Mary. Now it is our turn, our time to live, to hang on for dear life, for a dearer life and to let God dwell with us. It is almost time. God is coming home to us. Open the door and let him in.

Our readings begin with the last and the shortest of the vision promises that give hope and direction to the gospel readings. God is intent on giving a word of wild encouragement and expectation in spite of the political and historical plan of King Ahaz and his ministers. It is God who gives the sign, and the sign is a child named Emmanuel, God-with-us, but he will be with us in ways not expected. Originally the prophecy was given to a king on the throne of David; then it was connected to the gospel announcement to Joseph of the house of David, Joseph being Jesus' legal parent, earthly parent, and guardian; and then the promise evolved into the coming of the king who would bring justice to the whole world. The vision is not so much about Mary, the virgin, as about the nature of God's word and promise and how things come about in history and in God's dream for us. It chides us. Listen! Things are not going to work out as you plan and expect. Something else is in the works!

The psalm refrain commands us: let the Lord enter; he is the King of glory. This is a song of hope and close proximity to the face of God. And it has worldwide implications as well as reminding us that we must be sinless, with clean hands and a pure heart, if we are to stand in this place and see him. The blessing will be proffered and the reward given over, but we must ascend the mountain of the Lord; we must climb to be able to see the future; and we must together, as a race of human beings, seek the face of the God of our ancestors. The one who comes is maker of the universe, and all that dwells on the face of the earth belongs to him alone. We must be clear in our mind, heart, and desires, or else we will not see him right in front of us. The two individuals who most clearly reveal what this means and how this is enfleshed are Mary and Joseph, who are invited to let this extraordinary child enter into and transform their lives. And it is as though a great wind enters a small house, rattling the windows and shaking it to the foundation, knocking over anything that is not secured firmly. This child will disrupt each of their lives and ours if we are open to him.

This season of Advent has always had the character of quiet, stillness, even loveliness, as only the earth can be in winter. The weather in parts of the Northern Hemisphere can be brisk, dry, windy, even bitterly cold and snowy. The sky empties out, and there is a light that can only be called winter light. And yet this external world mirrors the interior of the soul of the church and our own spaces. We, too, like the world that waits for the seed to germinate and spring to come, lie low and believe in what we remember and have been told. There is an antiphon for Vespers in the old prayers of the Office that reveals the memory that has such power that it allows us to bear the cold and fallowness of winter: "On that day sweet wine will flow from the mountains, milk and honey from the hills, alleluia." This is the character of our receptivity. And sometimes in our waiting we need to be reminded that the heart of this season is not focused directly on us, but outward onto the one who comes to us, Christ the Lord. The writer Maria Boulding says:

> Advent is primarily about the coming of God, and only in a secondary way about our asking, seeking, waiting and longing. There is hope, because we are unconditionally loved, whatever may be our failures, our tepidity, or our secret despair. The word "Come" is a bearer of mystery. (*The Coming of God*)

This last week of Advent, especially, is marked by the exclamation, the pleading, the interruption, and the rueful declaration embodied in the sound "Oh." It is spoken accusatorily to King Ahaz by the prophet Isaiah in the formal address, "Listen, Oh house of David! Is it not enough for you to weary men, must you also weary my God?" The king has no time for the prophet, let alone the presence of Yahweh, the Holy One of Israel, meddling in affairs of state. Ahaz is embroiled in the siege of Jerusalem. The kings of Damascus and Samaria are leaning hard on the people and the land.

Isaiah describes it thus: "Take care you remain tranquil and do not fear; let not your courage fail before these two stumps of smoldering brands" (Isaiah 7:1–10). The language itself has all the echoes of Advent fare with its exhortation to live in the face of adversity and political strife, even violence, without fear, for God is the Lord of history and knows what is happening. God will have his own way with outward events that inwardly serve the larger purpose of salvation history and the care of God for his own people and all peoples.

Ahaz wants no part of Isaiah's prophecy or of the relationship of faith in Yahweh that Isaiah is pressing upon the king of Israel, the leader of the house of David. Ahaz is already making deals on earth, with the king of Assyria. He is paying homage to him, offering tithes and allegiances, bending to the power of another earthly king while he endeavors to bend history to his own agenda. King Ahaz is not about to wait on the kingdom of heaven or the will of Yahweh. So when Isaiah commands him to ask for a sign from God and says that it can "be as deep as the netherworld, or high as the sky," Ahaz refuses, but he refuses with deceit and false humility. Who is he to ask of God? He replies, "I will not tempt the Lord!" Of course, he has already gone long past tempting God by insulting him and turning aside for aid and support from other powers on earth, instead of from God's.

Isaiah is furious at the hypocrisy of King Ahaz and tells him what God's sign will be, in spite of whether he, the leader of the house of David, wants it or not. The Lord will give a sign, and this sign will be the adamant announcement that Yahweh is the Lord of heaven and earth, of the history of nations, and of personal lives, from the greatest in Israel to the least. The sign is the presence of an unborn child in a young woman, who already bears within her one who will be the presence of God so powerfully with the people that all will know the power of God is loose in the world. Ahaz's own child, Hezekiah, was definitely not the sign! History had revealed that he was more like his father, Ahaz, than anything God had in mind for his people. And so, the prophecy is linked to the hopes of the people of Israel for future liberation and salvation, for a Messiah who will be just and faithful, God-with-us, Emmanuel.

This child is the child Mary will bear into the world, protected by Joseph, a true believer and a descendant of the house of David. This is the sign, the gift of God. Matthew's gospel tells of the declaration of the angel to Joseph:

"Joseph, son of David, have no fear about taking Mary as your wife. It is by the Holy Spirit that she has conceived this child. She is to have a son and you are to name him Jesus because he will save his people from their sins." All this happened to fulfill what the Lord had said through the prophet:

"The virgin shall be with child
and give birth to a son,
and they shall call him Emmanuel,"

a name which means "God is with us." When Joseph awoke he did as the angel of the Lord had directed him and received her into his home as his wife. (Matthew 1:20–24)

It is Joseph, the true son of the house of David, who is more obedient and faithful than Ahaz ever was. Joseph hears the word of God in the dream, awakes, and does as he has been commanded, without questioning God or acting with false modesty. Joseph is directed by the messengers of God and always has been, for he is faithful to the promises. The sign is deeper than the netherworld and higher than the sky. It is made of the meeting of the Holy Spirit of God and a young woman who is only known in the world as "engaged to Joseph" but not yet married to him. The prophecy has grown with a life of its own, as any child in the womb grows, and will emerge to be something beyond Israel's hopes.

In an ancient Christmas carol sung best on Christmas Eve we hear the words: "The hopes and fears of all the years are met in thee tonight" ("O Little Town of Bethlehem"). One wonders if Joseph's initial response to awakening with the memory of the angel in his mind was "Oh, oh, oh!" Perhaps even Yahweh was weary of the people's lack of hope, lack of awareness, lack of belief. Perhaps one man of the house of David and one woman were enough, and God reached for them, and so, reached for all of us.

*The Lord of the Rings,* J. R. R. Tolkien's trilogy, has become a classic among those who read children's literature, fantasy, and magical tales. It weaves a world inhabited by creatures called hobbits who are good and gentle in a world of violence, intrigue, and danger. They have marvelous customs, one of them involving the ritual of gift-giving. They give new gifts to new friends and old treasures to old friends. The most cherished gifts are given to the oldest hobbits. Ancient gifts are the best of all, revealing the depth of friendship and love among hobbits. It works that way with our God too. Only the oldest and dearest treasures are passed on to those who are faithful longest and deepest. Mary and Joseph receive the gift that literally is the presence of God in flesh and Spirit, the gift that has been with God the longest, since the very beginning. It is the sign that God intended all along to give, whether we would ever come to appreciate it truly or not. This fourth Sunday of Advent presents us with a choice: to respond to the words and commands of the prophet Isaiah as did either Ahaz or Joseph.

And our response is described in the letter of Paul to the Romans, where Paul lays out his credentials as servant of Christ Jesus, as called to be an apostle and set apart to proclaim the gospel of God that God promised long ago through his prophets, as the Holy Scriptures record. And Paul's message, the gospel of God, is about this sign, this child, this human being who is Jesus Christ, God. The first few lines of the letter to the Romans are a statement of faith, a creed that is basic to the season and to early Christianity:

> ...concerning his Son, who was descended from David according to the flesh but was made Son of God in power, according to the spirit of holiness, by his resurrection from the dead: Jesus Christ our Lord. Through him we have been favored with apostleship, that we may spread his name and bring to obedient faith all the Gentiles, among whom are you who have been called to belong to Jesus Christ. (Romans 1:3–6)

This is the message, the proclamation of the gospel, the reality of all the Advent Scriptures, antiphons, and songs. It is about the coming of the Son of God in power and about we who are called, with Joseph and Mary, to belong to God, Jesus Christ our Lord. And so Paul ends his introductory greetings with a blessing for all who hear and take to heart his words, "To all in Rome, beloved of God and called to holiness, grace and peace from God our Father and the Lord Jesus Christ" (Romans 1:7). Because of the birth of this child, announced in so many ways this Sunday, we are the beloved of God and commanded to live with holiness, grace, and peace.

This letter is addressed to those in Rome, the center of power in the world at that time, a power that would persecute Christians and murder Paul, Peter, and so many of the disciples and followers of Jesus, yet not be able to stand against the coming of the Word of God into the world. The belief of those called to obedience changed history. That too is part of the promise, but it in part depends on the response to the Word of God. On this fourth Sunday of Advent we are confronted with our place in history and whether we will respond with obedience to the Word and awake from our sleep to make the dream of God come true in our flesh. God is with us! The time is at hand. Are we ready to give birth to the Holy One in our lives and history? We are invited into the company of Mary and Joseph, Isaiah and John the Baptist, Paul and all those who have believed and staked their lives on the promise.

Joseph and Mary did not retreat before the face of God, as Ahaz did — they turned to stand close together to receive God into the world, coming through them into history. In the last seven days of Advent, the church, through the singing of the "O Antiphons," tells us how to address, how to approach, the one to be born in our midst. The mood of Advent shifts drastically into one of wonder at Vespers on December 17, with the antiphon that brackets the Magnificat:

> O Wisdom from the Father's mouth,
> The Word of God is eternal love,
> Beneath whose firm yet gentle sway
> This world is governed from above.
> O Come! O Come!
> And teach us all
> The ways that lead to life.
>                     (An ancient rendering of the text)

And the O Antiphons will continue through the eve of Christmas. They hail the one to come in invocations, texts, and messianic titles that are couched in hope, longing, and intense concentration. They build in intensity, deepening our desire and focusing us on the Word of God made flesh among us. The titles are: "O Wisdom," "O Holy Word of God," "O Adonai," "O Root of Jesse" (or "Flower of Jesse's Stem"), "O Key of David," "O Daystar" (or "O Radiant Dawn"), "O King of All the Nations," "O Emmanuel." All the prayers beseech help and entreat God to come and instill in those who sing and listen to the music and words a sense of stillness, serenity, and heart's ease. What follows is one version of the O Antiphons that are used in my church in New Mexico:

> O Wisdom, O Holy Word of God, you govern all creation with your strong yet tender care. Come and show your people the way of salvation.

O Sacred Lord of Ancient Israel, who showed yourself to Moses in the burning bush, who gave him the holy law on Sinai mountain, come, stretch out your mighty hand to set us free.

O Flower of Jesse's Stem, you have been raised up as a sign for all peoples; kings stand silent in your presence; the nations bow down in worship before you. Come, let nothing keep you from coming to our aid.

O Key of David, O Royal Power of Israel controlling at your will the gate of heaven; come, break down the prison walls of death for those who dwell in darkness and the shadow of death; and lead your captive people into freedom.

O Radiant Dawn, splendor of eternal Light, sun of justice: come shine on those who dwell in darkness and the shadow of death.

O King of All the Nations, the only joy of every human heart; O Keystone of the mighty arch of human beings, come and save the creatures you have fashioned from the dust.

O Emmanuel, king and lawgiver, desire of the nations, Savior of all people, come and set us free, Lord our God.

There is an ancient Jewish story about promises and how they come true. This story is closely connected to the promise, the sign that Isaiah wishes to give to Ahaz, though he is reluctant to take hold of it, for it will change his life. The story is called "The King's Son."

✤ Once upon a time there was a king. He was loved by his wife, respected and a bit feared by his enemies and neighbors, and honored by his subjects, but he himself was miserable. He had no heir, no one to bear his name and continue his work in the kingdom. And so, he sent out a proclamation to all in the land that anyone who could help his wife become pregnant would be rewarded royally.

Many came forward with suggestions, cure-alls, potions, and all failed. The king grew angry and bitter. Now the proclamation read that those who tried to help them have a child and failed would be severely punished or killed and that if anyone succeeded they would be lavishly rewarded. Still people tried, and all failed and all died. The king grew black and despairing, and all in the kingdom mourned and suffered.

And then one day an old woman appeared in the court. The king and queen had seen her before. She was wise, a Jewish healer and prophet. She presented herself boldly before the king and spoke. "I promise you a child before the year is out." The king eyed her and reminded her of the penalty for failure. It did not faze her. She repeated her statement, "I promise you a child before the year is out, but," she added, "there is one thing you must do."

"What?" he challenged her, "What?"

"You must call out your troops, the army, every able-bodied man and woman and dig trenches and canals. Your people are dying of disease, without fresh water and sanitation. You must dig a canal for the fresh water and another, separate from it, for animal and human waste — and you must do this throughout the entire kingdom. When it is finished, you will have your heir." The king eyed the old woman, who waited for his response.

"All right, old woman, I will do it, but your word had best be good." She left and the king's decree was set in motion. Everyone worked, dug. It took almost three years for the canals to be built and for the system to operate. When it was finished, the king watched his wife, to see if there was a quickening, a swelling. There was nothing. The year passed and the old woman was dragged in before the king, who was furious with her. "Old woman," he said, "you lied to me. I want your life for your broken word."

"Fine," she replied, "and then you will never know what was the one thing more you needed to do to have your son."

The king froze. She had mentioned a son, specifically, this time. He eyed her again, harshly. "What do you mean?"

"The one more thing," she said.

"What is it?" he yelled at her.

She eyed him back and responded calmly, "You're not going to like it."

He yelled at her again: "I didn't like the last one either. Tell me."

"You must," she said, "gather all your nobles and landowners, the wealthy, and together you must redistribute the land among the poor so that everyone has their own small piece of land and can raise food."

The king's reaction was swift and exasperated. "That's impossible. Why should I do that?"

"Then," she continued calmly, "you will never have a son." The king fumed and was silent. Then, in a cold voice, he told the woman, "All right. I will do this thing, but if you have not told the truth this time, it will be your children who are orphaned."

"So be it," she replied and left.

This took time, lots of time, with negotiation, discussions, concessions, reorganization of the entire kingdom, its finances and priorities, but his wife encouraged him. Seven years passed and it was done. Again, the king watched his wife hopefully for any sign of quickening. Nothing. Enraged, he had the old woman dragged before him and condemned her to death right then and there, sputtering curses. She was quiet until he took a breath. "Go ahead and kill me," she said, "but you will never know what was the one last thing that you had to do to obtain a child who would bear your name and carry on your work in the kingdom."

The king could barely speak he was so livid with anger. "One more thing?!"

"Yes," the woman said, "you know things always come in threes. This one is the magic."

"What?" was all he asked.

"This is the hardest of all," she said.

"What could possibly be harder than getting my nobles to share their wealth and land?" the king spit back.

"Dismantle your army," was all she said.

The king mocked her and said, "What do you think, that I am crazy? I'll be overrun by my enemies."

"No," she replied, "your enemies respect you, but you are always getting involved in skirmishes and clashes outside the land, making alliances, and going to war elsewhere. And it is your people, your young men, who die and do not return to their families and wives. Your people need peace."

What could he do when he was so desperate for a child? He wept and almost whispered, "All right, woman. It will be done, but if there is no child I will kill you myself."

"So be it," she replied and left.

Years passed. The army was dismantled, alliances rewritten, clauses composed that stipulated no violence, no aggression. Ten years and the land rested and the people knew peace. And the king watched his wife, desperate, wildly. Nothing. No quickening. And the old woman was dragged in to die. The king approached her and she spoke, "Wait, before you kill me there is something I must say. Look around at your kingdom. Your people thrive and live to old age. The children are healthy and happy. Each family and clan has its own land and there is no robbery or thievery in the land. Visitors and strangers are welcomed and food shared. And the young live, not to fight wars or kill, but to raise children, to live, and to know happiness. And your people love you! You have no child, no one of your flesh who bears your name, but your people bless God for you. They give thanks for your wisdom and kindness, for the peace that you have brought to them. Your neighboring countries admire you and wonder how you have done this thing. Your name will go down in history as blessed, as just and honorable. And in the land, many name their children after you." The king stopped. He turned and looked at his wife, who nodded. The woman continued: "Your land was dead. Your heart was cold. Your wife was barren. Hope was banned from the kingdom. Now all that is changed. All quickens and stirs to life. Justice, peace, and a future for all are secured. That is all I have to say."

The king knew her words were true. She was spared. The kingdom prospered. Did the king and his queen have a son, a child of their own? It is not known. The promise came true. They say, in some Jewish communities, that the name of the king was Hezekiah, a son of King Ahaz. But others say that it doesn't matter because all the earth is still waiting for the old woman's promises to come true.

## Prayers and Reflections

At all costs we must renew in ourselves the desire and the hope for the great coming.          — Pierre Teilhard de Chardin

The hope Teilhard de Chardin speaks of is described in the two following texts:

By the tender mercy of our God, the dawn from on high will break upon us, to give light to those who sit in darkness and in the shadow of death, to guide our feet into the way of peace.

—Luke 1:78–79

With every power for good to stay and guide me,
  comforted and inspired beyond all fear,
I'll live these days with You in thought beside me,
  And pass, with You, into the coming year.

—Dietrich Bonhoeffer

# CYCLE B

---------- ✠ ----------

## First Sunday of Advent

*Isaiah 63:16–17, 19; 64:2–7*
*Psalm 80:2–3, 15–16, 18–19*
*1 Corinthians 1:3–9*
*Mark 13:33–37*

This is the year of Isaiah the prophet and the ancient texts that are so familiar yet evocative for people everywhere, regardless of religious beliefs. They speak of peace on earth and a life of justice and hope for all. The emphasis in the first readings is on prophecy, visions, and dreams of what might exist, and the wonder, amazement, and gracefulness that precede the birth of God on earth as a child in Bethlehem. The vision grows until it's almost unbelievable.

This is a season of hope. The figures of Advent radiate hope: Isaiah, John the Baptist, Mary and Joseph, and, of course, Jesus, the long-awaited one who is hope for all the nations. They all are intent on reminding us of who we are and the promises that call us back to God's dream of us, his own people, his children. We live in hope in these days, act in hope, pray with hope, and are a source of hope for others in the world, as we wait in joyful hope for the coming of our Savior Jesus Christ.

The dictionary defines hope as "a feeling of expectation and desire combined, a desire for certain events to happen or a person or thing or circumstance that gives cause for this," and the verb means "to desire, to expect and feel confident about." Emily Dickinson writes, "Hope is the thing with feathers which perches in the soul and sings the tune without the words and never stops at all." It is the song we sing this season that announces the incarnation and the birth of Christ in our hearts and communities.

Dan Schutte has composed a song for the season entitled "A Time

Will Come for Singing" (from his album *Gentle Night, Music for Advent and Christmas* [North American Liturgy Resources, 1977]) that sets the tone for us:

> A time will come for singing when all your tears are shed,
> when sorrow's chains are broken, and broken hearts will
>     mend.
> The deaf will hear your singing when silent tongues are
>     freed.
> The lame will join your dancing when blind eyes learn
>     to see.
>
> A time will come for singing when trees will raise their
>     boughs,
> when men lay down their armor, and hammer their swords
>     into plows,
> when beggars live as princes, and orphans find their homes,
> when prison cells are emptied, and hatred has grown old.
>
> A time will come for singing a hymn by hearts foretold,
> that kings have sought for ages, and treasured more than
>     gold.
> Its lyrics turn to silver when sung in harmony.
> The Lord of Love will teach us to sing its melody.

This season and cycle of readings are the story of how hope becomes visible and takes on flesh. It begins with the Word of God in the prophets' mouths, the Word that is sounded in our ears and makes its way to our hearts. These four weeks are time measured out to make another song, new music for the world's old and slow-beating heart. It is time for us to get ready, and we will need every one of these twenty-four days to prepare for the hope that is intent on coming into our world once again.

The other symbol besides song and poetry that is rife in this season is that of a face, the visage of the child of hope, God's own child. We are told in the reading from Isaiah that "for you have hidden your face from us and have delivered us up to our guilt." And yet the text reminds us of who and what our God is like and what our story has been, what God's story for us was supposed to be, in spite of what we do. And the vision begins with God, as "our father, our redeemer . . . named forever." And it is repeated again toward the end of the text: "Yet, O Lord, you are our father; we are the clay and you are the potter: we are all the work of your hands" (Isaiah

64:7). This is our original relationship, our beginning, yet we have consistently and deliberately turned our faces from what was hoped for us. And so we pray with Isaiah:

> Why do you let us wander, O Lord, from your ways,
>     and harden our hearts so that we fear you not?
> Return for the sake of your servants,
>     the tribes of your heritage.
> Oh, that you would rend the heavens and come down,
>     with the mountains quaking before you,
> While you wrought awesome deeds we could not hope for,
>     such as they had not heard of from of old.
> No ear has ever heard, no eye ever seen,
>     any God but you
>     doing such deeds for those who wait for him.
> Would that you might meet us doing right,
>     that we were mindful of you in our ways!
>
> —Isaiah 63:17–64:5

These last lines are the essence of these days, the yearning cries of humankind's heart and the fervent hope of the prophet: "Would that you might meet us doing right, / that we were mindful of you in our ways!" But the question before us is stark: Do we really want our God to come toward us to "meet us doing right," to approach us that closely, to remind us of what we were created to be?

There is a Hasidic story that speaks of the coming of the Messiah, the presence of justice, the presence of the Holy One among us so strongly that all would know the nearness of God and have to turn to acknowledge this power interrupting our usual routines and the world's history (a version of the story is found in *Shlomo's Stories: Selected Tales* [255–57]).

✤ Once upon a time Reb Baruch, who was the grandson of the Baal Shem (the Master of the Good Name and the founder of the Hasidism, who believed that one of the surest ways to call down the Messiah, to hasten his coming, and to stir the sparks of divine fire on earth was by dancing and telling stories), was praying. He had heard earlier in the day another story about Reb Avromole, the Trisker Reb who never ate or slept at all, living furiously and passionately, taking no time at all to just live like anyone else. Reb Baruch wondered, as he had so many times before, if it was true and if so, why did he chose to live this way? What drove him so? It was disturbing his prayer so much that he decided then and there to go see Reb Avromole, challenge him on his behavior, and see for himself if the stories were true. Off he set and found Reb Avromole, teaching to his disciples. Soon the Reb excused himself and beckoned Reb Baruch to follow. They walked and immediately Reb Baruch asked him: "Is it true that you neither eat nor sleep? Is it?"

The answer was simple and direct, "Yes."

Reb Baruch shot back, "Why?"

"Well," he said smiling mischievously, "I didn't sleep last night because I hadn't eaten anything yesterday and I didn't eat yesterday because I was so tired from not eating or sleeping before that."

Reb Baruch was serious and threatened him severely: "Tell me the truth or else."

"Or else what?" he retorted.

"Or else I'll kick you out of this world and not allow you into the next world" (and they say he could make good on such a threat).

Reb Avromole looked at him and knew he would not be able to wiggle out of answering the Baal Shem's grandson so easily as making a joke of the matter. "All right," he replied, "I will tell you a story. Once upon a time, it was long, long ago when I was just a boy about nine, my father came down very early and commanded me to go out immediately and get the horses for we were going for a ride. How strange, I thought, and yet, I jumped to obey for my father was such a busy man, teaching, seeing travelers who came from afar, preparing his sermons and classes, and praying. I barely saw him except when he came in late. He never came down in the morning until he had prayed and I had often gone to school by then.

"I knew it was important. Father wanted me to go with him, just me alone with him. I had the horses bridled and the wagon out as fast as I could. My father came out and jumped into the seat beside me, grabbed the reins, and we tore off down the main road. We hurtled along in silence, farther than I'd ever been before. The miles and the minutes flew by, and then at a small side road my father swerved off and we were going just as fast on a rutted road, overhung with trees that grew more and more wild. We came to a clearing and abruptly stopped. He jumped down, handed me the reins, and looked at me. 'Stay here and wait for me.' I looked at him, the fire in his eyes, the hope in his face.

"I waited and waited and he didn't come back. I had no idea where we were or where he'd gone, though I knew there was a shack nearby because there was smoke rising over the trees. It seemed that time stopped and I began to worry that he wouldn't be coming back and that I was left there alone. But then, my father appeared walking between the trees with another man. They were talking intently, oblivious of me. They were animated. They were the only people in the world it seemed to me.

"And the man with him was young and shining. No, that wasn't the right word. You know, people said my father's face shone and his eyes were like candles in the night. But next to my father even, this man burned, blazed, and was radiant. It was deep within him, shooting from his eyes. He was beautiful. I strained to hear what they were saying, but they were just out of range. Then they stopped just feet from me and faced each other. The young man looked straight into my father's face and said: 'Are you sure? Is this what you have to tell me? Are you sure?' And my father stared straight back and steadfastly said: 'Yes, I'm sure. This is what I must tell you. You must listen to me.'

"And then both of them burst into tears and threw their arms around each other and held on. It was terrible. It was as though they were family and they would be torn apart and never reunited again. My father wailed and the young man held him firmly. Finally they tore themselves away from each other and my father jumped into the wagon, grabbed the reins from my hands, wrenched the wagon around, and the horses bolted again under my father's shout. He never looked back. I did. The young man stood there weeping and I watched until the trees hid him from my eyes. My father said nothing.

"Once again the ride was frightening. We swerved onto the main road and raced toward home. I wanted to stop him, cry out, ask him who the man was and what was so terrible and important, but I didn't dare until we were within sight of home.

"I grabbed his arm and said, 'Papa, who was that?' He stopped the horses and turned to me, looking at me intently. 'That, my son, was Mashiach ben David, the Messiah!' He said it so silently, so truthfully that I knew it was so.

"'But, father, what did he want with us?'

"There were tears in my father's eyes and he told me that the Messiah wanted to know if he should come now. 'What did you say to him?'

"And my father looked at me and said, 'I told him not to come, not now, because no one was waiting for him. No one would be ready. I had to tell him that. No one was really waiting for him.'

"So, you see, Reb Baruch, that's what I live with always. If you had seen the face of the Messiah and you knew he wasn't coming because no one was waiting for him, would you eat, or sleep, or live like anyone else? Would you? Could you ever take a chance and ever sleep or eat again?"

Belief. Hope. Desire. Wanting God to come. Are we really waiting for God? Samuel Beckett's devastating play *Waiting for Godot* poses this problem in contemporary terms. Godot is a diminutive, endearing expression for God. Didi and Gogo are two figures, sad, really, who wait under the same tree every evening to see if Godot will come and give meaning to their empty lives. They wait, but it is a meaningless existence, with no real hope, no expectations. They do nothing in the meantime. They are killing time, before time runs out and kills them. Didi remarks at one point, "Habit is a great deadener." This isn't waiting, or being ready; in a sense this is existing without faith, without hope, without life really, graceless and empty. This is the distressing opposite of Advent's attentiveness and aliveness that we are invited to experience in these coming weeks.

The reading from 1 Corinthians begins with a prayer for this new year. The first words are a blessing: "Grace and peace from God our Father and the Lord Jesus Christ." This is the wish of the ages, the hope of all believers, the promise of God, the theme of Advent and all the church year, and the reason for the coming of God into our world. Now is the time for waiting for the revelation, for its deepening, for its transforming us, for letting the potter work on us again, strengthening us to be fired and readied for use as a thing of beauty.

We begin the season with reminders of God's faithfulness and the need once again to be grateful for God's gifts of speech, knowledge, and strength. We wait now for the "day of our Lord Jesus Christ," and we rely on God's own mercy, power, and strength to keep us blameless until God's presence moves in close to us, calling us to community, to fellowship and intimacy with God. We are told to remember the faithfulness of God and to endeavor to be witnesses to Christ's coming. It is Christ who comes to save us and Christ who will rouse his power; look down from heaven and see; care for us, the vine; protect what has been planted; and make us turn toward God once again (Psalm 80). Our hope is that then we will no more withdraw from God, who will give us new life, and once again we will call upon the name of the Lord and be saved, and we will see the face of God in our midst.

The gospel of Mark uses the words of Jesus to his disciples late in his life to call us back to home, to God's face, and to hope. The words are stark, demanding: "Be constantly on the watch! Stay awake! You do not know when the appointed time will come." We are told a miniparable, a story about a man who leaves on a journey and travels abroad leaving the servants in charge, each with his own task, and orders the one at the gate to watch with a sharp eye. We are called to be these servants, whose master is about to come home. We are to be gate-keepers, watchers for the dawn, those who send up the message and rouse the community.

"Look around you!" we are exhorted. We don't know when the master will arrive — dusk, midnight, when the cock crows, or at early dawn. We are not to be caught sleeping or engaged in our own affairs and negligent of our master's work. This will be the surprise that has never been seen before: the unexpected one who will make nations quake and remind us once again that God is mindful of our every moment.

We face four weeks of waiting, but this is the theme of Mark's entire gospel: be on guard. The world is not expecting what is coming and will be caught off-guard. We will be dismayed at the timing, place, and manner of God's arrival — the horrible death, the grounding among the poor and the broken-hearted of the earth. This is the way of Mark's story, full of surprises that are either comforting or disturbing depending on whether or not we are watchful and obedient servants. Einstein once said: "The only rational way of education is to be an example — if one can't help it, a warning example." This reading from Mark's gospel, which appears just before the arrest and crucifixion of Jesus, is such an example, a warning.

We have been left in charge! Martin Luther King Jr. told his followers: "Everybody can be great because anybody can serve.... [Y]ou only need a heart full of grace." Advent is time for us to acquire a heart full of grace, to practice being servants. And as Barbara Jordan said when asked why she pushed so hard at her work for jus-

tice: "When do any of us do enough?" Are we going to be caught
asleep this year?

This first Sunday seeks to orient us and set a tone of intensity; to
wrest us out of our lethargy, our self-absorption, our slipping into
the ways of the world that lure us away from faithfulness. The Jewish community lives with this hope, and they end many a thought
and conversation with the words: "May it come soon!" And many
of their stories are helps to stay awake, no matter how long, or how
soon we will be at it.

✤ Once upon a time two rebbes were sitting together and dreaming and praying, telling stories and wondering what it would be
like when the Messiah would come, finally. One of them, the
older one, looked at his younger disciple and said, "What do you
think it will be like, that day, that day when the Messiah arrives?"

The younger man thought about it for a moment, for he had
thought about it often and had imagined many scenes and possibilities. "It will be like any other day," he said. "People will get
up and go to work, kiss one another goodbye, wish each other
shalom on the street. Then, weary, they will go home, have their
dinners, tell each other their troubles, and go to bed. But then it
will happen. That day will come. Some will awake immediately.
They will know. They will sense it, tingling their souls, stirring
their hearts. They will race to their windows, throw them open,
and shout out into the streets below. 'Wake up! Wake up! What
in the world is happening? Do you feel it?' And then it will happen. Someone will yell back, 'Yes! It's the Messiah! He's coming!
He's already in the next village! Soon he will be here! Awake!
Awake! Throw off your sleep!'"

The older rebbe looked at his friend and his eyes were shining.
"Yes," he said, "that's exactly what it will be like, at least in the
beginning. It will be a day like any other. People will get up,
pray, go to work, kiss one another goodbye, and go out into the
street. They will do their business and bless one another with
the hope of Mashiach's coming. Tired, they will head home, eat,
put their children to bed, and then . . . and then, ah, that's when
it will be different than all the other days. No one, absolutely
no one, will be able to sleep. There will be tossing and turning,
people getting up and walking around, turning on lights to read,
get a glass of warm milk, talking to each other. No one at all will
be able to sleep. That's what it will be like."

It will start on a day like any other. Are we ready? Are we faithful servants, remembering our tasks, each of us, and hoping for our master's return soon? Do we "stand in life at midnight; we [who] are always on the threshold of a new dawn" (Martin Luther King Jr.)? The image of "withered leaves carried away on the wind" appears fleetingly in Isaiah's prayer. Trees have long been associated with this season and its culmination of Christmas and Epiphany. We take a tree and decorate it, with lights, ornaments, tinsel, even dried flowers in its branches to remind us of hope, of faithfulness, of being "ever-green" and fresh. Many churches bring trees into the sanctuary and add to them week by week and then plant them in the ground after the season is over. In the Native American traditions of the North and Southwest of the United States trees are called "the tall standing ones." They have a language all their own, and those who can understand this language are considered especially gifted and powerful within the community. For the trees can hear on the wind and in the weather the songs and languages of the birds that come from afar and those that nest year after year in their branches. They overhear travelers' songs and stories. They are watchers, those who see far and remember. Even their rings of yearly growth tell of times past and what they have known.

There are many stories connected to Advent and Christmas. Here is an ancient one from the Cherokee, though I have heard it told by Salish, by Iroquois, and by others too. Sometimes it is called "Why Are Some Trees Always Green?"

✜ Once upon a time when it was still very early upon the earth, the Great Spirit decided to visit the creatures of the earth, still new from creation. Everyone was told to stay awake and to watch and wait for seven nights. And those who stayed awake were promised gifts, gifts of power. They were all excited and determined to stay awake to get this power. They all began with chatter and wonder, questioning and suggestions on how to do it. Many thought it would be easy and boasted that they'd be able to do it.

Practically everybody made it through the first night, except for a few who slipped away and didn't dare show their faces. The second night they were beginning to think it would be easy until it grew very dark and there were no stars because of the thickness of the fog. It was getting harder, eyes were drooping and heads nodding, and jerking up again and again. By the third night no one was saying much of anything, but walking around, jumping up and down, leaning up against trees and rocks, splashing water on their faces, singing aloud, anything to stay awake. By the fourth night most were asleep, out cold, not even trying any more, exhausted. And the seventh night came and only a few were still awake. And the Great Spirit came, found them sleeping, looked at those still watching and waiting, and smiled. Among the animals only the owl and the panther had stayed awake, and so they were given the power to see in the dark, and from then on, they'd be night creatures, hunting in the dark, preying on those who had fallen asleep and had to rest at night.

Among the plants and trees there were a few more that had made it through all the nights: the pine, the evergreen, the spruce, the hemlock, the cedar, the laurel, and the holly had been watchful. These were the faithful ones, and they were given the power to stay green through all the seasons of the year. And their leaves would have great medicine for the healing of the nations. They would keep their leaves and needles while all the other plants and trees, bushes and grasses would lose them and have to fall asleep through the long snows until spring woke them up again. And so it is until this day.

All the tribes of the First Peoples send their young ones out at their time of coming of age to a mountain cliff, cave opening, or high place where they are to wait and watch. If they stay awake and aware, they are to be given great power for the healing of the nations, sight in the dark, and steadfastness through the seasons. Right before they leave they are told this story so that they know that they will be rewarded generously by the Great Spirit if they are faithful. They are to remember the owl and panther and the evergreen trees. And they know how much their people need the great medicine that only comes with such watchfulness and faithfulness. So stay awake! they are commanded, and their families and friends pray for and with them while they are gone. The greatest medicine of the Spirit is peace, peace among all, peace upon all, including all creation and earth itself, all our relations.

This is the season of our vision-quests, our prophecies coming true. Stay awake! We need this great medicine of the Spirit of God which is the grace and favor of the Father in the child of peace,

Jesus Christ the Lord. This is a time for singing, for staying faithful and seeing once again the face of God. Watch and wait, with a sharp eye!

# Second Sunday of Advent

*Isaiah 40:1–5, 9–11*
*Psalm 85:9–14*
*2 Peter 3:8–14*
*Mark 1:1–8*

The words of Isaiah spring from the tender regard of our God who is Father and Redeemer: "Comfort, give comfort to my people, speak tenderly to Jerusalem, and proclaim to her that her service is at an end, her guilt is expiated!" Our service is at an end! These are words of tenderness, and what is to come is delightful, life-sustaining, and immediate. The dream is coming true as only God can make it come true, and its effects will be seen in the earth itself: "Every mountain and hill shall be made low; the rugged land shall be made a plain, the rough country, a broad valley." It is time for a shift, a shake-up, a change, time for hope and comfort to break into our worlds. It is a time of growing wonder at the goodness of God. In the words of a prayer of St. Augustine: "Lord, when I look upon mine own life it seems you have led me so carefully, so tenderly, you can not have attended to none else; but when I see how wonderfully you have led the world and are leading it, I am amazed that you have had time to attend to such as I."

And it is the time of the voice that cries out in the desert, the voice of John the Baptist. For glory is near, and the Lord proclaims that all humankind will see this glory together, as revelation. The task immediately at hand is to prepare the way for our God, make a highway of holiness, and to cry out: "Here is your God!" And again we are given a description of this God: "Like a shepherd he feeds his flock; in his arms he gathers the lambs, carrying them in his bosom, and leading the ewes with care" (Isaiah 40:11). This God is even closer to his human children, holding them, like a father, carrying them like a mother holding her own close.

The responsorial psalm in some ways is a description of what is happening, what God has been doing all these long years since the reality of death was let loose in the world by our choice not to respond with obedience. It is a description of the one, a human being, who will let us see the kindness of our God and give us the gift of salvation, of saving face, and saving grace: "Kindness and truth shall meet; justice and peace shall kiss. Truth shall spring out of the earth, and justice shall look down from heaven." Again, even the land will respond to the Coming One's presence by yielding its increase, and justice will walk before him. This last reference to justice walking before the Coming One reminds us of John the Baptist, who went before the face of Jesus, told the truth to everyone, and was bold in God's cry for repentance.

And now in this cycle we return to the beginning of Mark's gospel, where he borrows the words of the prophet Isaiah to introduce the messenger of God who burst like a storm into Israel and Jerusalem's politics, economics, and religious life. He "appears" as though an apparition, a sign out of nowhere, out of the silence and the harsh barren regions of the Judean wilderness and desert. The description in Mark's gospel is that of revolution, of a shift in power and influence, a turning of a people again toward the covenant made in the desert. It is a ritual purification, cleansing, and strengthening for what is coming soon:

> Thus it was that John the Baptizer appeared in the desert proclaiming a baptism of repentance which led to the forgiveness of sins. All the Judean countryside and the people of Jerusalem went out to him in great numbers. They were being baptized by him in the Jordan as they confessed their sins.

What happened then is what needs to happen to us today, now in our age and nation. It is about repentance as individuals, but as a people as well, peoples of parishes, cities, national churches, and the universal church — the people of God. It is a preparatory step leading to our forgiveness, our being embraced by God again.

The description of John is traditional, classic of holy men and prophets trying to get others' attention in opposition to the existing order. He wears camel hair, a leather belt around his waist. His clothing is that of a slave, the meanest and most functional of garments: the belt served the purpose of holding the chains that often were tied around the slave's hands in front and then down to the ankles. John is slave to the Holy One and knows his place and who he is: "One more powerful than I is to come after me. I am not fit to stoop and untie his sandal straps." Removing the master's sandals, waiting on his word, and obeying are the work of a slave. Yet John obeys freely and fervently, alerting others to the nearness and power of the one who approaches. He explains himself simply: "I have baptized you in water; he will baptize you in the Holy Spirit." John works on a plane of tangible symbols, but the one who comes after gives from the source of power and transformation, the Holy Spirit.

The dream of God is starting to come true in fire, spirit, water, servanthood, obedience, and true worship that bends before the one to come and repentance. If the one to come is to be welcomed, embraced, and taken as ours, then we must be ready. We must have confessed, been forgiven, be repentant, changed, and ready for the Spirit of God to enter us and lay claim to us. Advent is about preparation, purification, and restoration of our lives and our world. In Hebrew it is called the work of *tikkum olam,* repairing the world. It is the true work of all believers. It is the concrete expression of how "justice walks before him."

Pragmatics of this second week are taken straight from the readings. We are to learn how to give comfort, to speak tenderly, to proclaim others' service and bondage ended, to prepare the way of the Lord with silence, listening to the Word of God with others, easing others' burdens, revealing the glory of the Lord, and crying out. It is work that is done individually and with others, sharing resources and contacts, imagination and sustained faithfulness. John spoke out, cried out for justice on behalf of others, for that is the root work of worship. The prophets are consistent in demanding that justice and worship be fused. It is as though each is a hand, and both must be used together if anything of real truth and durability is to be shaped. On this second Sunday of Advent we are summoned by John the Baptist to remember our own baptisms and our commitments to the truth, to the Word of the Lord in the Scriptures, to our role as God's people who serve the poor in the work for justice with them, so that truly there is good news to proclaim from the highest places on earth.

A journalist named Ann Medlock founded an award called "The Giraffe Project" to honor people who courageously spoke up on behalf of others and worked for justice, people who stuck their necks out on behalf of those who were being treated badly, unfairly. We need to look around us, see who should be given the Giraffe Award, encourage them in their work, and stand with them: people who work with immigrants caught in cold-hearted rules and systems that are intent on keeping people out rather than welcoming them into this country; people who are advocates on behalf of children on the street, laboring in fields and factories, as prostitutes bought and sold in markets around the world; those who work for treaties banning land mines, nuclear weapons, poison gases, and pesticides; those who work for the rights of farmworkers and those struggling in service industries at minimum wage. All these people in their daily lives and their dedication remember the dream of "kindness and truth meeting and justice and peace kissing, truth springing out of the earth while justice looks down from heaven" (Psalm 85). All of these people have a streak of the spirit of John the Baptizer in their souls and use their portion of spirit to prepare a way for God in our world. There is a Chinese saying that can teach us in small ways how to remember this dream of justice and peace kissing: "Putting on clothes, remember the weaver's work; eating daily food, remember the farmer's toil. Guide the blind over the bridge and the lame one over the threshold."

We are soon to come face-to-face with God, the one who plays with water, spirit, and fire. Our God will look like us, be one of us, and we must prepare the way: we must come face-to-face with one another and with ourselves, our sin, and our compliance with injustice and evil all around us. This is the work of John the Baptizer, who cries out and calls us to the waters of repentance, preparing us for the shepherd who will reach out to embrace us and gather us together as one community and family of God. Another Chinese saying reminds us: "We are no more virtuous without exhortation than does a bell sound without being struck."

The reading from the letter of Peter swings between exhortation and hope, instilling the fear of the Lord and a demand for change and emphasizing the perilous nature of time, including the present. A rather humorous story can put this in focus.

✣ Once upon a time a little boy was playing with his toys at the foot of the stairs in his parents' house. Towering above him was a great old grandfather clock that had been in the family for generations. It would chime the quarter-hour, the half-hour, the quarter-hour again, and then the hour, striking the number of hours. Just at the moment it began to strike the hour, the mechanism jammed, and it counted ten, eleven, twelve, and then continued past to thirteen, fourteen, fifteen, sixteen. The boy listened, for he had been practicing his new skill of counting, and looked up in amazement at the clock. He jumped up and ran excited into the family room where his mother and father were reading. He shouted, "Listen! It's later than it's ever been before! Come and see!"

Our readings are about that marvelous, surprising, and hard to believe reality — it is later than it's ever been before! Listen! Come and see!

We are given a lesson in time from God's vantage point: one day is as one thousand years to the Lord. This certainly puts us and our history, our theological and political issues, in perspective! And one thousand years is as a day: it is all one moment. God doesn't delay in making the promises come true, though from our angle it sometimes seems like a long delay. No, God is waiting and hoping and doing everything in his power to get us ready for what is coming so that we will not miss it, be caught inattentive, or worse, disbelieving and rejecting what is to come.

At our baptisms of water and the Spirit we committed ourselves to a lifestyle, a lifetime, of repentance, of coming to love, serve, honor, and obey God's will in our lives. Many of us are in sore need of God's patience and generosity, for we are not ready to meet God face-to-face, either in the person of Jesus Christ the Lord who will judge on that day ("the day of God when the heavens will be destroyed in flames and the elements will melt away in a blaze") or in other human beings in whom, "according to God's promise, the justice of God will reside."

Advent is the first season of the year liturgically and spiritually, out of synch with the rest of the world's time so that we can begin again, change our routines, and begin to "be holy in our conduct and devotion, looking for the coming of that day and trying to hasten it!" And the interim is crucial not just to its coming, but to its outcome. We are called "beloved" and told to live in the interim "without stain or defilement, and at peace in his sight." In some ways this Sunday is a rude awakening, a jarring reminder of how much we have forgotten and how once again, like the people of old, we have "wandered away from our God, like sheep oblivious to the sound of the shepherd's voice." Again a story can help us understand.

✢ Every now and then there is a story of a certain kind of problem on a freeway. The problem usually occurs at a spot where there are many overpasses of varying heights. Each overpass usu-

ally has a posting of how high the overpass is and what you
need for clearance, but one of the big rigs gets stuck under one,
wedged in tight. Nobody seems to know exactly what to do to
unwedge it, short of pushing it out the way it entered. Then a
small child, or in some cases an outpatient from a mental hospi-
tal, makes the obvious suggestion: let some air out of the tires.
Once that's done, the truck, now a couple of inches lower, can
squeeze through.

This Sunday, the presence of John the Baptist, the old words of
Isaiah, and the ringing call of Peter's message to his community all
serve the same purpose: to deflate us a little so that we can squeeze
into the season of repentance and lowliness.

It takes some letting go, some getting lower on the scale, some
deflation so that we can get a truer perspective on our lives and the
world around us. We have to learn to see the new heavens and new
earth that are already here in pockets and places: in a child, in community, in disciples, in the poor provided for generously, in sacrifice,
in a maid servant who waits on the Word of the Lord, in prophets
and kings who must learn to repent. Advent is preparation for seeing, for living with God face-to-face, and a time to look at ourselves
in light of God's time. And it begins with each of us individually
called to repent, to confess our sins, and to turn and wait for the
presence of justice that kisses peace — for then kindness and truth
will meet and embrace.

And we must all do this as a people being gathered and returning home, because we have been scattered and disoriented through
overly individualizing our relationships with God. On the island of
Barra, off the coast of Scotland, I heard a relevant story told by an
old woman who rarely left the island. She told me the story in an
old-age home where I went to tell stories and hear Mass in Irish.
Afterwards she took me aside and told me I could use this one because, she said, many folk like to do their praying on their own and
can't be bothered much with church and organized religion like they
used to.

✤ Once upon a time there was a pastor who inherited a church
on a large island, but that was about it — there was a church
building, but not much else. There were a few old souls who
came regularly, but most of the younger ones stayed away. They
were too busy with the fields and animals, with the new satellite

television dishes, videos, and their own business. And when the pastor would inquire after them in town or in the pub they'd excuse themselves with the explanation that they prayed better without all those people around them. They did better with their own quiet along the strand or by their own fireplace or kitchen table after everyone else had gone to bed.

So the pastor started visiting them one by one. He'd sit by the fire, drink tea, chat about the price of grain or sheep, and not mention religion. The fire would be crackling warm while the wind gusted outside, and the pastor would lean over and take a twig out of the fire. He was careful to take one that was glowing hot and burning well, and he would lay it on the edge of the stone fireplace and let it sit. He'd continue with the conversation and say not a word about the twig. And as they'd talk the twig would cool down; the glow would begin to fade; the twig would smoke and eventually die out. When that happened the pastor would stop in midsentence, look his parishioner in the eye, and put the twig back on the fire, holding it until it caught again. And then he'd take his leave.

The first man got the message. Next day a woman did. Pretty soon the story started getting around, and by the end of the month the church was packed.

Margaret smiled sweetly when she told me this and said, "I'm sure you'll find a way to use it, Dearie. It seems all your stories have a bit of that fire in them." She patted my hand and walked away, leaving me thoroughly delighted with this story, which I pass on to you. Advent is something we do together. We dream, repent, turn our faces toward God together.

There are warnings in this season, but they are always tempered with dreamings. So I will end with a story about dreams, and again about trees. The story is available as a children's book called *The Tale of the Three Trees,* a traditional Appalachian folktale, which I heard many years ago from a ninety-year-old woman during a long visit to the mountains of western Kentucky. It's a good way to get into Advent and reflect upon our lives and what God wants to do with us. This version was originally written for an article in *Church* magazine (winter 1992).

During the time I lived with the old lady, I watched her as she talked to trees and walked among them, and she told me everything she knew about them (which was substantial). Once, she even taught me to listen to the trees talking, the leaves and the bark of a couple of them rubbing and sighing and moaning softly against each other. She had only a few treasures in her house, and one of them was a box, carved intricately, sanded, and rubbed religiously practically every day that I was there. She explained that she had made the box for herself, after hearing a preacher tell this story. Since then I've heard the story told at storytelling fests, but never as I heard it that first time, sitting in that woman's spare bedroom, holding her handmade box.

✣  Once upon a time there were thousands of trees in this valley and holler — tall, elegant ones, pine, oak, fir, spruce, ash, lots of ash. The trees all had dreams. In late afternoons or on winter nights when they couldn't sleep for the sound of cracking ice and limbs, they'd tell each other their dreams. One tree wanted to travel, to see the world, even cross oceans (he'd heard about great waters from birds that nested in his pockets). Another wanted desperately to be a treasure box, to store fine jewels and be treasured by someone. Another couldn't really understand those dreams. She just wanted to be a tree, to climb toward the clouds, spend nights with her head in the stars and her roots all tangled up with others, waiting for the birds to return and the seasons to pass. She found each of the birds so different, so rich, so varied, she knew she'd never grow tired of just being a tree and growing old, real old.

But then the humans came [the old woman had said men] and they laid waste the hills, denuding them indiscriminately. They took all the trees, the ones with dreams and the ones without dreams. They cut them down, made lumber and splints and great logs, and hauled them all off the mountain. The trees were all broken in spirit, crushed, and reduced to nothing much.

One was carted away to another country and eventually sold cheaply to some fishermen and made into a boat for commercial use. It saw another part of the world, a small lake in a nondescript country. Another was sent off to some shepherds, sold just as cheaply for fence posts, but in fact it was never used for a fence post. Leftover, it was made into a feed box for animals sheltered in caves in the winter months. Not quite a treasure box! A third tree was left nearly whole and stacked in a municipal supply house, just collecting dust. So much for dreams, the trees all thought to themselves. So much for just being trees.

The old woman paused and looked at me hard, saying, "You know, when I was your age I was full of dreams, longings, and hopes, but they died — or more than likely other folk killed 'em, trampled on 'em, and ignored me and so helped the dreams to an early death. You'll see. But," she went on, "I still had a lot to learn about living and dreaming — as you do."

✢ Years went by and the boat was wearing out and the feed box was well used and the other tree was still there, stacked on the bottom of a pile. Then one night a young couple took shelter in a cave. Shepherds' kin had let them use it. The woman was blue with cold, in labor for hours even before she got there, riding a donkey. The cave was full of straw, manure, and lambs and goats and other critters in from the winter cold. She cried out and screamed and finally gave birth to a child, a boy. The father bent and lifted the body, wrapped him up, cleaned out the feed box, and placed the baby in it — a make-do crib. But somehow the feed box knew it held a treasure, a child, a real child. Oh, lambs had been in it before, and spiders and mice and even birds, but a child! Who might it be? What would it grow up to be? The box always wondered and remembered that night and the ones that followed, because the family stayed a good while.

Then all of a sudden they were gone one night, rushing, fearful, and in great distress, running for their lives. But the box remembered. It had had its treasure. And for the first time in years, the tree — now a treasure chest — wondered how its friends and their dreams were faring.

It was decades later when the boat, now worn and beginning to leak from constant use, was taken out again during one long night that turned into day. Without any preparation, the fishermen then took it out again. The boat was crowded and lopsided. There was a man asleep in the prow and all the others sat in the stern. The boat labored just to stay afloat and then, wouldn't you know it, a threatening storm came on hard and fast. The boat was sure it was going to be swamped and overturned. It would go down, never to come up again.

But the sleeping man awoke and stood up in the boat facing the wind and waves and sang to the sea and the storm, blessing God and telling the weather to mind its ways and be careful of his friends and their boat. And the wind listened! It died down, the waves settled, the sun came out, dancing on the water, and the boat marveled along with the fishermen in it.

Who was this man? He wasn't a fisherman. The earth, the air, and the water all responded to him lovingly. Suddenly the boat knew it had seen the world, the whole world, encompassed in a human face and body and in the eyes of awe and faith. It, too, remembered its other friends and hoped for their dreams to come true.

The third tree lay stacked and left alone. Then one morning other logs and planks were shifted and moved aside and some soldiers grabbed the lonely tree, dragging it out into the street, into bright daylight where it hadn't been in so long. It started to rejoice, but then recoiled in horror. What were they doing? They lifted the tree high and dropped it heavily onto the shoulders of a man. He was already bent and bleeding badly and in terrible shape. The tree was roped onto him, yoked, and he began to walk (if you could call it that!) through the streets of the city with a mob pushing and shoving, screaming and spitting and cursing at him all the way. It got worse. He staggered and they hit him; they pulled in somebody else to help him.

Then they reached a hill outside the city, a garbage dump, unroped him, and threw him and the tree on the ground. They yanked him and held him down as they drove spikes into him and through the tree. The tree couldn't believe this was happening to both of them. It was awful! Again the spikes went in, accompanied by laughing and jostling. Then the tree with the man nailed tightly to it was hauled up with ropes and shoved into place, a crossbar now, affixed to an upright beam.

Soon the tree was soaked with blood; pieces of the man's skin stuck to it. The man moved, tried to breathe, to shift his weight, but there was nothing the tree could do to help him. Who was he? Why did so many people hate him? Onlookers came and went, some with pity and care, most with curiosity and callousness, some even vicious and cruel.

He took a long time dying (at least the tree thought so). His friends came and lifted him down with a lot more tenderness than he'd been hung up. The tree was taken down too and left on the hill. It rained afterward; the sky got very dark; the ground shook; and there was a terrible feeling in the air. The tree was lost, forgotten, abused, having been used for something so beyond belief. "Why didn't I just die too?" thought the tree.

It went on like that for days and nights, and then the ground shook again. The tree sensed the earth shaking, but with delight, with fresh hope, with exultation.

He came early that morning, just after dark, walking barefoot on the ground, delicately, but surely as though he knew nothing would hurt him again. He stooped beside the tree and said, "Thank you for your compassion and for being my bed, even if it was one of pain." He knew it had been hard for the tree too. The tree started to bloom right there in front of him, couldn't help it, just had to. He was delighted and smiled, which made the tree bulge with sap and life. He broke off a twig to take with him and said he had always had a fondness for wood.

That was the story. She said, "You're a smart girl, put it together." I thought about it for months. But right before I left her house, she took out that box again and let me hold it. And she said (clearly she was preaching to me) that it was important that I get it right: "Remember your dreams. Remember the trees. Remember."

Remember God's dreams in Isaiah's words, in John's clarion call, in Peter's letter, in God face-to-face with us in Jesus Christ. Remember it's time for justice and peace to kiss and truth and kindness to embrace. Remember it's time for us to turn and face each other, ourselves, and God again. Remember, it's time to hasten that day!

# Third Sunday of Advent

*Isaiah 61:1–2, 10–11*
*Psalm: Luke 1:46–50, 53–54*
*1 Thessalonians 5:16–24*
*John 1:6–8, 19–28*

John is attracting attention and because the people are stirred up, even the authorities are taking notice. Hope is catching and it is loose in the land, set loose by words and the impassioned belief that God is paying attention to what is going on in history and that God has his own plans, as he always has had, for earth and those he has made to live in peace on his earth. And the lines are being drawn, witnesses called and gauntlets thrown down. It starts even before the child is born. John is his herald, his "point guard," his trumpet call, and his servant who tells the truth, but he is not the one the people have been awaiting. He is not the truth or the light, just a person who testifies, someone who gives his word publicly and stands on it so that others must decide for themselves who this person is who is heralded. And it is time for us to decide too.

Mark's gospel is confrontational, with questions that demand that we decide who we stand with, what we believe in, and how we will act. And since it is such a short gospel, the church often borrows from the gospel of John, equally aggressive and sure in its tone and announcements about Jesus, to supplement it during the seasons of this year's readings. The style of the gospels lends to the drama of the story and the intensity with which we are pushed to choose now where we stand in relation to the light that has come into the world. We are pushed to let the light come into our lives and world, our history, as once it came in the person of Jesus Christ.

This third Sunday is Gaudate Sunday, calling us to rejoice and exalt, and the first reading from Isaiah lists many causes for our rejoicing. The first portion of the reading is always applied to Jesus himself because in the synagogue in Nazareth he proclaims this passage as his mission and calling. It is the announcement that a prophet is in the people's midst, and Jesus uses the ancient formula of declaring that it is the Spirit of God that has summoned him and given him the words. But Jesus goes still further and says that the Spirit of God "is upon" him, has anointed him, and he carries that power and authority in his words and person. The message of what God is going to do, is already doing in Jesus' presence in the world and his person, is cause for the masses to rejoice exceedingly for it spells the end of their oppression, suffering, and humiliation. There are five parts to the altering of history, the saving of humanity, and the hard work of the Son of God among us.

"He has sent me to bring glad tidings to the lowly." This is the first priority, and it echoes the glad tidings of the angels to the shepherds keeping watch over their flock by night when Jesus is born. Originally these tidings and hope are given to "all those upon whom God's favor rests." Now it is simply "the lowly." The lowly are the bottom of the pile, the dregs of society. And the good news for all these people who have to work incredibly hard just to survive is simple: freedom! Freedom from poverty, starvation, homelessness, sickness, illiteracy, slavery, dehumanization, violence.

While the first step involves healing physical sufferings, the second is "to heal the brokenhearted," although Jesus leaves this phrase from Isaiah out of his proclamation and adds another. Along with the necessities for living with dignity will come hope and solace for those who are anxious, discouraged, terrified, lonely, and humiliated. These words often refer to the lowly and the poor who suffer all the indignities of injustice and oppression as well as the psychological, emotional, and religious traumas that plague people of all social levels and economic backgrounds.

Then we are told the next two steps in the program of reform and radical altering of society for those who rely on the Spirit of God: "To proclaim liberty to the captives and release to the prisoners." Just the mention of these two projects can instill fear and trepidation in many who hear the message. The reaction is "What? You have to be kidding! That's dangerous and stupid, asking for trouble, not fair." There is often especially strong reaction to the reference to prisoners. Amnesty and freedom are marvelous if you are the one who has done wrong, but other things altogether if you are intent on revenge or securing the stiffest penalty possible. But "captives" are mentioned first, and that would seem to be a reference to those caught in war, the innocents, those who do not benefit from either side's victories. These are slaves, as in the days of Egypt, in bondage to nations and powers, corporations and caste systems that keep people as statistics in socioeconomic and ethnic, racial and religious brackets, and not as human beings. And as for the prisoners, that category can include all those literally in jails and prisons for political and religious activities, human rights activists or agrarian reformers and educators, writers and community organizers of indigent and minority groups, as well as those imprisoned by unjust banking systems, high interest rates, unfair housing laws, low wages, underemployment, and those without the language, culture, or resources to survive in systems that function primarily for elite influential groups in a society. The "captives" and the "prisoners" are thus all the people in any society whose lives and circumstances are decided as much by their status (their lack of education, health care, inheritance, connections...) as by what they may have done or not done that is against the law. In any case, there is an edge, a radical transformation of society, a change of priorities announced in the words.

The last step has to do with a specifically religious reality: "To announce a year of favor from the Lord and a day of vindication by our God." This refers specifically to the Jubilee Year that was proclaimed by law, by God's design, originally every seven years, then every fifty years, for the Israelite people in honor and remembrance of their sojourn in Egypt. It was to be a year-long celebration of Sabbath, of liberation and promise for the land itself and for all those in the land of Israel, whether they were members of the covenant or not. All debts were to be canceled; all prisoners were to be freed and allowed to either go home or settle in the land. Land was to be redistributed so that no one was without, and people were to be able to buy back their family's heritage. The basic concept behind this was that no one owned land in perpetuity, for the land belonged first to God and was given in trust to the people as a whole. And there were to be no poor, no destitute, for no one was to know the experience of slavery that all had been subjected to in Egypt. The Jubilee was a built-in restorative principle that refocused the primacy of the people's relationship to God. It was the tangible moment of grace, of God's victory over evil, individual and national selfishness, and humanity's disobedience and idolatry. It was a glimpse of God's ultimate vindication in creating the earth and all people.

And this is what Advent is all about — the victory of God, the coming of justice into the world, the comfort of God, and a cause for rejoicing. And Isaiah's words continue telling us that "our God has clothed us in a robe of salvation and wrapped us in a mantle of justice." We are wrapped in this shining garment so that we can witness to others about the light of our God. What does our mantle of justice look like? We were, of course, wrapped in a white garment at our baptisms, clothed with heartfelt mercy by our God, a sign of our commitment to being faithful disciples of Jesus Christ and children of light.

In his letter to the Thessalonians, Paul emphasizes these points in a prayer that is reminiscent of our baptismal promises and consecration to God. First, it is a command to undertake specific duties, and then it is a prayer for all of us that ends in a confession of faith in Jesus Christ:

Do not stifle the spirit. Do not despise prophecies. Test everything; retain what is good. Avoid any semblance of evil.

May the God of peace make you perfect in holiness. May you be preserved whole and entire, spirit, soul, and body, irreproachable at the coming of our Lord Jesus Christ. He who calls us is trustworthy, therefore he will do it.

These words could refer immediately to the prophecies of Isaiah and to the anointing of the Spirit calling us to work to make these glad tidings come true and to hasten the day of God's victory over evil and our unfaithfulness. The images of Isaiah are intimate ones of a bridegroom crowned with glory and a bride wearing the wealth of her family and of earth springing forth like a garden blooming out of due course in winter. It is time out of time, not the usual pattern of life but a radical alteration. Jean Vanier, the founder of the L'Arche communities, has said: "Our hope is that the winter of humanity will gradually be transformed to the bursting forth of love, for it is to this that we are called."

But this description of Isaiah says nothing about a gradual transformation. Instead, it will be a time when justice and praise spring up before all the nations. It is a judgment that shines with glory and radiant hope for all who have waited and so fervently needed and hoped for justice and God's vindication. It is time for us to "rejoice heartily in the Lord, in our God who is the joy of our souls," for this is the new year, a year of grace and favor because of God's faithfulness to his promises and because Jesus Christ our hope is in the world and has sprung forth into humanity and dwells with us and will come again to embrace us all again.

And so we borrow the lowly woman Mary's song of praise and joy to sing on this Sunday so close to the appearance of God's son. This song is worship of God, acknowledgment of God's great deeds and the wonder God brings on earth even now to those who fear him. It echoes the angels' song at the beginning of the book of the prophet Isaiah when he hears the choirs of heaven singing: "Holy, holy, holy, Lord God of hosts."

Now the song of praise is in the mouth of the woman who declares the glory of God in our life and flesh. "My being proclaims the greatness of the Lord, my spirit finds joy in God my Savior." This is to be our attitude for the rest of the time before the birth of our Savior is experienced again in the power of the Spirit's grace and favor. We must not forget that this season is about the greatness of our God's love and mercy for us, seen in conjunction with our often faithless response and lack of gratitude. Faithfulness puts us out of step with all of history and yet our service of the glad tidings draws all the nations of the world into the time of God's graciousness.

But there is a warning element too: "The hungry he has given every good thing, while the rich he has sent empty away," and "his mercy is from age to age on those who fear him." Our choices are crucial.

With whom do we stand? We now come to John the Baptizer

again, this "man sent by God, so that through him all of us might believe — but only to testify to the light, for he himself was not the light" (John 1:6–8). This is the crux of the matter. Are we witnesses to the light? Do we testify to the light? The priests and Levites from Jerusalem, the temple authorities, want to know who John is, just as the world wants to know who we are and where our allegiances stand. And John refuses all their inquiries and suggestions. He is not the Messiah, not Elijah, not the prophet. He is not so easily fixed. He is, quoting Isaiah, only the voice, the voice crying out in the desert that echoes and is carried by the wind: "Make straight the way of the Lord!"

The whole tenor of the encounter is that of an inquisition, of a court of law, of threat and dangerous sparing between conflicting powers of the world and the Spirit. And those who are in power and those who serve them keep hounding John, needing a niche to put him in so that they can deal with him, dismiss him, or report on his intentions, report back to those who are heavily invested in their positions of authority over the people, religiously and spiritually. But John will not let them pigeon-hole him. He is adamant: the baptism he offers is preliminary, only a shadow of the power of the one he precedes. "There is one among you whom you do not recognize," he says. There is no recognition because there is no hope, no desire, no repentance, no transformation, no real praise of God.

John is clear about his own relationship as the voice, as the herald, as the prophet who precedes "the one who is to come after." His role is one of servant, of adoration, and of worship; nothing more. He is not worthy to kneel before the Coming One and unfasten his sandal strap. This is a man of power, of passionate devotion to the honor of God, of forceful words of condemnation and fear of the Lord toward an errant and soulless people grown lax and self-absorbed. They are blind to the light, refusing to believe in the promises of God, giving testimony to disbelief, disobedience, divided loyalties, and living in ways that serve more to dishearten others in need than to give them hope.

And so we are confronted by John and called to witness to the light, to give testimony that is just and true, and to be humble before the one who comes to do God's will. We are not "to stifle the Spirit or despise prophecies" as many of those at the time of John were doing, as many of us who claim to be religious still do.

There is a rather disturbing story that I tell not only during Advent but also in Lent that puts us in our place and allows us to

see ourselves, perhaps as John the Baptizer would see us if we were
questioning him today on who he is. It is about light, about justice,
and about what we are searching for in this season and who or what
we think is coming toward us. It is called "The Cottage of Candles," a Jewish story told by Howard Schwartz, who is probably the
most distinguished collector of Jewish tales. In telling the story, he
notes a line from Proverbs: "The soul of man is the lamp of God"
(Proverbs 20:27). This version is from a collection of tales by Zevu-
lon Qort, from Ben Zion Asherov from Afghanistan, found in the
Israeli Folktale Archives (7830). There are also similar stories told
in Latin America, such as one called "La Muerta." This is the way
I tell it.

✤ Once upon a time there was a young man who was passionately
interested in finding justice. He studied the concept legally and
religiously in all the traditions and was intrigued by it, wondering if it really existed in reality, if there was indeed any justice
on the earth. And so he set out to look for justice. He looked in
the places of power, palaces, institutions of law and education,
places of worship, and among those with wealth, prestige, and
influence, but he could not find justice. Oh, some people practiced acts of justice on occasion, but more often than not it was
because it suited them and their interests not because they believed in justice, and certainly not because they sought justice for
all peoples.

So next he went among those who were students of the law
and their teachers, masters and disciples of various faiths, and
the devout, no matter what their social status might be. And
again he was disappointed. It seemed to him that they were more
interested in defining the concept, discussing how it worked and
where it was used, and the penalties and rewards for its practice
or disobedience than in experiencing it and making it a reality in
the world around them.

And so next he went to the highways and byways, among the
ragged and destitute who wandered in search of justice, though
they certainly would never be able to say that was what they
needed and wanted. He visited and stayed in hovels and inns,
small villages and farms, in the local folks' homes, among the
poorest of the poor. He was distressed to find that though they
lacked justice, they were often more interested in acquiring material goods than the virtue and practice of justice. It seemed

that no matter who he was with — soldier, farmer, statesmen, merchant, man or woman, even children — generally, justice was not on their minds. And so he became disheartened as he grew older and traveled more and found little or no trace of justice.

He was heading home, finally, ready to give up, and on the way found himself in a deep, dark wood. He had been traveling for days and was hopelessly lost in the forest, with no sense of which way was home. And then he came into a clearing that had a rundown, ramshackle house standing lopsided in the high grass. He went and peered in one of the dusty windows and was surprised to see a great light coming from inside. It was blurred but was definitely a great shining light. He went to the door and was equally startled to find it ajar. He pushed and it swung open easily. He found himself in a place most strange, a room full of light. He wandered around and found that there was room after room after room of the lights.

There were endless floor-to-ceiling shelves that stretched, it seemed, forever. On the shelves were tiny oil candles, countless numbers of them. They burned, some brightly, furiously quick, slowly, sputtering and going out; others flaring up. He looked more closely and saw that the wicks were standing in containers. Most of them were clay or tin, though there were others made of silver, bronze, and gold. The wicks were short, stubby, thick, or thin depending on the kind of vessel they were standing in. And the oil was thick, slow burning, smoky, with some candles having many inches worth and others only a few drops. He was fascinated by the light and the utter silence and wandered from room to room, marveling at the number of the candles and the rooms that flowed one into the other. The place was certainly larger than what he could have imagined from outside.

And then as he was looking intently at some of the candles he was aware that he was not alone. Beside him was a figure, pale and white, tall and very quiet, dressed entirely in white, even with white hair and skin, with flowing robes and mantle. He turned with a bit of fear, but the figure was serene. He stuttered and said, "I've never seen anything like this. What is this place? I have traveled for years, traveled far and wide, and never have I seen anything like this before. I have been searching for justice and the search has taken me to distant lands and in places of wonder and dirt. Where am I?"

The figure looked at him and said, "This is the Cottage of Candles. Every candle you see here is the soul of a human being. All the humans alive now in the whole world are here. They live and they die. As you can see, some are strong and have many years ahead of them. Others have very little time, and some are dying even as we speak." And one on the shelf in front of them sputtered and went out.

The searcher for justice was stunned and silent, thinking of course what his own candle looked like, where it was. And he turned and asked, "And my own?"

"Yes," she said, "that is why you have been brought here. Come." And she took him deeper and deeper into the maze of rooms, finally stopping at a shelf of candles. She pointed to one at eye level. "That," she said, "is yours." She indicated one that stood in a simple clay vessel, but it stood in only a couple of drops of oil; its wick was bent and even now having difficulty standing.

He gasped! Was his life so soon to be finished? What had he done with his life? Looking for justice all these years and not finding it, had he wasted his life on something that didn't exist? He was appalled and frightened. And then he noticed a vessel of bronze right next to his own, its wick thick and strong, standing in many inches of pure-burning oil. He stuttered, almost unthinkingly, "Whose is that?"

She looked at him hard and answered, "That you are not given to know. Only your own."

He looked again at his candlewick and fear rose in his heart. How long did he have? If only he had just a bit more time, to live, to do all the things he hadn't had a chance to do while he was so intent on searching! "Oh, God!" he felt himself crying out, in despair or hope, not knowing just which it might be.

He turned and realized that once again he was alone, utterly alone. He looked around the room. There was no one. He looked in the room he had come from and there was no one. The figure, whoever it had been, was gone. He came back and looked again at his candle and at the one right beside it and a thought sprung into his mind, "What if . . . ?" No, he couldn't. But he looked again. That candle had so much oil. It stood so strongly in its bronze container, and the wick was tall, burning so slowly in comparison to his own. Just a drop or two. Just enough to give him a little time, to sort things out, to put things in order. It wouldn't matter for the other had so much. And so, he furtively looked around again — he was still alone. He picked up the other vessel and tipped it toward his own. He reminded himself, just a drop or two, nothing much. And as the oil began to slip toward his own candleholder, he was suddenly and forcibly grabbed. The figure was back, and she had an iron grip on his arm. The eyes in the face were deadly and the voice soft and serious, questioned him, "Is this the kind of justice you were looking for?" The grip tightened until he thought his arm would break. He was forced to his knees in pain, the eyes never leaving his face in accusation. And then, in an instant, everything vanished. Everything.

The figure was gone. The cottage of candles was gone. All the light was gone. He stood alone in the dark wood, and all he could hear was the moaning sound of the trees all around him. He was frozen in place. All he could think of was what he had tried to do and how much time he had left. And the sound of the trees whispering and sighing in the dark.

It's a story that stops us in our tracks. What kind of justice are we looking for? Are we looking for something we have concocted in our heads, an illusive dream, or do we work at practicing justice, beginning with the corporal works of mercy? The story is full of feelings and questions, much like John the Baptizer's presence engendered in the people of the temple, of Jerusalem, and all of Israel. Are we ready for the Anointed of the Lord, the Holy One of God, the light to come into our world? In the words of the story, "Is this the kind of justice you were looking for?"

But the brighter side of this Sunday can give us great cause to rejoice. There is another story that is often told during the Jewish festival of lights.

✤ Once upon a time when Abraham Ibn Ezra was traveling and preaching, he found himself visiting the king of Egypt. He was treated royally and ushered into a room with the most incredible paintings. These, he was told, were painted by the illustrious master Karaguz hundreds of years before. They were priceless, irreplaceable. Abraham noticed that one wall was conspicuously empty, and he motioned toward it. The king explained that Karaguz had died before he completed the paintings, and no one dared to match his skill and expertise. Abraham was silent a moment and then spoke boldly, "I can create something for that wall that will surpass by far the other paintings." The king was incredulous. "Allow me a few days, curtain off the area, and give me privacy. I need some things, rags, powdered silver, antimony." He went to work. He mixed a paste of the silver and antimony. He covered the wall with it and then worked hard rubbing it into the surface. After it dried, it was polished. And he called the sultan in to see. The king was stunned. It was true — the wall was beautiful. It was a mirror that reflected the other paintings, and now they seemed to be alive and moving, vibrant and so radiant. Now all the paintings looked truer.

This is what we are to do: reflect the light, witness and testify to the light, and rejoice at the presence of the light in the world, even if it is still hidden. Today we remember that God still wants to do great things for us and fill our spirits with joy. God wants to bless us and bring us mercy. And he uses the weak, the lowly, a simple peasant girl wrapped in light and freedom, a prophet from the desert robed in words of justice and passion. God wraps us in a mantle of justice and a robe of salvation through our baptism and wants us to shine forth with his light announcing and making ready the way. It is time to pray in the words of John Baillie, "O Light that never fades, as the light of day now streams through these windows and floods this room, so let me open to you the windows of my heart, that all my life may be filled by the radiance of your presence.... Let there be nothing within me to darken the brightness of the day."

# Fourth Sunday of Advent

*2 Samuel 7:1–5, 8–11, 16*
*Psalm 89:2–5, 27–29*
*Romans 16:25–27*
*Luke 1:26–38*

There is a Chinese saying that a good question is like beating a bell. It interrupts the silence and makes us listen. In the first reading from the book of Samuel the Lord puts a question to David through the prophet Nathan. David, we are told, is "settled in his palace" and resting from all his labors, wars, campaigns and that the Lord "has given him rest from his enemies on every side." David is living in the lap of luxury. While at leisure he begins to mull over his destiny and fortunes. He realizes that he is "living in a house of cedar while the ark of God dwells in a tent!" This statement reveals much about David. He does think of God, but only as an afterthought, long after his own comfort has been taken care of. He is musing aloud, and the prophet Nathan, in attendance, comments on his ruminations, saying, "Go, do whatever you have in mind, for the Lord is with you." It seems that Nathan thinks like the king on this matter. But that night the Lord visits Nathan, and it turns out that neither Nathan nor David understands the Lord at all, for God tells Nathan to tell "his servant David, 'Thus says the Lord: Should you build me a house to dwell in?'" That is the question that is like a bell pealing and chiming out, shattering the still air.

The Lord has a few more things to say, revealing and reminding the king of who he is, who put him there, and what his place is. David appears to have forgotten what God has done for him and that his task is to serve. It is God who moves history and causes kings to rise and fall and dynasties to remain in power. God's words through Nathan to David are a litany of important things that David should keep in mind when he thinks about his priorities and what he is doing for God. It is interesting to note that the Lord comes first to Nathan and then through him to David. Nathan is God's intermediary. David is put in his place with this speech or sermon:

> It was I who took you from the pasture and from the care of the flock to be commander of my people Israel. I have been with you wherever you went, and I have destroyed all your enemies before you. And I will make you famous like the great ones of the earth. I will fix a place for my people Israel; I will plant them so that they may dwell in their place without further disturbance. Neither shall the wicked continue to afflict them as they did of old, since the time I first appointed judges over my people Israel. I will give you rest from all your enemies. The Lord also reveals to you that he will establish a house for you. Your house and your kingdom shall endure forever before me; your throne shall stand firm forever. (2 Samuel 7:8–11, 16)

While David has architecture in mind, God is thinking in terms of something much broader, longer-lasting, and more dynamic — of

a house, a lineage, a secure dwelling place, and a peaceful domain.
David has it all wrong. Once again he has fallen into the trap of
forgetting who God is and forgetting that David is where he is today
and that the people are at peace because of God, not David. So
God, once again, tells the prophet to inform David and the people
of the promises of God and what God still intends to do for this
slow-hearted and slow-to-understand people. God will fix a place for
them and will give them rest, peace, and a house that will endure
forever and a name that will stand firm in spite of history, wars,
exile, and destruction of the monarchy. David has been told through
the prophet where he stands; even better, David should be kneeling
with God. The tone is solemn, declarative, and sure, each statement
beginning with, "It is I.... It was I.... I will...." This God is and
has been working in the past and is forming the future as surely
as creation was originally formed. It is all in the mind and hand of
God, who is the only king in Israel, no matter who sits on the throne
in His name, as the servant-leader of his people. God's goodness
surpasses whatever King David or anyone has in mind.

Traditionally, the composition of many of the psalms has been
assigned to David, and today's response is a fitting one. Awareness
invades David's soul, and he comes to realize that as much as the
Lord has been active in his life — from the time he was a simple
shepherd in the hills of Judea, through his battles and triumph as
king, in the shadows of his life when he would forget whom he
belonged to and served and when God took second place in his affections and attention — God is not finished with him yet and will
continue to act in his life, past his death, and on into the future generations. So David sings: "Forever I will sing the goodness of the
Lord." The psalm itself is a dialogue back and forth between God
and David. David begins and God responds with the reiteration of
his promises, telling David that one day he will call him "Father, my
God, the Rock, my savior." We too sing out the goodness of God
because long centuries later we have known more of the goodness
of our God than David, his chosen king, could ever have imagined.
It is our duty and gift to "forever...sing of the goodness of the
Lord."

In his letter to the Romans, Paul hints of the significance
of God's promises to David. Paul describes the gospel that he
preaches and proclaims, this gospel "which reveals the mystery hidden for many ages but now manifested through the writings of the
prophets, and at the command of the eternal God, made known to

all the Gentiles that they may believe and obey." This mystery, the meaning of all the promises, is a person who draws us into a relationship with God and initiates us into wisdom and strength. The mystery's heart is Jesus Christ, who is the goodness and the glory of God revealed to us. This is the one who gives rest from all our enemies and is with us, enduring and standing firm forever. This is God's kindness established among us. Before this mystery, before the goodness of God we must sing, worship, and adore. It is the only fitting response. The poet Rumi writes of this attitude we must have before God's goodness:

> Today like every other day, we wake up empty and
> frightened.
> Don't open the door to the study and begin reading.
> Take down a musical instrument.
> Let the beauty we love be what we do.
> There are hundreds of ways to kneel and kiss the ground.

The awesome power of God humbles itself before us, and we can only "kneel and kiss the ground" literally, seeking to live with gratitude and awe before God's presence in the world. But God's presence is hidden and we must learn to see. Wisdom, the Asians are fond of saying, is often nearer when we stoop than when we soar.

The gospel of Luke tells the ancient story of how God's promises to David came true in humbling and troubling ways. It is the familiar story heard often in this season on feasts of Mary, the story of the angel Gabriel and God's dialogue with Mary through the intermediary of the angel. We are told that she is betrothed to a man named Joseph of the house of David, that her name is Mary, and that she dwells in the lowly and mean town of Nazareth in Galilee.

The Buddhists say that we must remember that the lotus flower blooms in the mud. Mary, the virgin betrothed, is innocence and purity of attention, but hidden, known only to God's eye. And so she is greeted wondrously, so wondrously that the greeting deeply troubles her: "Rejoice, O highly favored daughter! The Lord is with you. Blessed are you among women." In her innocence, her lack of self-interest or self-absorption, she wonders what the greeting means. Ever since that moment, we have been wondering at its meaning and power. She is told that she is to conceive and bear a child. She is told how the promise of God to David is coming true in her lifetime, in her life, and in her flesh. As with God's revelation in the first-person singular to David through the prophet Nathan, the words of God to Mary are conveyed by Gabriel. They are about Mary's child and who he truly is and will be, though he is hidden mysteriously in her flesh and blood, in her womb. For Mary will be God's house in history, in the world, God's entrance way, his gate into humankind. We are told something of who this child is:

> You shall conceive and bear a son and give him the name Jesus. Great will be his dignity and he will be called Son of the Most High. The Lord God will give him the throne of David his father. He will rule over the house of Jacob forever and his reign will be without end. (Luke 1:31–33)

Every woman who becomes pregnant wonders at one time or another what their children will grow up to become, what they will do, how they will leave their mark on the world. They wonder too about themselves, about how their own person and hopes and dreams will be expressed in their children. Mary wonders how this will happen. She is not pregnant. She has not known Joseph or any man. She wonders who the father will be. She is told, in words and terms that are still as mysterious as they were when they were originally conceived and spoken:

> The Holy Spirit will come upon you and the power of the Most High will overshadow you; hence, the holy offspring to be born will be called the Son of God. (Luke 1:35)

The angel's vocabulary and syntax shift from the second person to the third person. The angel is describing the coming of the Spirit of God to the prophets throughout the long history of Israel's unfaithfulness and God's enduring and solicitous care and kindness in spite of their inattention and infidelities. From the very beginning this child is not Mary's but belongs to God; the child is given to the people who have waited and hoped for the promises to come true in their lifetimes or those of their children. The announcement is a weaving of the past and future together with Mary's own person, which becomes the link that turns the words into reality, into flesh and blood, into a force that will change all of history and renew it once again.

And so then the angel comes back to the present and tells Mary one piece of practical and necessary information. Her kinswoman Elizabeth is pregnant too, ahead of her by six months. Even though Elizabeth was thought to be sterile, she is now also part of God's impossibly wondrous dream for the earth's children. What the angel has described to Mary is impossible — except through belief, through the goodness of God, and through the power and overshadowing of the Holy Spirit. Once it seemed impossible for an oppressed groups of slaves to be drawn out of bondage and led to freedom and into a land flowing with milk and honey. Now God is again about setting the captives free and releasing prisoners. The impossible has been set in motion with the conception of John the Baptist, but now the vision must be brought to fruition through human free choice. Gabriel's dialogue with Mary awaits her word. Whether or not the dream comes true in history hangs on her response. The intimate communication of God with humankind — the discourse of the Word in flesh — hangs suspended in time.

The Holy Spirit will come upon her and overshadow her, but not without her assent, her heart and flesh given over as gift, as house to the Holy One of God. God is discreet and does not intrude. But Mary responds, knowing her place, as David did not: "I am the maidservant of the Lord. Let it be done to me as you say." As God kept repeating to David, "I am . . . ," now Mary speaks for all those mindful of God, "I am the maidservant of the Lord." We have the sense of her bowing, bending low, although the line that follows could be sung in joy, could be spoken as power being let loose: "Let it be done to me as you say." Let it be done. Let it come true, finally; let God in, to dwell, to stay, to establish forever his place of peace where all his people may rest from their afflictions and enemies. Let it be done. Let creation be healed and made whole again. Let us know again dialogue with God, as once we walked in the garden and spoke face-to-face. This time, though, let us obey and oblige God. Let it be done; let the house be built. And the angel left Mary, but the Word remained; the seed was planted; the incarnation was a reality; the promise was set in motion. Grace had entered into humankind and had a human face and form, taken from the woman Mary, maidservant of the Lord, daughter of kings, beloved of God.

Traditionally, in litanies Mary has been called Ark of the Covenant, Tower of Ivory, Seat of Wisdom, Mirror of Justice, Cause of Our Joy, Mystical Rose, Refuge of Sinners, Queen of the Prophets, Queen of the Martyrs, Mother of the Poor, Mother of Peace. There are many ways to describe Mary's relation to God in light of her giving birth to Jesus. She is the House of God, Mantle of Justice, Morning Star, Light of Freedom, Disciple, Virgin of Guadalupe, Hope of the Poor, Homeless Lady, Woman Running from Danger and Violence, Woman of the Word, Prophet of Her People, Waiting

Woman. As communities of faith we could write litanies to express our understanding of the mystery that "once hidden for ages" now has come to pass because of Mary's belief and her obedience.

But we rejoice over Mary because we share this glad tiding. We, too, like King David and Mary, are to be the house of God in the world today. As Mary bore Jesus in her flesh and blood in her time and place, we are invited to open our hearts and allow Jesus entrance in our flesh and blood in our time and place. We are called to take this Word of God to heart and delve deeply into its mysterious meaning and force here and now, today, at the end of the twentieth century.

William Bausch tells of a custom in the Middle Ages. At that time, monks and most of the populace could not read or write, but every morning in monasteries and chapels many of them would meet around a Bible. It would be opened, and in silence they would wait for the Word to be spoken and read aloud. The one who could read would slowly tell the story of God's words in the world, reading a single passage clearly so all could hear. He would finish, stand in silence before the book, bend in homage, and then back away from the stand with the book, standing at a slight distance. After a period of quiet, he would approach the book again and read the same passage. He would do this again and again, until all had departed and there was no one to listen to the Word of the Lord. Each monk or visitor left when they had secured what they needed to reflect upon for the day. The Word invaded their minds, hearts, and bodies, and they took it with them into their work, study, and interactions, as well as their prayer. With the Word within them, they were ready to live in the Spirit and let that Word transform their own flesh and blood.

Tagore, a poet of India, has written a prayer that speaks of this mystery of the Word:

> If you speak not, I will fill my heart with your silence and endure it. I will keep still and wait like the night with starry vigil and with head bent low with patience. The morning will surely come, the darkness will vanish and your voice will pour down in golden streams, breaking through the sky.

During Advent I once asked a group of people what time of day the Annunciation of Gabriel to Mary occurred and what that signified to them. The answers were varied. Many immediately responded "in the morning," either at dawn or midmorning prayer, in harmony with beginnings on earth. A few thought late afternoon, after the heat of day and toil had eased and there would be some breathing space. Most people thought the angel came when Mary was already stilled and reflective, waiting on God. Some said night, in a dream, in the dark, knowing solitude brought consciousness of God's reality and nearness. It seemed everyone wanted the encounter to be gentle, nonintrusive, like a faint whisper of wind, a soft breath on skin.

At the beginning of this cycle of readings we were warned to stay awake, be on guard, for we do not know when the Lord is coming. This is Advent, from the Latin *ad veniat*, meaning toward the one who comes — toward his face! And we were questioned: What if the Master returns at midnight, or cockcrow, at dawn or dusk? Will we be ready for his appearance? Did the angel come with God's invitation at dusk, in forgiving light, at the time of shadows, when it is sometimes easier to see with God's eyes? Or at the darkest part of the night when we often can't sleep because of worry, the need to pray, when we are all too aware of our humanity and mortality (it was during the dark of night, while shepherds were keeping watch over their flocks, that Gabriel and the host of heavenly visitors broke into song the night of this child's birth)? Or could it have been in early morning when the cock crowed with its echoes of Peter's betrayal three times? Was it at dawn, before the rest of the world knows it's light, but when the poor and homeless have been on the streets and are eagerly awaiting warmth and the sun to come and perhaps the kindness of a stranger who will give them something to drink or eat?

Was it like the sound of thunder and lightning cutting across the sky, heralding the coming close of the storm's power? Was it like the sound of a rattlesnake in the desert or wilderness, so near that you stop and listen with every sense heightened, waiting for the bite? For the announcement and conversation between Gabriel and Mary are loaded both politically and religiously. This is not just a singular or personal encounter. Jesus will be born into a royal line in a time when the lineage has been forced underground, when those in the royal family live in a territory that is occupied by enemies. What is being proposed is subversive and revolutionary, giving impetus once again to the people's long-dormant hopes and dreams of freedom and liberation, and the possibility of living out the glory of God and giving witness to God's presence among them. This is a troublesome proposition for a child born of a poor village girl in a border town far from the center of power, a town that has learned to accommodate and live in collusion with injustice and infidelity. It may have been like whispers in the night, hushed and confidential. But they were dangerous whispers, conspiratorial, bent on releasing the stranglehold of sin and evil and breathing a song of freedom into weary people bowed long under the yoke of oppression. "Let it be!" could have rang out victoriously, with quiet expectant confidence and wild hope. Yes, let it be — let it come to pass that life is full of grace again.

On this fourth Sunday of Advent, so close to the birth of the child, we are chided and reminded that this all happened months ago. Since this young woman bravely and courageously aligned herself with God's Spirit in history against the domination of the world's powers, God has been stirring in her flesh and taking shape from her flesh and blood, her heart and mind. As soon as she says "Yes," she and her unborn child are in danger from even her own people, who are expecting something altogether different in their reading of the law, the Scriptures, and justice. They will want to stone her and her unborn child to death as an abomination.

Mary is told not to fear, that she will bear a child, just as her grown child will bear his cross to his place of execution. His name will be Jesus, Joshua, and he is the one who will save us all from our sins. She is royalty by her connection to her child. They will both bear the burden of responsibility and care of their people, especially the poor and the lowly. Mary knows the promises, but there are a lot of surprises in this invitation: having it happen in Nazareth is one, and God's asking a favor of a no-account young girl is another. She hears and is asked to believe that now, with this new disposition of God, the sterile are made fruitful; the old give birth in the usual ways; the young and unmarried give birth without sexual encounter; and God is hidden and dwelling among his people not in palaces but in the poor.

John's conception was a thing to marvel at, but Jesus' conception alters all of history and human life both before and after. Mary's life (and Joseph's) will have no other focus but the child who will be the Son of the Most High God, the prophet to the nations, the light of the world. With Mary's acceptance, the season of light begins, and the darkness begins to scatter. And with our taking of the story to heart, the Word of the Lord to heart, it begins in us, with obedience as it did with Mary's assent. In Luke's gospel, Mary is the servant of the Lord, as Jesus is the suffering servant of Yahweh. Together they are images of discipleship, obedience, and faith. With

Mary we begin this season of light, believing the Word of God in the Scriptures and obeying just the one piece of information that we are given in our need — to go out into the world and make it possible for the Word of God to spread, for hope to be born again. It is only a week or less until the birth, until the dawn comes and the Son of Justice appears in the world as a child of the poor, befriended and adopted by a just man who breaks the harsh law and refuses to disassociate himself from those in need. The Son is born without shelter, in a cave in the fields with shepherds and animals, stars, earth, and angels as those who first see God's presence in the world more clearly, more intimately, and more humanely — so close at hand, hidden in a poor woman's flesh, sleeping beneath her heart all these months. This has been God's preferred dwelling place in the world.

We end with a story that begins at the time of David when he was dreaming of building a house for Yahweh. "The Walls of the Temple" brings us up to the present day, questioning where we think God dwells now.

✣ Once upon a time when David had been king for quite a while, when things were quiet in his domain and there were no battles to fight, he started dreaming every night. He dreamed that he would be taken to heaven and shown all the glories of that other world. He learned that that world was a mirror image of what this world below was supposed to be, before humans disobeyed. And he saw a temple in heaven, in the heavenly Jerusalem, that he secretly decided to copy and build on earth to the glory of God. And so, every night he memorized another piece of the building, the architecture, and its surrounding environs.

And then he started building it in his city, Jerusalem. He gathered all the people of the nation together, and he told them of the dream and what they would all build together. They held a national lottery, and each of four groups drew lots for what portion of the temple they would construct. The priests chose first and got the south wall and the area where the Ark was kept behind its great curtain that hid it from the eyes of others. Next the princes chose, and they received the north wall and the pillars and staircases. The merchants were next, and they got the east wall and the provision of oil for the lamps. Last, the poor got what was left, the west wall and the curtains of the temple. And work began.

Some of the groups went right to work. The priests collected money from the taxes of the people and their wealth and hired others to work on their wall. The princes gathered their excess jewelry and money and hired the best workers to build their wall. The merchants made deals, bargained and bartered, purchased their oil, and their wall went up. The poor, however, lagged way behind in their building because in addition to having to work on the other walls, they built their own wall themselves. But they did it with love and devotion, after they had worked all day or all week, and slowly it rose alongside the others. And finally the great temple was finished. It was dedicated to the Lord, and all gathered together to worship God in this magnificent place that they knew mirrored the one in the heavenly city of Jerusalem.

The poor were especially proud. Decades later, men would stand beside their children and grandchildren and point out a row of bricks, a segment of the wall, and whisper that they themselves had laid those bricks and that when they were children they had mixed the straw and mud and helped to build it. Mothers would stand beside the great curtains and show their daughters the finely detailed and tight stitching of yards and yards of cloth that they had painstakingly sewed during the long hours of the night while others slept. They would tell them how they had made the cloth from flax and wool, cotton and silk threads, and how they had helped dye the cloth. It was the poor's temple as much if not more than all the others.

Centuries later the temple was destroyed, burned and ground down to a pile of stones. Only the western wall remained. It is said that God couldn't bear for that wall to be destroyed and sent the angels to spread their wings over it, shadowing it with their strength and protection. That was the wall most precious to God because it had been built by the hands and sweat, the devotion and suffering, of the poor themselves.

Today, this Wailing Wall is one of the holiest places in Jerusalem, and people come to pray there, longing for the dwelling place of God, for peace to be restored to the city. Those who finish praying do not turn their backs on the wall, but like the medieval reader of the Scriptures, bow and back away from it, often with tears in their eyes, hoping for a day when there will be a place of peace, a dwelling place for God on earth, not just in a rebuilt temple but in the hearts of all human beings. People say that it is called the

Wailing Wall not just because of the tears of the people who long for God's coming but because often in the early morning air the wall is wet with dew. They say that the dew is the tears of the angels who mourn the destruction of the temple, but more the destruction of God's dwelling place among his children.

As Christians, we believe that God has restored the temple and that it is more beautiful than anything human hands could have fashioned, for now the Body of Christ is found in the bodies and faces of all those fashioned by God's hands. And we should remember that all this happened because, once long ago, when God asked a favor, a young woman welcomed God into her womb, her heart, and the earth on behalf of her people Israel and all people for all times. A Japanese haiku tells of time and history, of what is great and what remains: "The summer grass 'tis all that's left of ancient warriors' dreams." Because of Mary's obedience and fierce belief in God's promises given to her people, we have the stuff of dreams to rely on, the flesh and blood of God, the dwelling place of God among us still. Now it is our turn to say yes, to obey and sing out with Mary of the virgin heart and hope: "Let it be done...as you say. Let it be! Amen."

# CYCLE C

✛

## First Sunday of Advent

*Jeremiah 33:14–16*
*Psalm 25:4–5, 8–9, 10, 14*
*1 Thessalonians 3:12–4:2*
*Luke 21:25–28, 34–36*

The third cycle of readings begins at the end with the coming of the Son of Man in glory at the end of time. The first three Sundays of Advent in this cycle, especially this first Sunday, echo the previous Sunday, the feast of Christ the King. They reverberate with words of judgment, power, the right ordering of our lives, and different understandings of time. Yet these are balanced with hope, calls to repentance, encouragement, and exhortation. There is a balance of denunciations and annunciations.

At this time of the year the Hallmark Company sponsors television specials and produces cards that promote a sense of family, homecomings, and remembrances. This season does have its hallmarks, and the readings begin strongly with one that will be repeated often, shaping our prayer, our liturgical celebrations, our waiting, and our hope. Jeremiah the prophet begins: "The days are coming, says the Lord, when I will fulfill the promise I made to the house of Israel and Judah. In those days, in that time, I will raise up for David a just shoot. . . . " And the next sentence again refers to "in those days." We look to the end of Luke's gospel to catch a glimpse of what lies ahead. In fact, time will shift backwards and forwards in this season, shaking us out of our usual routines.

In the last days of November we Christians start another year, a new year, designated A.D., *anno Domini,* in the year of the Lord. We operate in a different time frame from the rest of the world. It can be termed salvation history, God's time, *kyrios* time, because we begin with the hope that the coming year will belong to God, that it will be characterized by God's presence in our lives and history, more so than the previous year. And what will mark this year are God's promises in the past — that this year they will come true. In our endings we find the substance of our present realities.

There are really three comings in this season: the coming of judgment and the reckoning of justice for all the world in history; the coming of the child of peace as God becomes human among us in history; and the coming of the Word of God to take root in our flesh and hearts as the Body of Christ today, redeeming all of time, changing all of history yet to come. It is time to put ourselves and history in perspective and ask whether we are ready for final judgment and for hearing the ultimate truth. This truth is about justice. The shoot that Jeremiah promises that will be raised up by God "will do what is right and just in the land." But, even more than that, all of Judah and Jerusalem will dwell secure and be given a new name, "The Lord our Justice."

In *Shobo-genzo Zuimonki*, Zen Master Dogen says that we should live each day, each hour, in the same frame of mind as that of a man falling from a horse! He teaches that at that moment, there is no time to relearn or undo the past, no time for recriminations or even for looking around. All depends in that instant on readiness. Another way of describing this readiness is expectant waiting, attentiveness to what is most important. This is Advent time; it is impassioned, intense, and focused. And so the gospel of Luke commands us to "stand up straight and raise your heads, for your ransom is near at hand." At the beginning of this new year we are exhorted to recommit ourselves to the coming of God, the coming of the kingdom of justice and peace, the coming of the Word that judges justly and saves everyone.

An old story told in many traditions sets the tone for Advent (keep in mind that the word means "coming").

✤ Once upon a time there was an old, old monk who had become the revered abbot of a monastery. One day a very young and enthusiastic monk came to question him about his life. "Father," he asked, "in all these years of prayer and discipline, of early rising and penance, have you become enlightened or holy?"

The old abbot broke into peals of laughter, saying, "If you have to ask, isn't it obvious? No, I've not become all that holy. And wisdom or enlightenment? I don't know. Sometimes it's hard enough just to survive day-to-day with some sort of gracefulness. To learn wisdom as well is asking for a lot."

But the young monk was serious and pushed him: "Then why do you stay? Have you learned nothing in all these years?"

The old monk eyed him seriously and answered, "Well, yes, I have learned one thing about God. Stay awake! You never know when God is going to decide to come and visit you. Stay awake! You never know when all your plans so carefully laid and detailed will be derailed, when your patterns and routines will be rudely interrupted. Stay awake! God loves to surprise you, catch you off guard, and throw you off balance, coming and insisting that He be allowed in to the center of your life. So, stay awake!"

That is the essence of Advent — stay awake; endeavor to stay awake.

And we're not specifically talking about awakening from sleep, but being awake: aware, focused, dedicated to one thing that roots our lives in God. In her book *Zen Seeds,* Abbess Aoyama Shundo, Roshi, writes:

> Shakyamuni Buddha said in *Yuikyo-gyo* (The Sutra of the Buddha's Last Teaching): "Monks, if you earnestly persevere, nothing is difficult. But, above all, you must strive with all your might, like ceaselessly flowing water wearing away a rock. If your practice becomes lax, it becomes as difficult as trying to start a fire by rubbing two sticks together but stopping before the wood gets hot. Earnest perseverance is true endeavor. . . ."
>
> In ancient times the job of keeping the fire going was a serious undertaking. One of the most important tasks of the woman in each household was to keep the fire burning continuously. To get a fire started, flints had to be struck to make sparks, or two sticks were rubbed together. There can be no pause in the latter method. Similarly, if our heart stopped to rest, we would die; the sun never takes a break. And religious practice should never pause. (73–74)

This is the stance of believers in Advent.

In his letter to the Thessalonians, Paul will pick up this refrain: "We beg and exhort you in the Lord Jesus Christ that, even as you learned from us how to conduct yourselves in a way pleasing to God — which you are indeed doing — so you must learn to make still greater progress. You know the instructions we gave you in the Lord Jesus" (1 Thessalonians 4:1–2). Yes, we all know the instructions, but now it is time to rededicate ourselves and focus intensely on the agenda of God for the world, the world where the Lord our Justice will choose to come and dwell among us. Advent is the time of intense apprenticeship to waiting on God, hoping for justice, staking our lives on the reckoning of history.

Advent rings out with the declaration of God for all to hear. Some day (in those days, at that time) all who dwell on the earth will come to know that "this" is not the way it was supposed to be; that what we do to one another, oftentimes even in God's own name, was never meant to be; that what nations do to one another will be judged in terms of truthfulness and justice for the poor. And this day "will come upon all who dwell on the face of the earth, so be on the watch. Pray constantly for the strength to escape whatever is in prospect, and to stand secure before the Son of Man" (Luke 21:35–36).

And we are reminded, even taught, that "there will be signs in the sun, the moon, and the stars, on earth, among nations, anguish, people distraught at the seas' turmoil and the roaring of the waves. There will be fright, terror, and anticipation at what is coming. All the power of heaven and earth will be shaken" (Luke 21:25–26). It can sound so awful that we want to run away and escape, to hide, but we are commanded to stand up straight and raise our heads, for this is the time of promises fulfilled for all those who wait on the Lord, for those who seek justice for the poor and those victimized by the powers of the world. Reckoning can bring rejoicing as well as remorse over what has been done and left undone. The world and history belong to God. As Christians we stake our lives on that reality, and "that day" will prove us true.

Advent calls us back to live in the in-between times, with integrity, single-heartedness, justice toward all, and true worship of God. On a practical note, we are told to "be on your guard lest your spirits become bloated with indulgence and drunkenness and worldly cares." These words of Luke's gospel sound a good deal like Jesus' exhortation to his disciples in the garden the night he was betrayed to the powers of the world of evil, the night he prayed for God's strength and Spirit to keep him faithful and obedient, the night he repeatedly went to his disciples to find them sleeping, when he had asked them to accompany him in his struggle to face the future. He would waken them and plead with them to pray to not succumb to the evil around them, the evil approaching them while they were unawares.

The strongest image of the gospel, besides the presence of the Son of Man, is this image of "that great day that will suddenly close in on you like a trap!" The words startle us and put the fear of the Lord into us. They make us nearly gasp with recognition of the power of this day and the presence of the Lord coming into the world of history to settle accounts and judge rightly for all concerned. This is the day that God takes back dominion over the world that was entrusted to us. This vision of the Son of Man is both warning and hope instilled in those who are faithful and hungry for justice and the security of all. This day proclaims that God — not any government, nation, or individual — has the last word.

The mention of traps should alarm us. We face twenty-four days before the feast of the birth of the child who will grow up to become the Son of Man. All the traps are there waiting for us, to snare us and keep us from being ready on that day. Some are barely perceptible — projects and agendas that our culture rather than our religion sets out to ensnare us during this season. In the Southwest many people still hunt with traps or set out traps on the outskirts of their property to keep the wilder creatures from getting to their gardens or their pets. These traps slam shut with fearsome violence, cutting limbs, catching unwitting animals in ferocious pain. Wolves, coyotes, foxes, even rabbits and dogs get caught. People also can be trapped — we walk into many traps unawares, because we are intent on other matters, so we don't look for the signs all around us. Then there is the "roulette" trap of the things we do over and over again, forgetting that inevitably we will run out of time, possibilities, or chances.

At the beginning of Advent, the beginning of another year, we are warned about the traps that lie before us. They have one thing in common, and that is luring us away from the core of our existence. They want to trap us in something that is superficial or in opposition to justice and the kingdom of God. We will be caught doing something we do not want exposed to the gaze of others, or we may be caught doing nothing at all except being selfish. The biggest trap of the season, of all our lives, seems to be selfish indulgence, as we crassly and constantly think of what we will be getting this Christmas, of the "stuff" we covet and scheme to get.

The gospel's words are even stronger. The gospel charges us with being bloated with indulgence, being filled up with something that is abhorrent to the Holy One, filled up with more than we need or can use, while others lack necessities. And drunkenness really means overindulgence, the satiety of food, drink, shopping, decorating, cooking, parties, the trappings of our culture's celebration that is based on greed and competitiveness. We can have too much of just about anything, all of those things that help us escape from and ignore the most important things: justice, truth, community, worship, integrity, sharing with others. Traps of saturation, lifestyles that make us appear more like stuffed turkeys or pigs with apples in our mouths than human beings.

We can concentrate on myriad details that have no genuine meaning and be caught up in organizations, meetings, and practices, also evil and sin. Most of all, we can get caught up in the trap of thinking, believing, and acting as if this is the way it's supposed to be. Worldly cares can become our god, our obsession, instead of worship and community, instead of the Word of the Lord and the transformation of the world into a place that provides security, safety, and peace for all.

In the gospel, Jesus is speaking of the destruction of the temple, of the center of the Jewish world, of any form of power and authority that is not God's. The readings are fraught with fear, treacherous doings, destruction of governments and structures, and radical changes in the ultimate reality. And yet the gospel summons us to hope, to deeper love, to liberation, and to a truer way of life. We are told to stand up, lift our eyes, and stand secure before the Son of Man, for our ransom is near at hand! This is sobering yet full of encouragement for those who have lived waiting for justice to come, for God to intercede on their behalf, for those who are believers in Jesus Christ, the Holy One of God who will accompany them and work with them for the kingdom of justice and peace on earth. Thomas Merton put Advent succinctly: "The Advent mystery is the beginning of the end of all in us that is not yet Christ."

Paul writes to his community and to us: "May the Lord increase you and make you overflow with love for one another and for all, even as our love does for you. May he strengthen your hearts, making them blameless and holy before our God and Father at the coming of the Lord Jesus with all his holy ones" (1 Thessalonians 3:12–13). This is where we stand and begin each year, turning once again to face the one who approaches us — at the end of time in the person of the Son of Man, and in just a few weeks as the child of peace who will grow up to be the way, the truth, and the life. This is our vocation, our destiny, our ultimate truth.

Abraham Lincoln, in replying once to someone who demanded that he take a particular course of action, claiming that "God was on his side," said, "Sir, my concern is not whether God is on our side; my great concern is to be on God's side, for God is always right." Is this our concern? Do our lives reflect the righteousness of the God we profess to believe in and follow? Do we live for what is eternal, everlasting, truest, and dearest? Do we remember that a day will come when God will scorn the world's priorities and stand on the side of those who fell victim to the ways of evil and injustice? Do others know by our behavior and decisions, our solidarity with the poor and those caught in the system's cracks and in the teeth of hard-hearted laws, that we stand as children of the light and that that light will once again burst upon the world, shattering the darkness and gloom of despair? The Son of Man stands solidly on the side of the poor and oppressed. But at this moment where are we? Now is the time, for "that" day will come upon all who dwell on earth.

The Son of Man is friend to the poor, to those in need of salvation, to those who align themselves with truth and justice, to those who are faithful in spite of the world's traps, to those who ask for forgiveness and extend mercy to others. The sense of standing up before the Son of Man is that of witnessing, of standing in a court of law, of speaking up on behalf of others, of confessing that Jesus Christ is Lord, that Christ is King, crowned with suffering and death. God has raised him up, a just shoot that has always done what is good and right in the land, for the people to take heart in and rely on as God's will for all people.

"A shoot will sprout. . . ." In Israel, in the garden of Gethsemane, there are ancient olive trees, some hundreds or even thousands of years old. On a visit there I watched gardeners prune the trees, and I picked up shoots to take home with me. These old trees are huge, sprawling, gnarled, and in all sorts of crannies there are shoots. Even where the wood is shaved and barren, there are small signs of life. The trees are still growing and capable of producing fruit. We also have years behind us, and there are pieces of us that are gnarled and dead. In this season of Advent, though, we are told that God is fulfilling his promises of old. A shoot will sprout, and justice will bud forth on the earth again. The promise is fulfilled in the person of Jesus, but it is also given as the Word of the Lord to us. We are to be shoots sprouting justice and bringing life out of dead wood and old visions and hopes. We are to be witnesses to another power in the world.

This power is that of the Son of Man. He once shared our own fate as human and mortal. Murdered unjustly, he suffered at the hands of nations and factions within his own religion and disciples and was betrayed by his friends and yet, at the same time, was the Lamb of God who willingly laid down his life for his friends. This man is the Lamb who (according to the book of Revelation) is worthy to break open the scrolls of the book of salvation and worthy to receive glory, power, and praise.

One day we will see it! The response to Psalm 25 is filled with the joy that will accompany that day. It is also filled with longing as we stand at the beginning of the year and fervently wait for his coming. "To you, O Lord, I lift my soul." As we sing it again and again we hang on to the note and extend our souls into time, reaching for "that" day. The psalm itself continues:

> Your ways, O Lord, make known to me;
>     teach me your paths,
> Guide me in your truth and teach me,
>     for you are God my savior,
>     and for you I wait all the day....
>
> Good and upright is the Lord;
>     thus he shows sinners the way.
> He guides the humble to justice,
>     he teaches the humble his way.

These last two lines introduce an attitude that characterizes those in the Scriptures who have captured the spirit and meaning of Advent: humility. They are the humble, those who are close to the earth and close to the promises of God, close to the heart of what it means to be human, close to the ground in their prayer, in their position in society, and in their way of viewing themselves. These are the ones who "keep God's covenant and his decrees," who are friends with the Lord because they fear God. These are the ones who stand secure before the Son of Man.

So we stand at the beginning and face the future, knowing that our God has stood with us in the past and invites us to share the destiny of divinity, justice and peace, promises and hopes fulfilled. Are we ready? Here is a humble story, a small story that questions us.

✤ The Sufi master and poet Jalaluddin Rumi was known for his passionate devotion to the Holy One, for his verses, and for the longing that he expressed in every action and prayer. Many, of course, sought to be one of his disciples and to be personally tutored in the ways of the mystic traditions of the dervishes.

One day a new seeker arrived and spoke to Rumi, "Master, I have come to present myself before you. Are you ready to teach me?"

Rumi, a master, indeed, in the art of discerning another's soul, eyed him long and deeply, then responded, "It all depends. Are you ready to learn from me?"

It all depends on the year ahead, on our lives, history itself, the will of God. And as we stand before the Son of Man and are eyed steadily, searchingly, truthfully, the question is the same: Are we ready to learn from the Son who is meek and humble of heart?

Are we ready to learn how to be apprentices, attentive, receptive to new ideas, creation, new ways to live with others, open to hospitality? Are we ready to seek courageous liberation from fears, routines, prejudices, petty meanness, and selfish indulgence? It is time for the discipline to begin, to start down this path, to lift our souls in offering, and to acknowledge whom we belong to and whom we stand with this year. There is an urgency in all the readings, a sense of hastening the day, of reading the signs of the times, frightening as they are.

Our world has its own signs of destruction and evil: the collapse of the Soviet bloc, the disintegration of myriad countries into nationalism and ethnic rivalry. A killing frenzy has been whipped up in eastern Europe and Africa; old hatreds are stirred blindly in Israel and Northern Ireland; and vicious conflict between Iraq and the United States continues. Closer to home, what is termed publicly as "compassion fatigue" has set in: the small-mindedness and mean-spiritedness of the tightening of welfare structures and immigration strictures. Whatever will happen in this year, we are called to stand up publicly and be seen for who we are and what we have done. We are called to confession, to assert our hope, to decide where we stand in the world — in it, but not of it. It is time again to choose and to pray for conversion.

The following short poem, "Earth Hard," can help take us into the season. It is by David Ignatow and is about standing up, but with a bit of a twist — before the Son of Man:

Earth hard to my heels
bear me up like a child
standing on its mother's belly.
I am a surprised guest to the air.

Advent is full of that freedom, that kind of adventure into the future, secure on the lap of God.

Advent tells us that we need reminding that we are to work for the Lord, that we are to watch over his domain and serve only him, that we need to awaken fully to the ultimate reality. We need to stand and face the world around us, secure in the knowledge that we belong to "the just shoot raised up by the Lord who does what is right and just in the land." We belong to those whose name is "The Lord our Justice." We face the season together, praying with Paul, "May the Lord increase you and make you overflow with love for one another and for all" (1 Thessalonians 3:12). God is coming toward us. It is time to go out to welcome him in with open hearts and arms. Come! Our ransom is near at hand!

# Second Sunday of Advent

*Baruch 5:1–9*
*Psalm 126:1–6*
*Philippians 1:4–6, 8–11*
*Luke 3:1–6*

Now we are introduced to the one who goes before, the prophet and herald, John the Baptizer. This towering giant of a prophet will dominate the readings for the next two Sundays. He goes before to prepare the way of truth. The readings last week dealt with time. Now we shift to where and how these things will come to pass, and next week we will be told precisely how to respond to these events. And this week's readings add another coming, that of homecoming, to the three primary comings of the season.

The prophet Baruch turns to his people who have endured exile and loss and encourages them to "take off your robe of mourning and misery; put on the splendor of glory from God forever!" We are instructed what to wear for the occasion: "Wrapped in the cloak of justice from God, bear on your head the miter that displays the glory of the eternal name." God is closer now, and he is preparing to show the world who we really are, to whom we belong, and what our true name is: "the peace of justice, the glory of God's worship."

The prophet Baruch's call is focused on the city of Jerusalem and, for us, on the church in the world. It is a call to rejoice and rise up. Our God was justice; now our God is the peace of justice. Justice is first of all judgment and truth-telling, revealing the nature of persons and events. Then justice is the coming of peace, of security, of possibility, of hope for all, of being "remembered by God." This peace coming from justice is for all the earth; in fact, the outlines and contours of the earth itself will mirror what is to happen to nations and to people's hearts:

> For God has commanded
>     that every lofty mountain be made low,
> And that the age-old depths and gorges
>     be filled to level ground,
>     that Israel may advance secure in the glory of God.
> The forests and every fragrant kind of tree
>     have overshadowed Israel at God's command.

The land itself will echo God's homecoming to his people and their return to their long-lost dwelling place. This homecoming is described in glowing terms, as coming "upon the heights of the city," one of the higher points in this region of desert, the Dead Sea, the Judean wilderness. All the lost ones will come home, exiles, aliens, outcasts, prisoners, slaves, from the east and the west. And it is God who is bringing them back, carrying them, "borne aloft in glory as on royal thrones!"

Their journey will be made easier because the land itself will aid them. The ground, the mountains, the hard places, the passes, the rivers and gorges — all will be leveled, filled in so that the people will be able to "advance secure in the glory of God." All creation will be shifted to serve them. The forests will form an honor guard, overshadowing them, shading them from harsh weather, bending to the people, and accompanying them with natural incense. The procession will be set in motion by one thing alone, "the Word of the Holy One," the command of God. If the people follow the "light of his glory," then the countenance of God and God's mercy and justice will accompany them. It is a procession, lit from within, stronger than the sun's or the stars' light. As once the people were led through the Exodus from Egypt through the desert to Sinai and then to the promised land with a pillar of cloud by day and fire by night, now they will be led by the very presence of God. They wear insignia, miters, and cloaks of justice, the livery of the King of glory, and they carry banners that proclaim a new power that holds sway over the earth.

This Sunday is the time of passage as we stand with the bitter taste of memory in our mouths and are called to sing in joy, dance the way back home, as many African Americans dance down the aisles with the offering of gifts, back and forth to Communion, in and out of church! It is time to look to our "glad rags," our clothing, and our vestments. Do we wear the garments of the works of mercy and the clothing of those who have remained faithful in the face of persecution and the disdain of the world's elite and power brokers? Whose company have we been keeping? Whose people are we?

When I visit Central America, I often work with communities and teach Scripture, give retreats and tell stories, and in return people give me gifts of clothing, weavings, serapes, ruanas, jackets, dresses, all handmade on back-strap looms hung between trees. The main color is often dark blue, but these garments are decorated with elaborate embroideries of flowers, beasts, birds, intricate patterns. The colors remain bright after long years of use, exposure to the sun, and washing on stones in streams. Sometimes a garment is made of older leftover pieces of material, taken from clothing that literally fell apart, each piece salvaged from something else. Nothing is wasted. I treasure these gifts and wear them when I teach or preach.

One day about eight years ago I was in an elevator in the parking garage of the Seattle airport. The elevator stopped, and about ten people got on, obviously all from the same family, refugees from Guatemala. I was wearing a blouse that had been given to me in the mid-1970s, nearly twenty years earlier, and it took a minute or two for me to realize that they were excited, whispering and talking in a Mayan dialect and pointing to me. The few who could shifted into Spanish and asked me where I got my shirt. I smiled and told them the name of the woman who had made it for me while I stayed in her village. Immediately there were smiles all around, at the recognition of the name and the clothing, the hand and the stitching, and the old friend. They were en route to Canada, staying with strangers through kindness.

Our meeting was a homecoming in the elevator of a parking

garage. With laughter and tears, we exchanged stories and telephone numbers and made plans to celebrate with dinner that night. Never have I been so aware of being "wrapped in the cloak of justice from God." To those who knew the language and could read the signs, my blouse proclaimed a company of justice and mercy across time and place, gathered from the north and the south at the Word of God, woven with the hope of a justice-filled peace. The responsorial psalm's refrain, "The Lord has done great things for us; we are filled with joy," was visible in the pieces of cloth that made me family. In spite of torture, persecution, massacres, hunger, and disappearances of friends and family, they were contemporary "captives of Zion, like dreamers, their mouths filled with laughter and their tongues with rejoicing." That night they shared the stories of tears and torn hearts over tortillas and beans, rice and fried ice cream, but they were carrying seeds to be sown, even literally, with seeds of corn, beans, and other plants from their homeland.

The words of the psalm, the words of the Guatemalans, and the words of Baruch were variations of the words of John the Baptizer and of the woman Mary. All were singers and sowers of hope in the places of violence and poverty. All had been filled with laughter and joy, singing and dancing. And all could sing:

> Restore our fortunes, O Lord,
>   like the torrents in the southern desert.
> Those that sow in tears
>   shall reap rejoicing. (Psalm 126:4–5)

One day there will be a reward for faithfulness, a harvest of hand-carried sheaves of wheat—food to celebrate the presence of God at work in the world in spite of the world's intents.

Paul reminds the community of believers in Philippi that he rejoices in every prayer he utters because "they have all continually helped promote the gospel from the very first day." What a statement! Could we be described with that kind of faithfulness, integrity, and single-minded focus in our own lives and communities? Is the good news preached to aliens (legal and illegal), to those who suffer disease, disabilities, debilitating prejudice, old age?

Paul is aware of only one thing, "that the Spirit who has begun the good work will carry it through to completion, right up to the day of Christ Jesus." Right up to the day. During all these days, in all these places, we are sure of one thing, the work to be done which Paul describes as "the harvest of justice." Much still needs to be completed. The readings from the Psalms and from Philippians can be said as prayers or as blessings as we depart, as daily reminders of the building intensity, and as prayers of petition at the offertory on behalf of the community in response to hearing the Word.

Paul prays that all of us will abound in understanding and wealth of experience, in the practice of corporal works of mercy, and in solidarity with communities in need. Paul prays that with a clear conscience and blameless conduct we will learn the value of things that really matter, right up to the very day of Christ, when God comes in glory to gather his own and to judge all peoples. Until then, there are many days when Jesus appears hidden in our midst as a poor child, unwanted by the community, someone who finds no room or accommodations in our towns and cities.

We often think of homecoming in terms of waiting. When we hear the word "homecoming" in the realm of religion, we think of the future, of death, of heaven, and of judgment on an individual level. To a certain extent that is valid, but it is truer yet to speak of homecoming here and now, where we live today. Paul Tillich wrote: "Our time is a time of waiting: Waiting is its special destiny. And every time is a time of waiting, waiting for the breaking in of eternity. All time, both history and the personal life, is expectation. Time itself is waiting, waiting not for another time, but for that which is eternal."

There is a Muslim story that can perhaps put this time and space of our waiting into focus as we wait for the day of Christ to come. On my first trip to Bethlehem, I stayed with a doctor and his family, and we told stories long into the nights. He was a Palestinian Christian, and his wife was Muslim. It was she who told me the story, supposedly one of the Prophet Muhammad's own sermons.

✤ Once upon a time there was a good Muslim, devoted, attentive to his religious duties, responsible for his family, obedient to the law. He prayed fervently and assiduously, never missing his personal devotions or public prayer. But often he was so intent on getting through all the prayers, making sure that he did them all that he didn't notice what Allah was doing right in front of him. While he read his prayerbook he neglected the glory of the sun rising right before his eyes, with streaks of silver, dusty blues, and crimsons inflaming the skies and declaring the creation of God. And this habit of unawareness overlapped into other areas of his life as well.

He knew that he must care for the poor and the orphan, and he did, often. He always came away feeling righteous and knowing that others would benefit from his generosity. But in all the years of providing food or paying his share toward public shelter and assistance, he never thought to ask himself why there were always so many in need, so many widows, orphans, poor, and prisoners. It never occurred to him that the presence of such poverty in the community declared the reality of a great deal of injustice being practiced there.

He knew that he must work responsibly and teach the demands of the Koran, so he taught his own children and contributed funds to the schools and academies of his village so that other children might be taught. But he often overlooked the sufferings and struggles of those around him, those disheartened by survival alone, caring for large families and elderly relatives, with no time for study and prayer. He concentrated on making sure that he was doing what was necessary for his salvation, his reward, and his holiness. And then he died.

When he got to the gates of heaven he was shocked to see that heaven was a great walled city, and the gates towering above him were firmly shut and locked. On the gates was posted a sign: "These doors open once every hundred years. STAY AWAKE!" He was stunned. No one down on earth in his lifetime had mentioned that the doors were locked and opened only every one hundred years! What was he to do? How long did he have to wait? Had they just recently opened? Would it be a couple of decades, weeks, a few minutes (with luck)? There was no way to know. So he went off to the side and sat down to wait.

First he prayed, reflecting on his life, trying to remember the words that he had raced through so often on earth. But he hadn't paid a lot of attention to their meaning then, and now he kept drifting. He'd fall asleep and then wake with a jolt and wonder how long he'd been dozing. There was nobody around, and he had nothing to do, and he began to drift off more and more, sleeping more deeply. Sometimes he'd get up and walk around, push the gates, and then sit down again. He slept like little children, taking naps in the afternoon. When they wake up they don't know who they are or where they are, and they are grumpy and panicky. More and more often he was like that, sleeping longer and becoming inert. Each time, as soon as he got his bearings, he'd check the door. Still firmly locked. How was time passing?

One day when he was sleeping soundly the doors began to open. They opened very slowly and very quietly until they were wide open. A breath of fresh air, incredibly pure air, wafted through the open gates, a cool breeze that gently woke him up. Eyes open, he started for the gate, lurching toward it. But the gate closed much faster than it had opened, slamming shut, hard and with a deafening noise. And the sign dropped down again, "These doors open once every hundred years. STAY AWAKE!"

The story makes people laugh at first. Then they stop laughing and decide they don't like the story. It saddens them, upsets them, putting in jeopardy many of their beliefs and practices. If this story is true, Oh, dear! It reveals such gaps between words and practices, assumptions and reality, prayer and rote mouthing of formulas. It raises disconcerting ideas about the afterlife and heaven. The discussion is always lively, but it takes a while before someone asks, "Are you sure he's in heaven? How come there are no other people and no one else comes along?" Ah! There's the rub. Oscar Romero, the murdered archbishop of San Salvador, said, "Christianity cannot be thought of except in terms of relationships with other persons, brothers and sisters in whom we make real the comradely love that we preach." Is the Spirit that Paul refers to in his letter at work in us, even now, here? Have we learned to value the things that really matter? Do we really have clear consciences and act blamelessly?

Things that really matter include our truthfulness and integrity, both personal and public. Do we demand that governments, organizations, even our own churches and parishes do what they are intended to do, serve others, especially those most in need of justice, and those whose very existence is imperiled? Personal prayer, liturgy, and spirituality are sources of strength and goads to express our worship of God by honoring the Body of Christ in the world as much as we do so in churches.

Things that really matter include engaging in our work, making economic choices, and setting political agendas in such a way to benefit those who are most destitute. Our choices should be made so that all might have the basic necessities before anyone gets special attention or opportunities for excess profit. We must think of the earth and its limited resources and our children's children's children and what we are leaving them or taking from them. We must work at restoring and converting energy sources and cleaning up the pollution and destruction of the last half-century.

After spending a month in the Philippines for the first time and experiencing the violent inequality, the wretchedness created by drugs and pornography, the pollution of water, air, and land, and the misery of so many alongside the decadence and affluence of so few, I came back to the United States understanding two simple realities in ways I never had before. First, I wanted to find out what was the least I needed to live on so that I could share more with others. Then I wanted to atone for the choices and the results of those decisions that my own government and history had made in my lifetime. If there is to be any harvest of justice in the next century, these matters cannot be ignored.

What if Christmas came only once every one hundred years? How would we prepare for the twelve days of Christmas? Would we get caught up in the mind-dulling and expensive overindulgence: the destructive use of energy for lighting, the excessive food and drink, the buying of gifts? I will never forget one Christmas eve at Midnight Mass when I was home visiting my parents' parish. It's in a wealthy suburb of Washington, D.C., and people arrived in mink coats and the newest luxury cars. I was uncomfortable to begin with, and then the celebrant began the homily with the words: "Don't feel guilty about your diamond tennis bracelets, your new Mercedes, your cruise to the islands. You deserve it on this day of giving gifts, and you worked hard for the ability to lavish such attention on your own families." I was stunned. My outrage grew more obvious at the general drift of the remarks. My father, even at eighty, knew what I was thinking, and at his end of the long pew he leaned forward, glared at me, and mouthed the words, "Don't you do or say anything or else." I didn't, and to this day I regret it. Promoting the gospel, doing the good work of God, living with a clear conscience and blameless conduct, and letting the harvest of justice ripen were mocked, and I participated so the feathers in my own family wouldn't get ruffled. After the liturgy I bolted out of the church wanting to cry. All I could think of was John the Baptist and what he would have said along the Potomac River in this day and age.

And that is the meaning of the appearance of John the Baptist on this second Sunday of Advent. The gospel acclamation puts it in a nutshell: "Prepare the way of the Lord, make straight his paths: all people shall see the salvation of God" (Luke 3:4, 6). Without a meeting with John the prophet, without preparation and hard work, there is no salvation to see, no pure joy, no hope rekindled or gifts shared in memory of the gift of Jesus Christ. The reading situates us in our world, as John was firmly planted in his place. Luke describes the lay of the land. It's the fifteenth year of the reign of Tiberius Caesar. According to Rome, with its military presence occupying the territory, power lies with Pontius Pilate. According to the Jewish ruling monarchy, power means Herod and Philip and Lysanias. In the area of religion, Annas and Caiaphas dominate, as they have for decades. These are the authorities, the elites, and everyone else is powerless and of no note.

All this is very specific. It's like saying, "In the sixth year of the presidency of Bill Clinton, when A (fill in any name you wish) was secretary of defense and so-and-so was governor of such-and-such state, and B was the representative from so-and-so district, and C was the mayor of such-and-such town, and in the twentieth year of the pontificate of John Paul II and the tenth year of rule of Bishop X, . . . the Word of God was spoken to John, the son of Zechariah, in the desert." This specificity can startle and wrench us out of our place and into a place where things can begin to change. The Word of God comes into the world in specific places and to specific people, usually beginning with a prophet, a person who is a voice for someone else and who proclaims the earth's shifting as forcefully and dynamically as an unexpected earthquake.

And we know that Zechariah, the priest who took his turn in the temple offering sacrifice, did not believe the voice of God in the messenger Gabriel and was struck temporarily dumb, speechless. It is Zechariah's child who is the voice, the herald, the one crying out in the desert the ancient command that interrupts rudely and joyously:

Make ready the way of the Lord,
    clear him a straight path.
Every valley shall be filled,
    and every mountain and hill shall be leveled.
The windings shall be made straight
    and the rough ways smooth,
    and all [of you] shall see the salvation of God.

We are yelled at: don't listen to the world's voice; listen to the one who cries out on behalf of the truth, of God, and of peace with justice. The peace of justice will be given to those who listen to the voice. John strides forth from the desert, where most do not venture or know how to live. Life in the desert pares things down to the essentials, to the mortality and limitedness of being human. The Word of God comes not in power, but in powerlessness, austerity, asceticism, and purity. This is God's place, and it comes to the flesh of those who are waiting. Stay awake!

Where is the Word of God appearing today? Whose flesh proclaims the coming of the Lord? Who is making a highway of holiness for our God's homecoming? Who is leveling the mighty and tearing down the structures of injustice and callousness and lifting up those bowed under the yoke of the mighty, the economic giants, and the heads of corporations, states, nations, and international banking institutions?

Where are the prophets among us? The message remains the same; only the places and the people who listen and hear the voice change. Who are they today? For there is always one among us, another whom we must reckon with. The Word of the Lord in the Scriptures comes to us as surely as the Word came to John. Just as this man John, the son of a mute priest, was the only one worth noting during his time, in our time what is worthwhile is the Word and those who preach it. Peace in justice will be given only to those who listen and heed the voice. Our God is approaching us and drawing near to all those who are working at the harvest of justice.

There is a story told in Africa called "Son of the Tribe," a version of which appears in *Tales of the City of God* by Carlos Vallejo (Prakash, India: Gujarat Sahitya, 1992, 80–84). It situates us here and now and cries out to us.

✤ Once upon a time a young man, still a child really, knew that the time was approaching for him to face the test that would either make him a man, an adult in his tribe, or would expose him as still needing to be taken care of and incapable of serving his community. He was afraid. What if he failed and had to live with the knowledge that everyone knew of his failure? For another whole year he would have to be just a child. He was anxious to face the test and get on with it.

The day came and he appeared before the elders. It was explained to him what he had to do. He listened carefully and intensely. "You are to go into the jungle alone, and you are to take no food or water or weapons, and you are to find four animals: a python, a rhinoceros, a lion, and an elephant. You are to look right at them, into their faces, and you are to stand and make sure that they see and eye you back. Then you are to come back here and report to us."

He thought to himself, "I can do this."

He nodded and set off. First, the hardest, the lion. He tracked a lion, stayed downwind and spied him at a distance, a couple of hundred yards, laying on a rock. The young man was sweating as he stood and waited for the wind to change direction. It did. The lion looked up, surveyed the horizon, and spied the young man. They looked at each other, and eventually the lion put his head down again, and slowly, quietly, the young man inched away. The first one was done.

The next one, still difficult, was the rhinoceros, which was big and ungainly, thunderous in his charge. The rhinos were dangerous when spooked or provoked and could move unbelievably fast for so much bulk. The young man knew where they watered. He found a tree and waited, sleeping off and on. Around midmorning one came, nervous. The rhino could smell him and charged the tree a couple of times. He hung on, and the tree was sturdy and held. They eyed each other. Now he just had to wait for it to drink and leave. It did, but it was late on the second day.

Then he made his way into a thicker part of the jungle and found a python wrapped around a tree. He eyed it, and the great snake began to unwrap itself from the tree. Once on the ground close to the young man, the snake eyed him back. The young man bolted and ran out into the clearing. The water looked so inviting. He was now thirsty, hungry, and tired, growing weaker by the hour. He wanted some water, but then he stopped himself, for the elders had said he was to have no water. He would not be able to live with himself if he drank and didn't tell the elders, even if he passed the rest of the test.

The last was the easiest, the elephant. He knew that elephants don't attack humans unless their young are threatened or they feel trapped and cornered. He knew where they ate and gathered. He tracked them through field after field and clearing after clearing. He couldn't find a one. Where could they all be? He was growing dizzy and weaker. He would have to go back soon, if he was to make it at all. He knew he was not allowed to die trying. He needed water.

Finally he knew he was going to fail. He could not find a single elephant. He wept in frustration and failure. And he returned home to his village. The elders met him, gave him food and water, and listened to his story.

He began, "I have failed. I took no food or water, no weapons. I found the lion, the rhinoceros, and the python, and I looked straight at them and they eyed me back, but as hard as I tried I could not find an elephant, not a single one. I have failed."

There was silence among the elders and then the chief spoke. "No, you have not failed. You could not find an elephant because we stampeded all of them the morning you left. The test was not just in seeing and being seen by the wild animals but in whether or not you would tell the truth. You have. Welcome home. Now you are a member of the tribe."

For us, the test is also our truth-telling, along with or in spite of everything and anything else we might be doing. Out test is the harvest of justice in the midst of everything else we are doing in preparation for the incarnation. May God, who has begun the good work in us, bring it to completion. Amen.

## Third Sunday of Advent

*Zephaniah 3:14–18*
*Psalm: Isaiah 12:2–6*
*Philippians 4:4–7*
*Luke 3:10–18*

"Shout for joy. Sing joyfully. Rejoice in the Lord always! I say it again. Rejoice!" The words of the prophet Zephaniah and the apostle Paul ring out. And the strains of the music of the traditional Advent song "O Come, O Come Emmanuel" take on rich depth and meaning as the one we await comes closer and nearer to us. The refrain is full of yearning and hopeful but not exuberant. It is a silent profession of faith based on hope. "Rejoice! Rejoice! Emmanuel shall come to you, O Israel." And the first stanza moves closer to the reality and to that hope becoming true in our hearts and world:

O come, O come, Emmanuel,
And ransom captive Israel,
That mourns in lonely exile here,
Until the Son of God appear.

Now we sing:

O come, O Dayspring from on high,
And cheer us by your drawing nigh.
Disperse the gloomy clouds of night,
And death's dark shadow put to flight.

Rejoice! This we must do. It is not just an option. It is a theological demand based on the reality of our faith. It is what we've
been waiting for these weeks: the advent of God into our world,
growing stronger daily. The incarnation is a reality, and the Word of
God is hidden in earth's flesh, history, and our lives. The prophet
Zephaniah declares to us: "The King of Israel, the Lord, is in your
midst; you have no further misfortune to fear." And the response
to the psalm text puts it even more clearly: "Cry out with joy and
gladness for among us is the great and Holy One of Israel." This is
our belief, so we live with this awareness. If not, it is time to wake
up to the fact that our God is among us and has been for ages past,
seen and unseen. This rejoicing has nothing whatsoever to do with
our feelings. It is based on our faith.

At the time of John the Baptist, the great and Holy One had
been in the world for thirty years. We believe that the great and
Holy One has been in our world for nearly two thousand years. In
our parishes and churches, we worship among believers who stake
their lives on the hope that the great and Holy One has been in
their corner of the world. The great and Holy One has been in my
life for fifty-three years and in my parish for more than two hundred
and seventy-five years. How long for you? So, Paul says it again: "I
say to you, Rejoice! The Lord himself is near." This is definitely
cause for rejoicing!

It is now the third week of waiting. In the old days before Vatican II, this Sunday was called Gaudate Sunday, from the Latin
"to rejoice." As the third candle, the one wrapped in pink or rose-
colored cloth, is lit, the tenor of the season shifts perceptibly into
more apparent joy. What we wait for is nearer. How near? As near
as the first streaks of dawn are to the sun's explosion on the horizon, just as the first light begins to assert itself ever so slowly and

meekly into the darkest and coldest moment of night. This "crack of dawn" is a crack in the night's defenses, and the light begins its entrance. Along the line of the earth a faint color of roses or crimson appears, often so soft as to look like the flush on the cheeks of children or the ranges of the color of human skin. It is fleeting, a few moments' glimpse of glory that mirrors our joy, our expectation and hope. The Son of Justice is this close.

As always in this season, the focus is on the "other," the one hidden in our midst who walks among us, watching, waiting for us to see, to recognize and respond. So today is the day to sing back to God, confidently and unafraid. Does our God have cause to sing over us? Are we like the remnant, the faithful ones of the time of Zephaniah who stayed true and learned to sing in the midst of affliction and exile? Do we believe that our God will bring us home to "renew us in his love" and that our enemies have been turned back? God is in our midst! As the Venerable Bede wrote, "Christ is the Morning Star, who, when the night of this world is past, gives to his saints the promise of the light of life, and opens everlasting day."

But if the great and Holy One of God is in our midst, how do we know what this awesome presence looks like, especially given that we look at the world through eyes often covered over by the milky film of weak faith? A story suggests where and how to look. About three years ago, a young boy approached me after a workshop and said he had a story to tell me, but he'd only tell it to me if I promised to tell it in public once a year. I was intrigued (and I'm always looking for a good story!), so I agreed. This is his story.

✢ Once upon a time there was a little boy who had been going to Sunday school for years. After hearing about God for so long, he decided it was time to go look for God himself. He thought the journey might be long, so he found an old gym bag that was his father's; he stocked up on root beer, granola bars, and Snackwells; and then he set off, without telling his mother he was going. He was about six years old. Well, he hadn't gotten very far when he got tired and decided to rest a while.

There was a park right there, and he cut across the grass to a bench. There was only one other person in the park, an old, old woman who was sitting on the bench. He climbed up beside her. The two sat there and didn't say anything for the longest time. Then he turned to her and asked her if she was thirsty.

She smiled at him and nodded. Out came the root beer. They shared and sat in silence. Then they ate the cookies and granola bars and finished the root beer. They were together about an hour, and she didn't say anything at all, just smiled at him every once in a while. So he talked. He told her stories of his mom and dad, brothers and sisters, first year at school, his pets, everything.

Time passed and he thought of his mother at home. He realized that she'd be furious at him for going off without telling her, so he decided he had better go home. He got down from the bench and picked up his empty bag. They had finished everything. He said goodbye to the old woman and turned to go away. He took a few steps and stopped. He thought to himself, "She has such a lovely smile. I want to see it again." So he turned around, ran up to her, put his arms around her, and gave her a big hug and kiss. Her face broke out into that magnificent smile. He smiled back and headed for home.

His mother was waiting for him at the door, frantic. She grabbed hold of him and shook him, "Where were you? I told you never to go off without telling me. Where have you been? I've been worried sick."

He looked at her and smiled broadly, "You didn't have to worry. I spent the afternoon in the park with God!" Momentarily stunned, his mother was speechless. He continued thoughtfully, "You know, I never thought she'd be so old and so quiet . . . and thirsty."

Meanwhile, the old woman had gotten up very slowly from her bench, picked up her cane, and headed for home. Her son, about forty-five years old, was waiting for her, frantic. "Mother," he said, "how many times do I have to tell you not to go off on your own without telling me? I've been looking for you everywhere and was just about to call the paramedics and the police again. You can't just go wandering off. Where have you been?"

Her face was radiant. She smiled at him and said, "Oh, you needn't have worried. I spent the afternoon in the park with God."

Her son was stunned and thought to himself, "Oh, dear. She's much worse than before."

But she continued, rather thoughtfully, "You know, I didn't expect him to be so young and so talkative . . . and to love root beer!"

Everyone laughs, of course, when they hear the end of the story. It's almost too cute, and yet both the boy and the old woman are onto something theological and true — the great and Holy One of God is in our midst! They have recognized the meaning of the incarnation, our God become flesh and dwelling among us. Have we? What are we expecting? Where are we looking and what are we seeing?

In his letter to the Philippians, Paul exhorts us: "Everyone should see how unselfish you are.... Dismiss all anxiety from your minds." Rejoice! In a sense he's asking us if we are a cause for others' rejoicing. Does everyone, especially those most in need, see and experience our generosity, our sharing, our compassion, and our care? The early church was characterized by its sense of community, its sharing of resources, houses, food, finances. No one was allowed to go in need of the basic necessities of human dignity and life, for this was how they cared for the Body of Christ in their midst.

Especially in this season of the incarnation, we are challenged to make sure there are "no poor among us." We are to feed the hungry, clothe and shelter the forsaken, provide medicine and education for those without, and hope to God in our midst. To take in the orphan, the single-parent family, the lonely elderly, the stranger and traveler, the displaced refugee family, and the woman pregnant and without resources is to take in God. Can we see what is right there in front of us? For all the world is waiting — for the song of hope and victory, salvation and the presence of God, for the story of God's marvelous deeds among all nations. Do our lives sing out, "Shout with exultation, O city of Zion, for great in your midst is the Holy One of Israel!"? Does everyone see how unselfish we are?

How are we to become the cause of others' rejoicing in this season? How are we to give God cause for singing? The crowds listening to and hearing John the Baptizer's preaching and call to repentance ask the question for us in the first lines of the gospel: "What ought we to do?" And John's answers are a primer on how to wait, how to level the mountains and fill in the valleys, how to prepare a highway for our God, straightening out the roads and pathways of our lives in the world.

Three groups pose the same question to him: the crowds, tax collectors, and soldiers. The first group is the crowd. These people, who include the bulk of humanity, show how power functions in the world. John's commands are simple, direct, and challenging. To the crowds he says, "Let the one with two coats give to the one who has none. The one who has food should do the same." Blunt. This is the beginning of justice: basic sharing of human resources, specifically food and shelter. This is the beginning of repentance that will lead to the forgiveness of sins. William Blake puts it simply too: "If we would not share the little we have, / We would not give although we had everything at our command." This is not generosity; this is justice. The demand of justice is that we share with others, that we make up what is lacking from our excess, and that all begin to stand on the same footing. Or, in the words of the prophet Mary of Nazareth: "He fills the starving with good things, and sends the rich away empty." This marvel signals the nearness of the one we await.

Next came the tax collectors. These members of the Jewish community were in collusion economically and sociologically with the Roman invading and occupational forces. They made a profit from the misery of their own people's heavy burdens of taxation. To them John the Baptist replied: "Exact nothing over and above your fixed amount." In other words, practice honesty, integrity; think of fairness instead of profit margins, greed, or thievery. Do not use the systems to steal from others and to better yourself at the expense of others with less access to power. A Persian proverb puts it succinctly: "Live within your harvest."

In a sense, all of us are tax collectors. We all deal with money, taxes, the economic realities of the World Bank, interest rates, finance charges on credit cards, mortgage loans, overextension of our personal or corporate resources. John tells us to live so as to declare that life is not about personal wealth, getting ahead, having the best, selling your soul to the existing market structures. Instead, live truthfully with your eyes on justice. Live in such a way that you give others cause for rejoicing at the simple honesty of your dealings with them.

Finally, the soldiers quiz him. To them John gives three directives: "Do not bully anyone. Denounce no one falsely. Be content with your pay." The three commands are intertwined. Do not use your power, your force, your weapons in the employ of the state to make the burden of another more violent, heavier, or demeaning. Do not threaten physically, psychologically, or religiously. Use your force, your presence, to defend and keep others from harm. Resist nonviolently, but do no harm. The second command warns against the use of power to harm the innocent or the defenseless. There is to be no aggression, no making of enemies. And, finally, be content with your pay. Learn to live within limits, with discipline, in the present. *Muy contento* is a phrase that is added to many blessings or descriptions of life in many countries of Latin America. In essence, it is a desire or a prayer to live fully and gratefully just because life is, and that is more than enough. No matter what government or economic system we find ourselves within, this call to repentance begins internally, with an attitude shift and a vision of another power, another reality that is the truest force in the world. And it is "other": it is of God and God's promises of a peace with justice.

E. F. Schumacher, in his classic book *Small Is Beautiful*, wrote:

Every people ask: "What can I actually do?" We can, each of us, work to put our own inner house in order. The guidance we need for this work cannot be found in science or technology, the value of which utterly depends on the ends they serve; but it can still be found in the traditional wisdom of mankind. That is a personal shift of priorities.

But John the Baptizer is speaking to crowds and groups of people, and so his intent goes beyond personal transformation of consciousness or behavior. John is about justice, security for all, the fullness of life, the ultimate truth of existence, and the meaning of all creation. John's commands begin at the roots of systems, structures, governments, the military, and business, and they affect everything from nationalism to ecology and religion itself. In his book *A Continuous Harmony*, Wendell Berry puts it in economic and ecological terms:

But the change of mind I am talking about involves not just a change of knowledge, but also a change of attitude toward our essential ignorance, a change in our bearing in the face of mystery. The principle of ecology, if we will take it to heart, should keep us aware that our lives depend upon other lives and upon processes and energies in one interlocking system that, though we can destroy it, we can neither fully understand nor fully control. And our great dangerousness is that, locked in our selfish and myopic economics, we have been willing to change or destroy far beyond our power to understand.

John is "the prophet of the Most High who goes before the one who will give light to those in darkness, those who dwell in the shadow of death, and guide us into the way of peace" (Benedictus). John's agenda is about repentance, reparation, and restitution, as well as hope for an altogether different future born of grace and the power of the Spirit. John is intent on stirring society to change. If John were preaching to us today, he would say things like:

Cancel the Third World's debt and pour in aid equivalent to the interest those countries have paid over and above the principle. Usury is a mortal sin that destroys hope in people. The money that goes into the military steals from the poor and kills them. The violence of the streets and in your homes is born of the violence of your nation's policies abroad. Don't you dare terrorize and hold captive another nation by denying it food and medicine. Don't squander your wealth on weapons or research ways to annihilate whole peoples and portions of the earth. Everything you don't actually need belongs by right to those who do need.

"How much must we share?" would probably be one of our questions during this season. Perhaps John would respond with two questions more to the point: "How can you live in such a way that your tolerance for others' misery does not penetrate your heart? How can you declare that you believe in God or have your own spirituality when it does not include every human being having one coat to cover their nakedness and one piece of bread, one meal a day?" These questions interlock economics and armaments, wealth and weapons, and expose them as idolatrous. John would say: "Are you mercenaries or are you the children of mercy? What are you doing when you pay one person more than a quarter of a million dollars as a spokesperson for a product, while you pay all those who labor to make those products insulting and degrading wages?" John reminds each of us and all of us of one reality: "You know what you ought to do!" Unwanted words perhaps, but necessary ones that go before the Word.

To put it in the words of a poet (William Blake), we do not have to look far:

For Mercy has a human heart,
Pity a human face,
And Love, the human form divine,
And Peace, the human dress.

And all must love the human form,
In heathen, Turk, or Jew;
Where Mercy, Love, and Pity dwell
There God is dwelling too.

The reaction to John's preaching is dramatic. People in the crowd begin to wonder if John is the one. They are full of anticipation, hope. They sense the intensity building. They recognize truth and begin to look for the promises to come true, here and now, and they question him. (This is the season of questions!) But John is quick to respond. He emphasizes that he baptizes only in water. What is coming is fire and spirit, mightier by far than his simple beginnings. In fact, John, the thundering prophet of the Holy One, is not worthy to stoop, to kneel, before this one who is coming, to untie his sandal strap, to be his servant. If this is true of John, then what of us? A marvelous description of John would be a line by G. C. Lichtenberg: "When my spirit soars, my body falls on its knees." John also waits and shares the anticipation and excitement of the crowds.

The Jews had little cause to rejoice, living in occupied territory under the heel of the Roman government, living in dire poverty and daily brutality from the elements as well as those who had power over them. John's words stirred up expectations of liberation, of deliverance and salvation. His prophecies were about righting wrongs, about exposing all to the truth of God. John goes on to describe the one who will follow: "His winnowing-fan is in his hand to clear his threshing floor and gather the wheat into his granary, but the chaff he will burn in unquenchable fire" (Luke 3:17). This description, and our initial reaction to it without reflection, can lead us to a simplistic interpretation that John is talking about two groups of people, the saved and the lost. But John's words refer, instead, to a process of purification, of making holy, of becoming sacrifice.

The imagery is that of a harvest of food. Our God is first interested in feeding people, in making earth grow and bring forth every kind of plant and living thing, and in sustaining all. Our God abhors war and destruction. But our God, especially in the person of the one who is coming among us and is in our midst already, also knows that "the seed must die in order to bear fruit." The judgment is a lifelong affair. We are in the process of growing and becoming wheat; the chaff is being burned away as peoples, communities, and the human race itself. A friend of mine called it "the refining of the blessed." He says, "We all have our chaff, our dross, our waste. We all have our winnowing. And it is the fire of Christ that will burn it away. The burdens we carry do not make us unfit for Advent's message. In fact, they qualify us as prime candidates. The only exit from Dante's *Purgatorio* was a wall of fire. Once the pain was burned away by love, the other side was Paradise, sheer joy" (Frank O'Loughlin).

Or, in the words of Simone Weil in *Waiting for God:*

When an apprentice gets hurt, or complains of being tired, the workmen and peasants have this fine expression: "It is the trade entering his body." Each time that we have some pain to go through, we can say to ourselves quite truly that it is the universe, the order, and the beauty of the world and the obedience of creation of God that are entering our body.

John is setting in motion a process, a transformation, that will be lent impetus by the fire and the Spirit of the one who comes after him. John himself is not the Word; he is only the voice announcing the coming of the Word. This is the good news that he preaches to the people and to us. Now is the time for the doing of justice, restitution, and reparation, of transformation and of becoming holy like the great and Holy One of God who dwells among us, hidden in our midst even now. John is saying: NOW, repent, change, be true and just, for you are the children of God, brothers and sisters to each other. Wait on God. Look to what is coming. Don't slack off. Live intensely. Prepare and let God prepare you; make yourselves over. This will usher in "God's own peace, which is beyond all understanding, that will stand guard over our hearts and minds, in Christ Jesus" (Philippians 4:7).

Anthony de Mello tells a story that situates us face-to-face with John, in preparation for the one coming after him.

✤ Once upon a time one of the disciples spoke to another disciple, in fear and anxiety. "This man worries me and I don't know whether I can trust him." He was new to the group.

The older disciple answered, "That's all right. Even the Master says to reflect on his words, study them, practice them, and test their truth before you believe in them, or in him."

But the other disciple responded, "Oh, it's not so much his words that trouble me. They often bring enlightenment. It's his presence. He burns so much in me."

This is mild fire, old fire, in comparison to what is coming!

There is another story, more to the point, that describes how we are bound to each other. It was told by Jack Quinn in a new journal of the Irish Dominicans called *Spirituality*. Entitled "Just a Thought," it reminds us of the nature of John's communal call to repentance.

✤ One night during the last world war, an Irishman serving in the British Army, and stationed somewhere in Asia, was ordered to take his men and destroy several rubber plantations, so that they would be of no value to the advancing enemy.

He carried out his orders. The plantations were razed to the ground with flame-throwers, and all the installations were left a smoldering mass.

About the time the war ended, this man's father died in Ireland, and as his sole heir, he expected to benefit considerably from his father's estate. You can imagine his astonishment and disappointment when he arrived home to get details of his inheritance, to be told that in fact his father had died in very poor circumstances.

Seemingly, just before the war, he had been advised to invest in rubber plantations. He had acted on the advice and invested practically everything he had, in the very plantations his son, unknowingly but with great diligence, had later destroyed. The son had in fact been destroying his own inheritance.

But the end of our story need not be so tragic. Our God is about renewal, regeneration, re-creation, restoring covenants, and surprising us ever anew. It is the Sunday to rejoice exceedingly. We have great cause to rejoice and to practice our singing and bring joy to others. We are encouraged in the words of Meister Eckhart: "Be ready at all times for the gifts of God and always for new ones!" These are good words to heed, because, "Ready or not, here he comes!" This is the good news that John preaches to us.

# Fourth Sunday of Advent

*Micah 5:1–4*
*Psalm 80:2–3, 15–16, 18–19*
*Hebrews 10:5–10*
*Luke 1:39–45*

This is where it begins. This is the doorway, the entrance for God among the small ones, the least of the earth, those who don't count. God loves to hide, to visit, and to stay in places we usually seek to avoid like the plague, such as Bethlehem, a no-account place, to rule from below, from the base of justice. A place of peace and lowliness, a humble place whose reach will be vast and great. Bethlehem-Ephrathah, "too small to be among the clans of Judah," is like Mary, lowly, unnoticed, just another veiled and cloaked woman in occupied territory whose womb is now home for the great and Holy One among us. The seeds of revolution, the cracks in the firmament, the broken seams of history are so small in the beginning and yet so radical. Our God believes that downward mobility is the way to usher in hope and to become truly human. It is time for the lowly to be exalted and the mighty put down from their thrones (Luke 1:52). Or as Marie Dennis Grosso puts it: "That the mothers of Iraq may find solace; the impoverished of Peru may have just access to the necessities of life; the blacks of South Africa may know justice; the war-weary communities of El Salvador may find true peace; the Earth may be healed" (from "Partnership in the Approaching Miracle," *Sojourners* [December 1991]: 29).

One thing to remember is that all these readings are first about God, about God's gift to us in Jesus Christ, and only after that does the light focus on Mary or on us. It is God who keeps interfering in history through his promises and the prophets. The lack of responsibility on the part of humans makes a mess of our history. God is always intent on setting it true again, true to its original meaning and creation, its original blessing. God is interested in the insignificant, the poor, the merciful, the hungry of body and soul, the makers of peace, the pure, those passionate and persecuted on behalf of others. And so the promises are clear: "From you ... insignificant Bethlehem, otherwise condemned to oblivion, ... shall come forth for me one who is to be ruler in Israel; whose origin is from of old, from ancient times" (Micah 5:2). This is the Lord speaking, telling of the one who comes forth "for me," for God, for God's will and design. The secrets of God are found deeply, truly, and humanly in this one who "will stand firm and shepherd his flock by the strength of the Lord, in the majestic name of the Lord, his God" (Micah 5:4).

David, the mightiest king of Israel's history, came from this humble place. Even so, in the eighth century before Christ, the prophet Micah expresses disappointment in his own kingdom, its history, its failure in faithfulness. In his distress, Micah is anxious for another king who will once again remind Israel of its destiny and its holy calling to be God's own people. And so the promise is inserted into the prophecy in parentheses, like an afterthought that must be taken into consideration along with the hope: "(Therefore the Lord will give them up, until the time when she who is to give birth has borne, And the rest of his brethren shall return to the children of Israel.)" (Micah 5:3). These lines describe the town of Bethlehem, the people of Israel, the remnant that remains true in the midst of sin and evil, and also any woman who experiences the long nine months of pregnancy that ushers in a child and hope.

Sometimes a very simple thing will remind us of what God looks for and what God uses in his great plans for us. When I was doing a parish mission in Dallas, someone clipped this short piece from the *Dallas Morning News* of December 14, 1997. It is delightful and to the point.

## Tall Tale

When our three young sons were each given an elf ornament for the Christmas tree, they began a yearly contest to see who could place his ornament highest on the tree. (It's a boy thing.)

Our oldest son, Scott, won for several years. When he finally got his elf on the top of the tree, we knew the contest was over. Wrong. The next year, our middle son, Kevin, taped his ornament to the ceiling above the tree. End of contest, we thought. Wrong again.

The next year, we could not find the ornament of our youngest son, Mark. It must be on the roof, we decided. Wrong again. We finally found Mark's elf on the very lowest branch of the tree — with a note attached: "For whoever exalts himself will be humbled and whoever humbles himself will be exalted" (Matthew 23:12).

Needless to say, that ended the contest.

*Mrs. Bill L. Campbell, Denton, Texas*

Translated into contemporary reality, the truth still rings out and makes sense for those who can hear the prophecy and believe in its power and meaning. Do we believe that it is with the lowly and humble of the world that our God loves to visit, to hide away, and to dwell?

This is the last Sunday of waiting. Our urgency is expressed in Psalm 80 and its prayer-refrain: "Lord, make us turn to you; let us

see your face, . . . and we shall be saved." And we will see the face of
God in a way no one ever expected, literally in the body of a human
being born of a woman and the overshadowing of the Spirit of
God. The child will have the strength of God, the power and protection of God. This is the Son of Man, "whom you [God] yourself
made strong." His presence among us will teach us how to stand
firm and to pray once again as those who are rightfully God's own
people.

The central reading for this Sunday, more than the gospel, is the
portion from the letter to the Hebrews. Here is the ultimate truth
of what it means to be human, of who this long-awaited child really
is, and of why he has come among us.

On coming into the world Jesus said:

> Sacrifice and offering you did not desire,
>     but a body you have prepared for me;
> Holocausts and sin offerings you took no delight in.
> Then I said, "As is written of me in the book,
>     I have come to do your will, O God."
>                                         (Hebrews 10:5–7)

This is the crux of the good news, the crux of salvation, the heart
of Jesus' person — "I have come to do your will, O God." "The
offering of the body of Jesus Christ once and for all" — obeying
even unto death, death on a cross — is the sacrifice that saves us and
makes us holy.

The text "Sacrifice and offering you did not desire, / but a body
you have prepared for me" is a line from Psalm 40:7. Martin Buber
once translated the second line to mean "but an ear you have drilled
for me," as one would drill a hole in stone or a well in the ground.
Often it is translated with more gentleness, using phrases like "but
ears open to obedience you gave me," as in the New American Bible.
However translated, it emphasizes Jesus' obedience to the will of
God, his relationship to God, his mission, and our calling as his disciples. This is the mystery of the incarnation: God prepared a body
for his Son, prepared flesh for his dwelling among us as a human
being, mortal and vulnerable, and yet powerful in the strength of
God. This body stands between the old covenant with its sacrifices
that were insufficient to save and the new covenant that is found
in the body and blood of Jesus. Much is hidden in the secret ren-
derings of this mystery. Somehow, in Jesus all of us are redeemed,

made graceful and holy again. Once again, we know how to obey and what it means to be human.

The best story I've heard so far about the meaning of the incarnation is a simple, anonymous one. It speaks volumes about a line from St. Peter Chrysologus: "God saw the world falling to ruin because of fear and immediately acted to call it back with love. God invited it by grace, preserved it by love, and embraced it with compassion."

✤ Once upon a time there was a young man working hard in a corporation. He was moving up in the corporate structure and thinking that it might be time for him to invite his boss and the other vice presidents of the corporation to a dinner party at his house. But he had a young son, only six, and he knew how hard it would be for him to behave himself at a dinner party. Finally, it was decided. There would be a formal dinner party, catered, with waiters and servers, cocktails and hors d'oeuvres before, and an elegant meal.

The man sat down at the table for days before and showed his young son the place setting with its extra forks, spoons, water and wine glasses. He showed him what each was for and explained that he would be served at the table and that he was not to reach for anything and to be very silent and good because this was such an important day for his father.

The evening arrived and things were going extremely well. Cocktails had been served and the meal had begun. Water and wine were in abundance on the table, the soup had been served, and conversation was lively. The man glanced at his son and smiled at him. He was doing just fine. But within minutes, the boy forgot his father's instructions. He was hungry, and he saw a basket full of rolls, not that far from his reach. Without thinking, he reached for one and knocked over his water glass. Then, dismayed, he pulled back and knocked over his neighbor's wine glass, right into the rolls and soup.

The son was horrified and remembered what his father had said. He looked in terror at his father. The father saw the terror on his young son's face. Immediately he knocked over his water glass, followed by his own wine glass, and then he laughed. He said to his son, embracing him, "Come on, let's clean it up together."

Ah, that is incarnation. It begins in lowly Bethlehem, in the humble beginnings of the one who will obey God and in Mary, a young woman from Nazareth of Galilee, betrothed to a man named Joseph of the house of David.

This fourth Sunday of Advent includes both the story of the Annunciation — the story of the angel Gabriel coming to ask the favor of Mary and Mary's obedience — and the story of the Visitation, of Mary going in haste to the hill country of Judah to see her pregnant cousin, Elizabeth. The Visitation is about Mary en route to Elizabeth, encountering her and seeking asylum with her, and it is also about the encounter of two unborn children, John and the long-awaited one who is the hope of the ages. This is the story of how God travels and gets loose in the world.

Luke's gospel is the gospel of the suffering servants, who are obedient to justice and to the will of the Spirit of God. And so, on this last Sunday before the birth of the child, we are told the story of how the Spirit moves throughout the world through believers, the first of whom is Mary. We are told that "Mary set out, proceeding in haste," an echo of the people of Israel who set out for freedom, proceeding in haste to escape the slavery of Egypt.

Mary journeyed to the hill country, an arduous trip of about ninety miles, to the outskirts of Jerusalem, the fringes of power, to Zechariah's house. She traveled along the Jordan River south, along the Dead Sea, and up the steep hills into the villages that extended up the mountainous area west of Jerusalem. This was a dangerous, physically exhausting trip either on foot or by donkey. A scant fifteen miles a day was grueling on Mary's missionary journey, the first of many into the world.

She enters Zechariah's house and greets Elizabeth. Mary utters the traditional greeting, the blessing of all Jews, "Shalom." And her voice is no longer her own. Her voice is the voice of the Spirit in her, sounding in the air, "Peace be with you!" However it was uttered — wearily, as a prayer, in welcome and delight, mysteriously, barely a whisper — it resounded throughout all time and space. The Jewish community believes that when Yahweh spoke on Sinai everyone at the foot of the mountain heard the voice and that every Jew since has heard that voice. Similarly, Mary's words of greeting, the voice of the Word of God within her, has echoed down the centuries and throughout the universe ever since. Her greeting is the same as the greeting of Jesus after the resurrection, when he enters the locked room where his disciples are hidden in fear. Mary and Jesus both use the words of Micah, "The child shall be peace." This is the peace of God, hidden in the flesh and words of Mary his mother. The voice of the Spirit of God within her stirs the child in Elizabeth's womb to life. At its sound, Elizabeth is filled with the Spirit of God and cries out! This is traditionally the description of one who is possessed by God, one who has been made a prophet. Elizabeth responds first with a blessing: "Blessed are you among women and blessed is the fruit of your womb." Many women in Israel say that this is a traditional blessing for a woman who is pregnant, for all Jews live in the hope that this child, every child, will be the Messiah.

But Elizabeth next asks a revealing question. The outpouring of the Spirit triggered by Mary's greeting with the word "Shalom" has brought knowledge, understanding, and revelation. Elizabeth asks in awe, "But who am I that the mother of my Lord should come to me?" She wonders, just like the old woman in the park and the young boy who shared his root beer! Elizabeth sees Mary for who she is, and the child for who he is, and responds in faith. Unlike her husband, who doubted the angel Gabriel's announcement because it strained his limits of belief and hope, Elizabeth responds with awe in the face of Mary's obedience and belief.

Mary's presence and her one word of greeting, "Shalom," brought the reality of joy to Elizabeth's body and to the body of her child dancing in her womb. John has also heard the voice, as any child in the womb hears music and voices. John knows this is the one he has been born to herald, and he will wait to hear that voice again and to see Jesus face-to-face.

Elizabeth breaks into prophecy, blessing Mary for her belief and her obedience: "Blessed is she who trusted that the Lord's words to her would be fulfilled." This first beatitude of Luke's gospel is directed at Mary, who is the first disciple of her child, who will save all people. The blessing is also directed toward all people who will obey and take the Word of the Lord to heart in their lives and flesh and carry the Word into their history. Blessed are all those who believe in the promises and stake their lives on the words coming true. Blessed are all who hasten the reality by their actions and responses. Mary sets out in haste, for she is both fleeing danger and intent on making the words reality. She is shadowed by fear from the beginning, for if her village, her community, finds out she is pregnant they will stone her and her unborn to death. Elizabeth's house is sanctuary, now for two pregnant women and two children who, once born, will know violence and fear, as their mothers knew it from the beginning.

Beginnings are terribly fragile, even dangerous. So much can happen to abort them, disfigure them, edge them with pain and doubt. But here the beginnings are in the flesh of two women who know how to believe, who are as strong as the children they will bear into the world. Their strength is born of the Spirit and practiced daily in faithfulness, imagination, and raw courage. The Other is now among us, in the flesh of Mary who will never be alone again and neither will we. This is the Visitation: two women in distress, given up to the will of God and the bold stirrings of prophecy and joy, strong signs of the presence of the Spirit.

This is how God comes: to the small of the earth, the minorities, the lowly, those fearful of "righteous" folk, the ones we'd never think to listen to or notice much. Elizabeth's question to Mary is also a question for us: "Who am I that the mother of my Lord should come to visit me?" Who are *we* that the mother of my Lord should come to visit *us*? Who are we that the Word of the Lord comes to us in the voice, the greeting, and the words of another?

The Visitation of Mary and Jesus to Elizabeth and John pose some pressing questions on the world. Whom are we listening to? Whose voice greets us with peace? Whom do we go to visit? Whom do we aid in times of distress and need? Who are caught in the web of the world's distrust, exclusion, and violence? Does our voice stir joy, the Spirit's power, and prophecy? Who is listening to us? Where do we stand with those termed illegal, sinners, expendable, unwanted, whether they are unborn, poor, feared, or condemned to death? What is stirring inside us during this week? What is readying itself to be born in us? Is there room in us for God, for the Word made flesh? Are we emptying out space and preparing room for the Word?

God is here. And the domain of peace that shall reach to the ends of the earth one day is here. It's been here in the blessed: the old, the barren, the useless, the unmarried and pregnant, the virgin, the poor and the lowly, the children not wanted, the children of the poor, the strangers on our roads looking for sanctuary.

It's close, near at hand in the flesh of the Other, of others right here in front of us. In the words of Thomas Merton "Peace sleeps beneath your paper flesh like dynamite!" The Spirit is stirring, and hope is trying to get born in us, kicking to get free, to emerge into the open. A contemporary story from Japan (a version of it is found in *Zen Seeds* by Roshi Aoyama Shundo) helps elucidate this.

✱  Reiko Kitahara, a young Christian woman, the daughter of a professor who lived in Tokyo at the end of World War II, moved to an area that had been bombed to rubble, where a desperately poor shantytown had sprung up. It was called Ant Town, and it was the home of ragpickers, people with nothing who would leave every morning in the dark to scour the streets, alleys, and garbage dumps of Tokyo for rags, cloth, anything to use, sell, or make into something else that might be useful. She gathered the children of the ragpickers together and was their teacher. Reiko also visited the old, infirm, and the sick, whom she tended with delicacy.

   She would stand at the edge of Ant Town in the morning dark as the ragpickers all left for their hard, empty days of scrounging for leftovers. She would send them off with a greeting and blessing for a prosperous and good day and then would be standing there in the dark when they returned, welcoming them home and blessing them again. They loved her and looked forward to seeing her face and hearing the sound of her voice, and they cherished her smile and her compassion. She became known as the Blessed Virgin of Ant Town.

   After a few years, she grew sick and contracted tuberculosis. She stayed because this was her home; these were her people; and it was here that she wanted to die. She lived in a shack, like all the others. It was brutally hot and close in the summer heat and freezing in the winter winds. Like the others, she had no medicine, no blankets, and little food. She was visited only by those whom she had first visited. She died young and compassionate, beloved of the people. When they went to bury her, they found a notebook under her pillow. They'd seen her take it out often and wondered what was written in it. The calligrapher Mitsuo Aida opened it and read the only words that were written there: "Aren't you going to smile right now?" This was her reminder to herself when she was in pain and was dying: the need for joy, the need for others to see and sense her inner belief and trust, the need to share that when she had nothing else to give.

   The roshi quotes Shakyamuni Buddha's list of "Seven Offerings That Cost Nothing," one of which is a smiling face. The latter wrote that he "wished that everyone would smile and accept all other people in the way that a mother smiles on her children and opens her arms to embrace them" (*Zen Seeds,* 104). And the calligrapher Mitsuo wrote this poem in Reiko's memory:

> With just your being there,
> The atmosphere somehow brightens.
> With just your being there,
> Everyone feels at ease.
> I yearn to be just like you. (*Zen Seeds,* 102)

This Sunday reminds us of the necessity of obeying like Mary, of lending our bodies to God so that the Word might enter our worlds. This week will be full of visitations, welcomings, greetings, travel, and strangers among us still in need of sanctuary. Like Mary, we must take the Word that has been given to us and bring it out into the world. We must bring the hospitality of God to all. Ralph Waldo Emerson said: "Hospitality consists in a little fire, a little food, and an immense quiet" (cited in a magnificent cookbook, *From a Monastery Kitchen,* comp. Elise Boulding with the assistance of Brother Victor Avila [New York: Harper and Row, 1976], 23). Mary spent three months with Elizabeth sharing just this and letting the Word take on more and more of her flesh. Another quote that is very timely for this Sunday is: "The Christian life is a journey.... Therefore do not wait for great strength before setting out, for immobility will weaken you further. Do not wait to see very clearly before starting; one has to walk toward the light" (in *The Choice Is Always Ours,* ed. Dorothy Berkley Phillips).

This is a good time to begin our story of Christmas this year. As Elizabeth said to Mary and to all of us who believe: "Blessed is she who trusted that the Lord's words to her would be fulfilled." It is up to us now to make the Word come true. God wants our flesh to come into the world this year. It is the moment for us to respond with the words of the Psalmist and with the words of Jesus: "I have come to do your will, O God." Perhaps our voice will stir the heart of God to great joy and bring delight to God again.

# FEAST DAYS

✤

# Feast of the Immaculate Conception
## *December 8*

*Genesis 3:9–15, 20*
*Psalm 98:1–4*
*Ephesians 1:3–6, 11–12*
*Luke 1:26–38*

The meaning of the feast of Mary as the Immaculate Conception is hard to define precisely. Even the church itself has taken centuries to try to put it into language that leads us into the mystery of God's singular grace and gift to Mary from the moment she was conceived in the "eye of God" and then conceived on earth. We are told that John the Baptizer was called (as were some of the prophets) from his mother's womb, but Mary is chosen even before that, and she is favored by God in a unique manner. She is "conceived without sin." The mystery that surrounds her coming into the world is found deep in the heart of God's hidden plan from before creation. Human beings are described in theological language as having been born with original sin. Although this often sounds like it is a thing, something tangible that we inherit from our parents as we are conceived in the womb, it's not. Rather, original sin is a concept to help us understand what it means to be human, to sin, to die, and to be free as well as to be flawed and incomplete.

The church believes that Mary — by the singular grace and favor of God — is human, is free, and will die, yet that she was created somehow more finely tuned to the will of God and open to obedience because of the intervention of her child's power of redemption and resurrection. Buddhist doctrine incorporates the concept of "our original face," the essence and the truth of who each of us is before we are born. This holds true no matter what we choose or how we develop or what we become. It is our ultimate reality and possibility. Our original face knows both freedom and sin because we are all human beings, but Mary's original face knows more of freedom and truth than of sin.

The readings remind us again and again that the Immaculate Conception is the marvelous work of our merciful God and that, by Mary's child's life, passion, death, and resurrection, all of us are called and chosen to be blameless and holy in this life and to know the mystery of Mary's own conception in our life as Christians. Like all mysteries, the meaning is found not so much in the definition of the dogma but in the belief and experience of Mary and in the incorporation of that experience into our own choices and lives.

The first reading from the book of Genesis takes us back to our beginnings. Many of the stories in Genesis fall into the category of stories that explain how things got to be a certain way. Particularly when reading the creation accounts, it is important to remember the first and cardinal rule of all stories: all stories are true; some of them actually happened. The emphasis in the stories of Scripture is not on factual accounts of historical events, but on the realities that we experience now in our lives of faith and the layers of meaning that are hidden in the stories. They are like mother lodes in a mine, with layers upon layers. As we sift through the different meanings, we grow in understanding of the theological concepts that are being presented. We will begin with three points in this reading of Genesis, one for each of the three cycles of readings.

This story, like many others in Cycle A, is a vision. It tells of a vision that failed and the judgments that accompanied that failure long ago when Adam and Eve — and so all of us as human beings — ate of the tree of knowledge of good and evil and so of the tree of life and death. Joseph Campbell once said that "a myth is a story that never happened because it is still happening now." It doesn't really matter if what is told in the Genesis story actually happened to two specific individual human beings. What matters is that the story is still happening to us now. It is a story of the universal experience of the human race.

Adam and Eve, and all of us, refuse to take responsibility for their (our) actions and their consequences. This is a vision in retrospect, seeking to explain how evil got into the world; how deception, lying, lack of responsibility, blaming others for one's own choices, even death and suffering came to be an ever-present and powerful reality for all human beings. It can be seen as a vision of bleakness, of a hard and cold dose of reality that shocks us into awareness of sin and evil and of the fact that we are the ones who chose evil, and this in a world that God intended and fashioned as good. This is the way it has been for eons.

The vision ends with naming. The woman, wife to Adam, is named Eve, "the mother of all the living." Even in the midst of this suffering, which is a consequence of knowing good and evil and choosing the evil, disobeying the command of God and coming to know separation, enmity, fear, and threat, Eve still becomes life-giving and engendering. Life is crucial. No matter what happens, this thrust toward life will continue. This is the point of all the visions in the Scriptures — how to restore life, nurture it, and bring it back into perspective and enhance it no matter what has happened. Our God, the maker and keeper of all things, is the God of life!

This particular piece of the Genesis story is hard to deal with because it is fraught with issues of knowledge, self-awareness, consciousness, sexuality, obedience, and blame; human beings are being questioned by God. In some ways, it is a sad and pathetic story, presenting human beings as faithless, gutless, whining, quick to blame others, childish, cowardly. God asks them why they chose to disobey. And they don't really answer; rather, they seek to excuse themselves. The focus is on Adam, who has sinned and eaten of the tree. Now he is hiding in the garden and aware of himself for the first time as separate — from God, from the woman Eve, from his own body, and from all other creatures in the garden, such as the snake. He also seems separate from the earth itself. Aloneness has entered the picture and with it, distance and alienation, estrangement and disorientation.

Human beings have begun to hide, to disguise ourselves and be deceitful with God and with one another, seeking to cover up not just our nakedness but what we choose to do in response to God's summons to obey the law of the garden. It was a law that had held everything in balance. Now the balance has been broken, and there is collusion with what is not of God. It is a story of trickery, deceit, behavior that selfishly turns inward. It is about fear, insecurity, knowing now what is obedience (good) and what is disobedience (evil). It is a story of dissonance, disharmony, disjointedness, broken words and trust betrayed, refusal to relate with integrity.

The story contains what we often read as a threat; instead, it is really a promise to restore the balance with the serpent. We are told that there is enmity between human beings and the serpent (not an animal, but a symbol for what is not of God's making, a symbol of our choice of that which twists and distorts reality — evil). One day the harmony will be restored, the balance righted between the woman and all creation, between her offspring and the offspring of those who chose evil. We, as Christians, believe that the balance was righted and the process of creation was begun again in Jesus and continues in Jesus' brothers and sisters, all of us who are reborn and made holy in baptism. This piece of the story ends with Adam and Eve, the father and mother of all the living, waiting in hope for the promise to come true, for their sin to be redeemed and their relationship with God restored.

The most important question in the reading is asked in verse 9: "Where are you?" This is God's first question to humankind after our choice to distance ourselves from God's vision for all created in the image and likeness of God. The question has nothing to do with geography or space. It is concerned with relationship, with awareness and conversion: Are you with me now? Where are you in relation to your brother and sister, your loved ones and your enemies? Where are you in relation to your responsibilities? Where are you in relation to the very earth and resources that you have taken for your own possession and use? The question could just as easily be stated: What have you done? What are you doing? What will you do now that you have loosed death into the world and you will taste of both death and life? Or, God could have said: Why are you hiding from me? Why are you running away from yourself and what you have done? Why are you hiding from the truth?

God's second question, "Who told you you were naked?" reveals a further level of consciousness, of vulnerability, of evil as a consequence of choice. And the blame begins. We deflect and disown our mistakes, sin, and evil, creating enemies that we can scapegoat and then punish for our own inhumanity and weaknesses. The serpent becomes what we know it as today, a creature that crawls on its belly, feared by humans who try to kill it or escape from its presence.

God's two questions point out that the Genesis story is a reminder of our failures, our fall from grace, our mortality and disobedience. This disobedience is a refusal to worship and acknowledge God as the being who has the right to command us; it is our attempt to act as gods in our own right.

The story ends with Adam and Eve living outside of the garden, dwelling in time, as we all know it. Eve, our mother, the mother of all the living, will now die. We also will die as a consequence of knowing good and evil and life and death, because we are all human and all of us are Adam and Eve. At the end of the story, though, the God of the living interferes in their lives, even as they are fearful and trying to hide from God. There is a hint that this God of ours will always be coming after us, seeking us with words ("Where are you?") and with the words of the prophets and sages. There is also a hint that one day the Word made flesh will come to dwell with us, outside the garden. Someday, hopefully, we will not be afraid and will turn to face God and answer truthfully: "Here I am, Lord; I come to do your will. I will obey." Our story begins when we begin to respond to the reality of what it means to be human and to be in relation to God, no matter what we have done.

And so, we turn and pray: "Sing to the Lord a new song, for he has done marvelous deeds" (Psalm 98:1). We who are made in the image of this God are called to watch and imitate what God does rather than doing what we choose to do. The psalm praises God who, no matter what we do, keeps doing great things for us, marvelous deeds in spite of our inhumanity to one another, our lack of regard for creation and its innate laws. The psalm's words are a universal call to announce God's presence in history, over all time, in the whole world. No piece of history or earth can escape God's goodness, kindness, and faithfulness. All can come to know this God; all can sing of the glory that is given to us; and all can come to rejoice at the Lord's work in us.

It is a new song because life is always redeemable with this God. The marvelous deeds begun in our creation — free will, our imaging of the Holy One, the invitation to intimacy, and the asking of freely given love rather than a demand — are continued. Justice and kindness continue in spite of what we have done, in spite of our slowness in learning the wisdom and ways of God. And another new song is to come, the song of Jesus, born of Mary the singer of God's praises and of God's kindness toward the faithful and those in need.

The opening blessing of the letter of Paul to the Ephesians catapults us through time into the present, after the birth, life, obedience, death, and resurrection of Jesus. This is the new song, the story's kick and twist of fate, dreamed up and enacted by God, who interfered so many times in history, trying to prepare a people to accept the Word, the truth, and the life. The marvelous things are beyond telling. They are known by belief and response as they have been a part of the story and over time become known. And we know! We know that

> God has bestowed on us in Christ every spiritual blessing in the heavens! God chose us in him before the world began, to be holy and blameless in his sight, to be full of love; likewise he predestined us through Christ Jesus to be his adopted sons — such was his will and pleasure — that all might praise the divine favor he has bestowed on us in his beloved.
>
> In him we were chosen; for in the decree of God, who administers everything according to his will and counsel, we were predestined to praise his glory by being the first to hope in Christ. (Ephesians 1:3–6, 11–12)

This was the gift God intended to give to the world even before creation began and human beings stumbled and fell over our own feet and wrenched our hearts away from the original dream. We were created to be human, like God, and called to be holy, like Jesus. Like Jesus, we were intended to be God's beloved, to be blameless in our behavior, and to be responsible for one another, all adopted children of God. God's pleasure has always been in his creation, in our lives, in the gifts that he bestows upon us, and most exceedingly in the gift of Jesus Christ, who is the presence of God among us. Our humanity is made complete, is redeemed by our praising God, by our hoping in God's glory, by hoping in Jesus Christ.

The church reminds us that on every feast of Mary we are included in what we sing of her and praise in her, for the work of God that shines forth in this woman of obedience, faithfulness, and truth is seeded in each and all of us by the gift of the Spirit in Jesus and in our baptisms. Along with Mary, we are called and chosen to be holy and blameless in his sight, to be full of love, to be the sons and daughters of God. This was the intent at the beginning. This is what we were all created for. This is what gives God pleasure. With Mary, we are called to be among the first to praise God and hope in Christ's glory shared with us in life, death, and resurrection.

And so we come to another story, about our beginning in the Spirit of God born in Jesus and the coming of God into the garden of the world again, asking: "Where are you? Are you with me now? Are you obedient this time?" From now on there will be another story, interwoven in the strands of the history of sin, evil, and the world's power, the power of the serpent that crawls on its belly, eats dirt, and reeks of death, not life. And the Spirit of God will seep through the world, through history, through all of creation, like rich, vibrant sap, re-creating, redeeming, bringing light and hope, security and protection for those who believe and obey.

When Mary hears the angel's words, "Rejoice! O highly favored daughter! The Lord is with you. Blessed are you among women," she is troubled. But the angel's words ring out, "Do not fear, Mary. You have found favor with God." This favor, this blessing, is just the beginning of God's great works in this woman who is his beloved daughter and who will be asked to be the mother of his beloved Son.

Now it is time for the human race to stand up and look God in the eye again and walk with him in the garden. Mary is told what we come to believe. This child will be savior (Jesus). Great will be his dignity, and great will be the dignity of all those who come after him. He will be called the Son of the Most High — and so will all of us who believe in him — and there will be a real kingdom of justice and peace that will last forever, in spite of evil. It will stand sure against anything human beings can do because it is born of God's Spirit and seeded in the flesh of all humankind.

Of course, Mary doesn't know all of this. She clings to the Word of God. She obeys. She clings to the child that is given to her, bestowed on her by God. She obeys, overshadowed by the Spirit as the Spirit overshadowed the people in the desert, the prophets of God, and the kings of old. Amazing grace is about to be let loose in the world, but it has to be given and accepted freely. Long, long after the Garden of Eden, Mary answers rightly: "Here I am, Lord, I am your maidservant. I am yours. Let it be done to me as you say. I agree. I say yes." Now God is back where God always wanted to be — with us. The angel leaves her, but the seed of life and hope, the trail of glory, stays.

This is the meaning of incarnation: God's will is being made flesh, taking the flesh, freely given, of Mary's body and soul. According to the gospel, this feast day is incarnation, not annunciation. It is the feast of the woman who is the mother of all the living, those who live now in Christ. It is the feast of the woman of the Word of God who lives on it and obeys it so completely that it comes true. It is the feast of the woman who is God-bearer, the Theotokis; this seems a more appropriate title than the more oblique Lady of the Immaculate Conception. Mary was conceived without sin, and she conceives a child by the power of the Spirit and her obedience. Like Jesus, she gives back as sacrifice and gift the body given her by God.

In our language, culture, and time, the term "Immaculate Conception" has too many negative and limiting references to sexuality, all of which negate the theological reality at the heart of the Scriptures and God's interruption into Mary's life. This is the story of God's creation, of the goodness and marvelous wonder of God. Theology is not primarily about biology or sexuality. It is about faithfulness and the essence of what it means to be human, made in the image and likeness of God. Theology is also about incarnation, about God taking on our flesh and humanity and offering us the possibility of being more like God than we could ever imagine.

The stories of Mary and our stories are more about liberation and freedom, obedience and hope, community and wholeness. The story of today's readings is more about the Trinity and our relation to the Father, the overshadowing of the Spirit, and the child born of Mary and God, than it is about the moment of Mary's conception. Mary is great because of what God has done for her, and God wants to do the same for us, make us great and holy. Whatever we say of Mary is meant to come true of us as well. We sing of Mary, but Mary as our sister and our mother would like to be able to sing of us as well.

In the office of readings for December 20, there is a reading from the homilies of St. Bernard entitled "In Praise of the Virgin Mother":

> You have heard that you shall conceive and bear a Son; you have heard that you shall conceive, not of man, but of the Holy Spirit. The angel is waiting for your answer: it is time for him to return to God who sent him. We too are waiting, O Lady, for the word of pity, even we who are overwhelmed by the sentence of damnation.
>
> And behold, to you the price of our salvation is offered. If you consent, straightway shall we be freed. In the eternal Word of God were we all made, and lo! we die; by one little word of yours in answer shall we all be made alive.
>
> Adam asks this of you, O loving Virgin, poor Adam, exiled as he is from paradise with all his poor wretched children; Abraham begs this of you, and David; this all the holy fathers implore, even your fathers, who themselves are dwelling in the valley of the shadow of death; this the whole world is waiting for, kneeling at your feet.
>
> And rightly so, for on your lips is hanging the consolation of the wretched, the redemption of the captive, the speedy de-

liverance of all who otherwise are lost; in a word, the salvation of all Adam's children, of all your race.

Answer, O Virgin, answer the angel speedily; rather, through the angels, answer your Lord. Speak the word, and receive the Word; offer what is yours, and conceive what is of God; give what is temporal, and embrace what is eternal.

Why delay? Why tremble? Believe, speak, receive! Let your humility put on boldness, and your modesty be clothed with truth. Not now should your virginal simplicity forget prudence! In this one thing alone, O prudent Virgin, fear not presumption; for although modesty that is silent is pleasing, more needful now is the loving-kindness of your word.

Open, O Blessed Virgin, your heart to faith; open your lips to speak; open your bosom to your Maker, Behold! the Desired of the nations is outside, knocking at your door. Oh! if by your delay he should pass by, and again in sorrow you should have to begin to seek for him whom your soul loves! Arise, then, run and open. Arise by faith, run by the devotion of your heart, open by your word. "And Mary said: Behold the handmaid of the Lord: be it done to me according to your word." (from homily 4.8–9, taken from the *Divine Office, Approved for Use in Australia, England & Wales, Ireland, New Zealand, Scotland, Advent, Christmastide & Weeks 1–9 of the Year* [London: Collins, 1974], 141–42)

St. Bernard speaks personally to Mary at that moment nearly two thousand years ago when she was asked a favor by God. We can reread the text as though it were directed to each of us, called to respond like Mary originally did. She surrendered. She worshiped and embraced the will of God for all humankind. God has done a marvelous deed in the creation of Mary, in her conception and birth, and Mary responds gratefully and completely.

There is a parable found in the writings of Zenkei Shibayama, who was the abbot of the Nazenji Monastery in Kyoto. I heard it from a Buddhist nun who had attended a retreat on the Scriptures of Advent and Christmas. She told me this was how she imagined Mary.

✠ Once upon a time there was a dove, gentle and simple, who dearly loved the forest where she lived. She loved nothing better than to fly over the forest and smell the trees and the air, watch the clouds dance and disappear, see the weather patterns change, and ride the currents of the wind. She would dip down into the streams of clear water and dart in and out among the shadows and grasses. And then one day as she was watching her beloved forest from above she was horrified to see that a fire had started at the edge of the forest.

She immediately flew to a nearby stream, filled her beak with a few drops of water and flew back to drop them on the fire. She did this repeatedly, crying out the danger to the animals, birds, and creatures of the woods. Most fled before the onslaught of the fire, and when some realized what it was she was trying to do, they mocked her or pitied her. Some cried out to her to save herself and to be careful or she would get caught herself in the fire and be burned to death. But she was so concerned about her beloved dwelling place on earth that she went back to the stream again and again, bringing a few drops of water to drop on the raging flames. And the fire continued to spread. Her wings were blackened, her lungs choked with smoke and, finally, she fell exhausted from the air, into the fire and died.

The other animals were angry or cynical, saying that she was stupid, that she could have no effect on the fire, that she didn't have to die, that her pathetic tries were all in vain.

The nun stopped here and told me that this is where the story originally ended, but that she had resisted the dove having to die; it was all so unnecessary and futile. Without thinking (perhaps inspired by the Spirit) I responded, "Ah, but the Great Spirit, God, saw what the dove had tried to do, saw the love that the dove had for the forest and all its creatures and so, in his great mercy, sent rain and put out the fire and saved the forest." She laughed delightedly and said that there were teachers in her Soto tradition that taught exactly that ending of the parable. She added that this is how she viewed Mary after the retreat's stories and reflections. I looked at her and hoped she'd continue to hold dear that image.

Mary is the dove that so loved the earth and her dwelling place that she was willing to die for it, and so God, in his mercy, sent rain to save what she loved. The Buddhist nun went on to tell me of Kuan Yin, the Buddha of compassion who often carries long ropes to throw to sinners and those in great distress and pulls them to safety. This is our Mary, the beloved of God who loved so well and freely chose to love, to respond to God's invitation to save the earth.

In Mary, God knew that those created in his image would learn once again to obey, to surrender to the heart of what it means to be human, and to live with amazing grace.

Later that evening, after I'd spoken to the Buddhist nun, I was reading the office and found this passage of Isaiah 45:8:

> Let justice descend, O heavens, like dew from above,
>     like gentle rain let the skies drop it down.
> Let the earth open and salvation bud forth;
>     let justice also spring up!
> I, the Lord, have created this.

"I the Lord have created this." The heart of the mystery of the Immaculate Conception of Mary is just this fact: "I, the Lord, have created this." It is the first of many great and marvelous deeds that God continues to do and seeks to share with us. But we must be obedient as Mary was and respond to God's question, "Where are you?" with her words, "I am the maidservant of the Lord. Let it be done to me as you say."

Let us pray to Mary in the words of the Coptic liturgy:

> Hail Mary, the most beautiful dove, which carried the
>     Word of God for us.
> We greet you with the Archangel Gabriel saying:
> Hail Mary, full of grace, the Lord is with you.
> Hail, O Virgin, the glory of our race; you have borne
>     Emmanuel for us.
> We pray that you will remember us before the Lord Jesus
>     Christ,
> that He will forgive us our sins.

This is Mary of Nazareth, the mother of all those baptized and alive in Christ Jesus her son. Because of her obedience we are all called to be "holy and blameless in God's sight, to be full of love ... that [we] all might praise the divine favor he has bestowed on us in his beloved" (Ephesians 1:4, 6). We rejoice in Mary and in God's gift to her, as blessing for all the human race.

# Feast of Our Lady of Guadalupe
## *December 12*

*Revelation 11:19, 12:1–6, 10*
*Psalm Response: Luke 1:46–55*
*Luke 1:39–47*

This is the feast of the Americas. While the feast of the Immaculate Conception is the feast of the church in the United States, the feast of Nuestra Señora la Virgen de Guadalupe is that of the patroness of North and South America. On this day we remember Mary's appearance as a young, indigenous, pregnant woman to Juan Diego Cuatitlatoatzin (his commemoration is December 9) on the hill of Tonanzin, which is in present-day Mexico City. This woman, Guadalupe, woman of the poor, woman of the Americas, is the bridge between the North and the South, rich and poor, Hispanics and Anglos and the indigenous. She is the woman of hope and of the hidden presence of God in our midst. This woman is in the tradition of the prophets of old, and she heralds her child with her vibrant Magnificat of praise and with the *cinto,* the black sash around her waist announcing she is pregnant to all who know the language of Aztec symbols. She is hidden among the poor, the oppressed, the slaves, and all those on the roads outside the cities, much like John the Baptist was. She is the underground hidden river, the source of joy and hope. She is the sign of God who has come in human flesh among us, like John who baptized in the waters of the Jordan River. She calls us to repentance, to care for the poor, and to work for justice now. She and John echo many of the same beliefs and traditions.

In her, the children of God are waiting to be born. They are looking for a place that welcomes them on earth, a community that cares for the poor, the refugees, the ones cast out of the kingdoms of this world, as the indigenous peoples were persecuted, hounded, and destroyed by the conquering armies of invasion. This is still the experience of many in the Americas today. Our Lady of Guadalupe lives between the North and the South, indigenous and immigrant, conquered and conqueror, as John the Baptist lived between the Older and Newer Testaments. She too is this bridge strung across suffering to hope, this resting place of roses and spring in winter, of joy in the midst of despair, brokenheartedness, and shared poverty. She is a servant, like Isaiah and her son Jesus. Her words are of tenderness and healing, of peace to come. Her promise is her presence among us, with her child's nearness to those who are in need and pain. As she cradles him under her heart, she makes a place for all her children.

She is the dark one, the light, the candle burning more and more brightly in the midst of winter, coming with solace, with comfort and touch, with silent glory and regard for all the small ones of the earth. She is the strongest, most enduring prophet of Advent, this woman of hope. She was ready and waiting, the watch woman at the gate, the first to see, the first to say yes, and the first to be open to the Word. She is waiting with us for the birth of her child.

Guadalupe's feast day sometimes falls on Gaudate Sunday itself and more often than not in the third week of Advent, the week of joy. A fitting way to welcome her is to rejoice, to sing her welcome, pregnant with her child, her Savior and Lord, and ours. Along with John the Baptist, she goes before the face of the Lord, showing us how to be heralds of the good news, rejoicing in the presence of God among us, waiting for the fullness of time to bloom and appear in our midst as a child, as the kindness of God bending down to earth to sing to us.

There is a tradition in New Mexico and much of the Southwest and in many Latin American countries called *las mañanitas.* Everyone rises before dawn, around four in the morning, and goes to church to pray and offer Mary a morning serenade and to sing her praises with music, with mariachis, with prayer and silence. Afterwards there is a fiesta, a meal with chocolate, bread, and *menudo.* And there are always red roses, so many of them, reminding us of the revelation, the gift wrapped in Juan Diego's *tilma,* his cloak, and sent to the bishop of Mexico City. Her gift announced who she was and what she wanted, a church built on the outskirts of the city, where her children who had been orphaned, enslaved, raped, and burdened by their conquerors could come to pray. She proclaimed that she was not La Conquistadora, the conqueror, but La Morenita, the little dark one, beloved of God, an indigenous Indian woman.

She is called Guadalupe for a number of reasons. The story is told that the bishop's interpreter did not understand Juan Diego's dialect and thought that he said Guadalupe, connecting her immediately to a shrine in Spain. The Indians of Mexico say that "Guadalupe" means "source of underground hidden waters" and that the name is appropriate, not only geographically (because Mexico City is situated on top of an underground river) but also theologically (because she is the source of life, the one who carries within her own body the Water of Life). For many, she is fondly called Lupe, a diminutive form of her name; Lupe also means wolf, an animal that is more hidden than seen, fiercely faithful to its mate and its young ones, and shy of human beings because of their violence.

For the Spaniards, this woman standing on the earth with the rays of the sun at her back was evocative of the woman of the book of Revelation, she who is clothed with the sun, the moon, and the stars. But for the indigenous people, she was the mother of the one who was to outshine all their gods and to lovingly heal the wounds and violence of the invasion that sought to destroy their culture and their very existence. She was to reach out to both cultures and peoples and bring them together in her embrace, making of them a new people, a people born into shared bloodlines, and bound into the blood of her firstborn son, Jesus.

The first reading today is from the book of Revelation. It describes who this woman is, not only on earth but in the sky:

> God's temple in heaven opened and in the temple could be seen the ark of his covenant. (11:19a)

> A great sign appeared in the sky, a woman clothed with the sun, with the moon under her feet, and on her head a crown of twelve stars. Because she was with child, she wailed aloud in pain as she labored to give birth. (12:1–2)

When the Israelites were traveling in the desert for forty years, the Ark of the Covenant was God's dwelling place, his residence. Mary has also been called the Ark of the Covenant, the dwelling place, the residence of God in her flesh. She is the woman about to give birth, struggling in pain, wailing and crying out loud for deliverance, for her child to be released into the world. And she is a sign. She is the church, all of us conceived by the Spirit, born of the Word of God, obedient to the will of the Father, struggling to release the power of God into the world of history.

As the reading continues, we are shown another sign:

> Then another sign appeared in the sky: it was a huge dragon, flaming red, with seven heads and ten horns; on his heads were seven diadems. His tail swept a third of the stars from the sky

and hurled them down to earth. The dragon stood before the woman about to give birth, ready to devour her child when it should be born. (12:3–4)

This terrible image is threatening to life, murderous in intent. Again, it is a sign not just of the dangerous nature of the birth of this child into the world and history but of the danger for all who are bound to this child in his struggle to set the world free, to bring it new life and the redeeming grace of a new creation. All creation is a part of this struggle, from the stars to the desert. And the struggle continues with the vision:

She gave birth to a son — a boy destined to shepherd all the nations with an iron rod. Her child was snatched up to God and to his throne. The woman herself fled into the desert, where a special place had been prepared for her by God. (12:5–6)

This is the incarnation, the birth of God into human flesh, the birth of Jesus the Lord of the nations and of all time. This child will grow up to shepherd the nations, to gather the lost and the scattered of the earth back into the arms of God, bringing peace with justice. He will be snatched up to God, after being crucified and cast outside the city gates. He will rise gloriously to God's throne where he will continue to shepherd, to judge, and to bring justice to the earth.

The reading tells us that the woman fled for safety into the desert, that place in the Judeo-Christian tradition that is the privileged site of intimacy with God. Again, this is the image of the church, all those who prefer the desert to the world. As Jesus struggled with the Hinderer (the devil) in the desert, he was tempted, but afterward he was ministered to by the wild creatures of earth and the angels of the air. The church dwells in the world but is not of the world. The church's heart is always in the desert, where God can speak to our hearts and purify us and make us a people that belongs to God alone.

Then the scribe of the book of Revelation continues:

Then I heard a loud voice in heaven say:

"Now have salvation and power come,
    the reign of our God and the authority of the Anointed
    One." (12:10a)

With the birth of this child, the mystery of the incarnation becomes reality. God becomes flesh and blood; the gates of heaven spring open; and earth and heaven are one again. There is a new domain, a new authority, another power, and there is salvation. We are rescued, freed, and given the fullness of life.

The reading is very appropriate for the feast of Guadalupe. When Guadalupe appeared to Juan Diego, a poor peasant on his way to Mass, a long walk from his village, she comes in light, with music and the smell of flowers and spring. It is winter, but she stands with her bare feet on the earth. She is small, like many of the indigenous people, dark and dressed simply in the clothes of Juan Diego's tribe. She tells him that she is his compassionate mother, the mother of pity who sees and hears the cries and distress of her people in bondage and that she loves him dearly, tenderly. She questions him, "Am I not your mother?" She is the mother of all who dwelled in this land before the coming of those who would force them into slavery and murder them. She is one of them. She stands with them before the dragon of violence, murder, rape, pillage, and slavery. She will always be with them, a refuge and solace, a healer and a comforter.

She asks Juan Diego to go into the city, to approach the bishop and tell him to build a church for all her people, not in the city, but out on the road, away from the powers of the world. She tells him that she is the mother of all her children and that she wants the bishop to attend to the sufferings of her dearest and most vulnerable children, Juan Diego's people, of whom she is one herself. With the birth of her child will come an advent, a coming together of enemies, of victim and oppressor. The violence, the indignities, the slavery must stop. The powerful must start acting like children of the mother of the Savior, with justice and mercy. This is what she wants. This is the will of her child, the will of God. This is what the reign of our God looks like, the reconciling of enemies, the binding up of wounds, the asking of forgiveness, the prayers of rejoicing, and the hope for the peoples of the Americas. There will always be a struggle between those who are born of her child, the suffering servant who resists evil with the force of love, and those who are born of the dragon, intent on violence and the destruction of creation itself. We know where God stands in this struggle, and we know that the Mother of God stands always trying to give birth to God in us. Although she is always in danger, she is always under the wing of God's power. We are invited to stand with her.

There is an ancient hymn to Mary called the Akathist Hymn to the Virgin that fits perfectly into Advent and into today's readings, especially those from the book of Revelation. This old prayer, attributed to Romanus the Melodist, is from a prayer card given to me at a Ruthinian Orthodox liturgy.

> Hail to you through whom joy will shine out!
> Hail, redemption of fallen Adam!
> Hail, deliverance of the tears of Eve!
> Hail, height unattainable by human thought!
> Hail, depth invisible even to the eyes of angels! . . .
>
> Hail, lightning that lights up our souls!
> Hail, star that causest the sun to appear!
> Hail, thou through whom the creation becomes human!
> Hail, bridge that conveys us from earth to heaven!
> Hail, access of mortals to God!
> Hail, defense against invisible enemies!
> Hail, key to the gates of paradise!
> Hail, radiant blaze of grace!
>
> Hail, thou through whom we are clothed in glory!
> Hail, pillar of the fire guiding those in darkness!
> Hail, key to the kingdom of Christ!
> Hail, impregnable wall of the kingdom!
> Hail, thou through whom we obtain our victories!
> Hail, healing of my body!
> Hail, salvation of my soul!

While this prayer is a bit more elaborate than the simple greeting of the Hail Mary, "full of grace, the Lord is with you, blessed are you among women and blessed is the fruit of your womb, Jesus" (from today's gospel reading), it captures the feeling of a portion of the eastern church that honors Mary as the first of the saints, the first of the prophets, and the first of the martyrs and doctors of the church. It pulls us out of our usual ways of thinking of Mary and of addressing her. In this hymn Mary is more symbolic than human, perhaps even more church than woman; she is the instrument of God's design for all creation.

The responsorial psalm is the song of Mary the woman, poor, unknown, from a small inconspicuous village in occupied territory. And does she sing! Her song of joy seeps through every inch of her flesh and rings in her bones. She begins with herself and her particular relationship with God, but she also sings herself as one of many, of the blessed lowly servants of earth for whom God loves to do great things. She praises God who has noticed her and notices all those who fear him. She proclaims what the poor fervently hope for and need to believe in, that God is on their side, attentive to their cries, and intent on righting the balance of power so it will be in their favor. It is a summation of all the prophets' visions put to music. The music is not just what pours forth from her mouth; it sings through her bones and will take the form of a firstborn child, the exaltation of God. Today, we are invited to sing of Mary and to sing with Mary, to sing the praises and the holiness of our God.

The reading from Luke begins after the angel leaves, when the terror of what others might do to her sets in. She seeks sanctuary with a distant relative who is long past the child-bearing age but experiencing the unexpected birth and joy of a child. She must go in haste. No one can know of her pregnancy until there is space in the world and in other people's hearts for him to be born. She must hide out among those who will understand and shelter her. She goes to Elizabeth, who is in her sixth month, pregnant with the prophet John. They already know his name, given to them by the angel Gabriel (they share the angel in common too) before Zechariah's heart stumbled and he was struck dumb. The child to be born will be "the voice crying out in the wilderness!"

Mary enters with the customary greeting of peace, Shalom. The very sound of her voice causes a rift in the universe. This is the voice of one who is obedient to God's word and will. This is the voice of the woman whose child is the Word of God enfleshed, sleeping in her womb, the stirring of a tiny note of hope. The sound of her voice reverberates in Elizabeth's soul, causing her to cry out. Elizabeth is seized by God and prophesies in the ancient tradition of her people. Her words to Mary are a double blessing, one upon her as the chosen one of all the women of earth and one on her child to be born. Elizabeth recognizes in an instant that this young unmarried woman, running for her life and that of her child, is more than she appears. She is the mother of the long-awaited one who will bring justice and the presence of God to her people. She is the mother of the Savior, the Liberator of Israel, the Prophet of God. Elizabeth sees Mary! And in that moment of seeing in her mind, heart, and soul, her whole body responds.

And the child John, who is called from his mother's womb, as many of the ancient prophets were, hears that voice and its echoes of the Spirit of God and awakes. John, "the voice from the desert," responds wholeheartedly to Mary's voice. He kicks, dances for joy. He knows that voice! He will wait all his life to hear it again. Elizabeth's double blessing now becomes a trinity. She pronounces Mary as trusting in God's Word. She cries out, "Blessed is she who trusted that the Lord's words to her would be fulfilled." Elizabeth's beatitude is stated in the third person. It is first of all for Mary, but it is also a blessing for all those who would be her children, her fellow-followers and disciples of her child, the Word. It is a blessing for all of us who celebrate this season by turning again to the words of the promises of God that have come true and still are coming true in us.

Now Mary sings her response to Elizabeth's blessing. She blesses God. The familiar words can never be sung enough, felt deeply enough, be prayed through us enough. She chants, sharing her song with us: "My being proclaims the greatness of the Lord; my spirit finds joy in God my savior." It is the rallying song of all her people, of those who have remained faithful and who yearn for the promises to come true. She has much to sing about, for the reign of God begins in her; the power of God gathers its strength in her womb; the redemption of all creation is but a seed within her waiting to bud forth. For now, though, it is hidden, and the only ones who know are she and Elizabeth, John who is yet to be born, and all the angels of heaven.

She is a bridge between heaven and earth, standing on the ground of a hill outside Jerusalem and standing again on earth on a hill outside Mexico City. She also bridges two continents, many cultures, and many peoples. When her voice comes softly to Juan Diego, there will be the most delicious singing of unearthly birds in the air all around them.

This is the day of Mary's cry of rejoicing, of prophecy, of denouncing injustice and announcing what her child will do for us all, as God has already done for her in her lowliness and poverty. The Magnificat, the song of incarnation, is the opening of the crack in the doorway so that the Word of God might enter into the whole world. Likewise, the Virgin of Guadalupe is the crack in the world's hate, so that reconciliation and peace might enter between the invaders and the indigenous world they have devastated. Guadalupe will hold both together in her flesh as she once held all of heaven and earth together in her body.

The Virgin of Guadalupe is the John the Baptist of the Americas and its peoples. Her cry is to care for the poor, to repent of injustice and invasion, and to restore dignity and hope among all her children. It is the fundamental imperative of the gospel of her child, Jesus. By clearly siding with the poor, those who reveal the face of God in our midst today, Guadalupe clearly announces the message of Isaiah.

In the Muslim tradition, a Sufi story is often connected to Mary. Called "The Sigh," it reveals much about the woman of Guadalupe.

✤ Once upon a time there was a man who was devoted to Allah in his prayers and ritual, at the mosque, in his home and work. He sought to be faithful and keep Allah in mind no matter what he was doing — traveling, eating, conversing with others. And he never missed the prayers. Five times a day he would drop everything as soon as he heard the summons from the minaret, and he would hastily close up his shop and run to the mosque for the prayers.

Well, one day it seemed as if hell itself was conspiring to keep him from getting to the mosque for the community's prayers. The summons sounded on the wind from the minaret, but he was with a particularly difficult customer. He did everything he could to pull himself away. After offering to cut the price in half and still not getting the man to decide, he threw the goods into the man's hands and pushed him out the door, locking it and following him. Then he raced down the street, knowing that he was going to be late.

Then he was accosted by a beggar, a particularly demanding and aggressive beggar. In his haste to leave his shop, he had left his coin purse behind. Finally, in desperation, he pulled off his finely crafted shoes and threw them into the beggar's outstretched hands, with a blessing prayer upon him, and off he went, running as fast as he could in his stocking feet.

Then he ran into a crowd, an unruly group that was fast turning into a mob. He tried fighting his way through — he could see the minaret just a few blocks from him over the heads of the crowd, but he couldn't get through the press of bodies. He pulled back out of the crowd and ran extra blocks down side streets to get around them. Finally, he arrived at the mosque to see the last of the worshipers exiting. He had missed the prayers altogether. He was near tears.

He approached the last man who was putting on his shoes and queried him, "Am I so late? Are the prayers really finished?" The man looked up and nodded affirmatively. With that, the man from the shop let out a terrible, broken-spirited sigh.

The other stopped, looked at him, and offered a suggestion: "Sir," he said, "you know that in our tradition you can barter and trade for prayers."

"Yes," the first man agreed, wondering what was being offered.

"I tell you what — I attended the entire prayer that you missed. I'll trade you my prayers today for your sigh." The man from the shop was delighted with the offer and immediately agreed. They shook hands and bowed to one another. He returned to his shop, rejoicing over his good fortune to have met such a generous person who would trade his prayers with him.

Until he went home that night and went to bed. In a dream the archangel Gabriel visited him. Gabriel looked down on him in pity and told him, "That was a terrible deal you made today. Don't you know that your sigh was worth more than all the prayers that man has ever said in his life?" And even in his dream, the man wept.

The story is told often among the Sufi, one of the mystical groups of wandering dervishes who sing and dance and write poetry, entrancing their way into the immediate presence of the Holy One. They say that that sigh is crucial. It is a gift, a blessing. And they say that Mary the Virgin, the mother of the prophet Jesus, knew that sigh often, as her only prayer. We could say that Mary is that sigh. She is that prayer that is more pleasing to God than any or all of the words we will ever utter. She looked upon her child, rejected, persecuted, tormented, crucified on a garbage dump outside the City of Peace, and she could only sigh.

Today, she still looks upon all her other children and all the victims of injustice, those tortured and imprisoned, those starving to death, and all she can still do is sigh over us, praying that the Spirit of God will move our hearts and transform us into children like her firstborn, Jesus. On this feast of Our Lady of Guadalupe, we ask ourselves: Do we live so that she looks upon us and sighs, or do we live causing her to sing out the glory of God now alive and free in us?

Another story tells of roses, the symbol of Guadalupe. In the

Guadalupe story, the peasant Juan Diego picked wild roses on a hillside out of season, arranged them lovingly, and then wrapped them inside his *tilma*. When Diego stood before the bishop, the roses fell out on the floor. The bishop thought the roses were the sign, not knowing that the lady's picture was imprinted in bright colors on the *tilma*. The gift of roses to the Virgin and to friends symbolizes intimacy, compassion, the love that is true between the friends of God. Told by Willi Hoffsuemmer, the following story about the poet Rainer Maria Rilke appeared in a collection of stories from the Philippines.

✤ While he was living in Paris, poet Rainer Maria Rilke used to take a walk every afternoon, and daily he passed by an old lady begging along the footpath. The elderly lady sat there stoically and silently and showed no sign of gratitude for the alms the passersby gave her.

One day, the poet was strolling along with a young lady friend, and much to her astonishment he gave the elderly lady no alms. She wondered why. He said in answer to the question he could feel, "A person must give something to her heart and not to her hand."

On one of the next days Rilke appeared with a small, half-opened rose in his hand. Naturally, the young lady thought it was for her. How thoughtful of him! But, no, he laid the rose in the hand of the beggar lady.

And then something wonderful happened. The beggar lady stood up, reached out, and took Rilke's hand and kissed it. She clutched the rose to her heart and disappeared. She stayed away for a whole week. And then she came back and sat there as lifeless and cold as before. "What do you think she lived on during that time?" asked Rilke's young companion.

"On the rose," he answered.

The Lady of Guadalupe has known for over four hundred and fifty years that all of us, really, live on roses. Today we are reminded to sigh over the world and its brokenness and to give roses, not only to Guadalupe but also to those she would single out if visiting earth today.

# The Birth of the Lord
## Christmas Mass at Midnight

Isaiah 9:1–6
Psalm 96:1–3, 11–13
Titus 2:11–14
Luke 2:1–14

Here it is, the night of nights! Light comes to shatter the darkness. Despair and oppression are dispelled, and dawn heralds life and freedom. Joy is let loose upon the earth, and it is time to share in the goodness of the Lord. This child opens a space in the world that will expand into a sanctuary, a place of grace and security, built on justice and righteousness for all peoples. One day the child's dominion will have no end. The place is earth, home. Its new name is Peace.

The crack in the universe begins to be noticed in Nazareth, with a trail that grows brighter in Bethlehem, far away from the halls of power. The holy breaks in, in the light of angels and in a song of freedom and joy. Signs tell that there will be a child, an unknown and unnoticed child of the poor, a baby wrapped in swaddling clothes and lying in a manger. This child is the Messiah, the Savior, the Glory of God breathing and sleeping among us.

The first to know are shepherds tending their flocks on the outskirts of town. It seems that fringes, margins, and boundaries are where our God gets in first, in places we wouldn't expect. This night, especially, we are to stay alert, to stay up all night if necessary, and to listen for the echo of the song that was sung into the universe so long ago. Some say it is the first song, hummed into existence when God, the Maker of all things, sighed and breathed over the empty dark at the dawn of time. The words become more distinct and clear this night: "Glory to God in the highest; peace on earth for God is blessing humankind. Glory to God in the highest; peace on earth to all of good will. God's favor rests on us. Glory to God in the highest."

This dear night God was born of a woman, Mary, and was tended by a dreamer, Joseph. This dear night our God wants to be born of us, all men and women who believe in the Word that has been given to us in dreams and visions of faith. This dear night may God find us awake, with our hearts open so that this space inside us might become a haven of peace for all our weary waiting world. Amen. What is the import of this night? This night's story is known and acted out by children in every country, dressing up as shepherds, wise ones, Mary and Joseph, angels and innkeepers. Yet what does it mean for us? There is a story from China that might help us look at this familiar night in more startling terms. It is called "The Honorable Gentleman Ye" by Shen Tzu.

✤ Once upon a time there was a wealthy man, an only son of elderly parents. He grew up fascinated with dragons. He read every story on dragons and collected books on them. He painted pictures of them, made kites and origami figures shaped like them. His knowledge of dragons grew apace as he grew up. And his fascination evolved into a fantastic collection of dragons: jade, netsuki size (about an inch or two high, intricately carved), great stone ones for home and garden, scrolls and screens in bright fiery colors, porcelain, and burnished metals.

But it was more than just collecting that interested him, for the honorable gentleman Ye truly was a gentleman, befriending others, especially strangers, living honorably, truthfully, expounding on and living out the values of the Great Dragon himself. Dragons were known to be ancient and wise in experience, always protecting and defending the innocent and weak against those more powerful and thoughtless. Dragons also shadowed those who did evil and reckoned a way to make justice come.

Ye was faithful and devoted to the Great Dragon and taught others to live with devotion to the old ways. His veneration was known far and wide; in fact, it rose up to the attention of the Great Dragon himself, who was impressed by the honorable gentleman Ye's defense of the Great Dragon's person and astute attention to his ways on the earth. It had been a long time since anyone had really taken the Great Dragon's presence and reality seriously, and the more he thought about it the more he wanted to reward Ye for such faithfulness. Finally, he lit upon the perfect gift: he would go himself and thank him for his devotion and worship! Yes, that was an apt reward.

The Great Dragon leapt down from the heavens and landed right next to the honorable gentleman Ye's great house and garden. He wrapped his great body and long tail around the house and with one great eye peered in one of the windows of the faithful gentleman's house, to see if he had caught him at home. He was in. There was such a thundering and rocking of the whole house that Ye ran outside to see what was the matter. He was terrified at the sight before him. The Great Dragon was shimmering in the light, the color of fire and rainbows, ice and light, of enormous size, tail waving (in delight) and fire flowing from his nostrils, his eyes flashing and so excited to see his friend, the honorable gentleman Ye.

But Ye was terrified out of his mind and ran from the Great Dragon. He was stark raving mad. They say he is running still and that the Great Dragon was so hurt by his reaction that he barely ever comes to earth anymore and when he does he always comes in disguise. Now the Great Dragon knows that humans, even those devoted to his person and worship, cannot take the sight of him, and he is greatly saddened.

A commentary on the story by Carlos Vallejo, S.J., asks, "What would happen if God would some day peer though the window of our house?"

God comes to earth to visit, and everyone is taken aback. This is not exactly what we expected or hoped for, not our image of what God should be. We retreat in distress, confusion, or nonrecognition. And so the first reading of Midnight Mass on Christmas Day is to startle us and throw us off guard; it is meant to make us wonder who this child really is among us now. The first part of the Isaian prophecy is more than exultant rejoicing; it is exuberant freedom, liberation, and wild celebration:

> The people who walked in darkness
>     have seen a great light;
> Upon those who dwelt in the land of gloom
>     a light has shone.
> You have brought them abundant joy
>     and great rejoicing.
>
> As they rejoice before you as at the harvest,
>     as men make merry when dividing spoils.
> For the yoke that burdened them,
>     the pole on their shoulder,
> And the rod of their taskmaster
>     you have smashed, as on the day of Midian.

For every boot that tramped in battle, . . .
will be burned as fuel for flames.

This is freedom from war and violence; from slavery, injustice,
and oppression as once God led his people out of bondage in Egypt
into the promised land. Now there is harvest, release, straightening up and walking, putting the memories of horror behind. Light
bursts darkness, explodes, shatters the gloom. The images are that of
a slave bent double who jumps up, throwing off the yoke, and the
rod of the slave driver being smashed. This is force and power let
loose. All the accouterments of war and oppression are now burned
and destroyed forever. Light reigns, and lightheartedness born of
great endurance suffuses the captives' faces and hearts. This is a
night for a bound and bent people to break into dance. Why? The
response is breathtaking and simple: "For a child is born to us, a
son is given to us: upon his shoulder dominion rests." The pole
that broke the back of the slave and the power that leaned on the
poor are now shifted. The shoulders of a child now carry dominion
and power.

All the Christmas readings contain intimations and echoes of the
cross, of the mystery of passion and death that shadows this child.
This one in particular is strong: that of a yoke of dominion resting
upon his shoulders. For Jesus will bear his cross, be burdened with
grief and sorrow and the sin of the world, and be yoked to the
wood that will be his deathbed. His dominion will be heavy, yet
also vast and forever peaceful. Is this an echo of Jesus' words, "Take
my yoke upon your shoulders for my yoke is easy and my burden
light and you will find rest"?

And then the child is named: Wonder Counselor, God-Hero, Father Forever, Prince of Peace. When we hear such names, we often
react without thinking about their depth of meaning. A *counselor*
may remind us of someone who listens, validates our lives and experiences, gives us the freedom to express our emotions, dreams,
fears, someone who accepts us as we examine our lives. On the other
hand, a counselor does not allow us to blame others or get away
with a refusal to take responsibility for what we have done or the
choices we are making in our lives. Counselors make us hear what
we say aloud. They put us in relation to others, healing those broken pieces of our lives. But there are other meanings, perhaps more
to the issue of the word "counselor." A counselor in a court of law
is bound to the defense of both the law and the client, balancing

justice and mercy. And in the Middle Ages a counselor was often a fool, one who could tell the truth to the king and make him hear and see the consequences of his behavior and mistakes, perhaps using unorthodox and even strange wiles to make him see himself in another light.

And this, our counselor, is a *Wonder-Counselor!* He is adept in the discernment of wonder, of awe and reverence, respect and dignity. What puts us in awe? What humbles us and empties our soul of all but hope, worship, and gratitude? Nature, beauty, art, children, love, release from debt, gratuitous generosity. . . . All these things this child is adept at revealing and calling forth. Thus Wonder-Counselor is the first of the names given to him.

The next is *God-Hero.* Every nation has its epics, the stories of those who liberated others from oppression and delivered them up to safety and hope. Usually heroes have to experience great trials and sufferings in order to be able to do this, putting themselves in jeopardy for others, with great-hearted passionate love and devotion. Likewise, our God-Hero will do this graciously, lovingly, with forgiveness even for enemies and friends who betray. This God-Hero will be God, divine and human, bound in life and death to those he threw in his lot with.

The next title is *Father Forever.* How can a child be a father, with a fatherhood that lasts forever? Obviously, this is not about biology but about strength, intimacy, and love. We think of the words from John's gospel, when Jesus is questioned by one of his disciples, "Where is the Father? Show us the Father!" And Jesus replies, "Thomas! Have you been with me all this time and you still don't see? If you see me, you see the Father!" This image of God in flesh and blood tells of adoption, of becoming children of Spirit and love, of God grasping humankind in the body of his beloved child. This child will live only to obey and revere God who is his and our Father Forever. He will know God as no human before has ever known or been known by God.

The title *Prince of Peace* evokes a sense of a God-centered refuge for those upon whom God's favor and Spirit rest and stay. Jesus will bring peace with justice and freedom from sin and evil. In this child will be peace, abiding, true, and universal. No more violence, hate, alienation, or separation from God or from one another. This child belongs to God and to the people. All this begins this night.

The response to the psalm is the words spoken by the angel to the shepherds in announcing the child born in Bethlehem: "Today is born our Savior, Christ the Lord." It is a battle cry of hope, of peace and exultation, of freedom and belief. We stake our lives on this and give our hearts over in absolute wonder and shared joy. And we sing a new song, learned from the sounds of hope and freedom, from angels' voices and obedient hearts. All are commanded to join in the song of gladness — all nations and peoples, the earth and sea, all of creation. Everything exults before the Lord. All of creation is called to dance, to go before this Lord who will rule the world with justice and constancy, enduring justice and mercy.

Paul describes this night in a simple statement: "The grace of God has appeared offering salvation to all!" This child will come bearing both glory and suffering, a mission and work to do. Paul puts it succinctly, "It was he who sacrificed himself for us, to redeem us from all unrighteousness and to cleanse for himself a people of his own, eager to do what is right." This is another echo of Advent and our hopes that God will come and meet us doing what is right and just. This child is our blessed hope, and his work will be to teach us how to live justly and temperately and to train us how to reject godless ways and worldly desires.

This is a night that reminds us that a human child, so mortal and subject to suffering and pain, is a child born of God, for the people, and there is something about this child that is undying, death-defying. He is joy, the presence of God, the harvest of a long-awaited promise. This power, this strength, this peace of God is given to us: "For unto us a child is given, unto us a son is born." God gets closer and closer to us, touchable in a new-born. This happens tonight. Now! Not just once upon a time. Now! This child comes to rule the world with justice. This child is what God looks like, what the Holy looks like in human flesh, in our flesh.

Luke's version of the Christmas story, read at every Midnight Mass, tries to situate this night in its political and religious context. We know it as the tale of the census, a decree by Caesar Augustus ordering a census of the whole world. Augustus, emperor of Rome, had decreed that Rome's rule over most of the Mediterranean nations would be a time of salvation for all, a time of peace and prosperity when all would reap great blessings. An inscription from 9 B.C.E., found in the city of Priene in western Asia Minor, reads as follows:

> Because providence that has ordered our life in a divine way
> ... and since the Caesar through his appearance [epiphany]

has exceeded the hope of all former good news [gospels = evangelia], surpassing not only the benefactors who came before him, but also leaving no hope that anyone in the future would surpass him, and since for the world the birthday of the god was the beginning of his good news [gospels], [may it therefore be decided that]...(cited in Helmut Koestler, "A Political Christmas Story," *Bible Review* [October 1994]: 23)

Luke's story is a highly charged political presentation in opposition to prevailing Roman propaganda, an affront to the ruling power who is the Emperor Domitian (81–96 C.E.). The emperor also had other names, including Savior, Son of God, Caesar, and Lord, so Luke's account and choice of words to describe this child contradicted contemporary beliefs and political pronouncements. The order from Augustus to count all the people in the world, as though people of other nations were cattle or pigs belonging to Rome, disordered the world and forced people to take to the roads, to return to their own towns to register. And so the birth of Jesus begins with a forced march, a harrowing journey for Joseph and his very pregnant wife Mary, from the town of Nazareth in Galilee to Judea, to David's town of Bethlehem. While they are in town, along with thousands of other political, national, and religious refugees, in the midst of chaos, "she gave birth to her first born son and wrapped him in swaddling clothes and laid him in a manger, because there was no room for them in the inn."

This description is crucial, not quaint or cute. This is a child of a despised, poor, conquered nation, an expendable people considered to have as much dignity as an animal. We are told that the place of birth is outside of town because there is "no room for them in the inn." Luke's gospel is a story of journeys and what happens along the way. One of Jesus' most famous stories of a traveler appears only in Luke — the parable of the Good Samaritan, an outsider who lifts up a Jew, despised, beaten, and near death, and takes him to an inn (Luke 10:34). And Jesus' last meal will be in an inn, a borrowed upper room, where he will leave himself as bread and wine for the world's hungry and weak (Luke 22:11).

We hear that Mary wraps him in swaddling clothes and lays him in a manger, a feeding trough for animals, packed with hay. At the end of his life, he will again be wrapped in shrouds and laid in a borrowed tomb. In between, he will be bread, food for the poor, especially for sinners like the lost son who comes to his senses when he begins thinking about stealing food given to pigs. This manger is the first "tabernacle," the house of bread, the altar and table for a feast of freedom and justice. Those invited are not ones we would expect: "Shepherds in the locality, living in the fields and keeping night watch by turns over their flock." Thomas Merton writes of this night: "Into this world, this demented Inn, in which there is absolutely no room for Him at all, Christ comes uninvited." Tonight, as on that night, the child, the Christ, comes to our world.

The poor shepherds are visited by an angel, as earlier Gabriel came to Mary. The appearance sounds like Isaiah's description read earlier tonight, "The angel of the Lord appeared to them, as the glory of the Lord shone around them, and they were very much afraid." But no fear! Not on this night! The announcement is resounding in the night sky:

> You have nothing to fear! I come to proclaim good news to you — tidings of great joy to be shared by the whole people. This day in David's city a savior has been born to you, the Messiah and Lord. Let this be a sign to you: in a manger you will find an infant wrapped in swaddling clothes.

Then there is an interruption, and Gabriel is joined by a multitude of heavenly creatures, praising God and singing, "Glory to God in high heaven, peace on earth to those on whom his favor rests."

The sign is a child born in David's city, but outside the realms of existing power, outside the city and the temple. The child comes into the world among animals, among shepherds who were outcasts, among the poor and the angels of God. Glory dwells best in poverty on this earth, it seems. God hides in a child, in lowliness, in places of exclusion, in caves, and among all those who can recognize him as their own, "those on whom his favor rests." God's favor began with Mary, the lowly and obedient servant; then Joseph, obedient and risking all to serve two others; then shepherds, the poor, the uncouth. They are the ones singled out to receive the gift of peace. Our way into that group is crucial. We must grow small, be humble and bent, surrendering to God in the poor, taking care of the children and the unwanted, those in need of protection, those who find there is no room for them in the economic structures of the world.

In his homily on Christmas Eve, 1978, Oscar Romero said:

> No one can celebrate a genuine Christmas without being truly poor. The self-sufficient, the proud, those who, because they

have everything, look down on others, those who have no
need even of God — for them there will be no Christmas.
Only the poor, the hungry, those who need someone to come
on their behalf, will have that someone. That someone is God,
Emmanuel, God-with-us. Without poverty of spirit there can
be no abundance of God. (From a Christmas card from El
Salvador, 1997)

Radiance and the light of angels direct us toward God's chosen
place on earth, a place of poverty created by power, by structures
and governments unnecessarily bolstering their own egos and thus
degrading other human beings. My grandmother has told me a story
of World War I, when she was just a child.

✤ It was Christmas in 1914 and the war was young. More than
eight hundred thousand had been killed, and it looked like
Christmas would be just another day of killing among Christians
on the German front. A British soldier on guard duty thought
he heard a familiar song in the cold dark night as he crawled
along the trenches: "Stille Nacht, heilige Nacht." He began to
sing back, "Silent Night, Holy Night." As he passed by, another
joined him and another until there was a chorus on their side of
the trench.

Then the German soldiers started another song, "O Tannen-
baum," and the English replied with "Hark the Herald Angels
Sing." Back and forth across the trenches, they sang carols
to each other. Then signs were hastily scribbled and held up:
"Merry Christmas" in German and English. And then it happened. The war stopped. First, one brave and tired soldier crept
under the barbed wire and crawled across the space that separated the two armies. He brought some sardines with him. More
and more soldiers crawled out into the space, bringing bottles
of wine, chocolate, packages from home, cookies. They shared
pictures of families, wives, and children, photographs of home,
and tin cups of wine, cigarettes, and more songs. The officers
of both sides were stunned but could do nothing. All night the
war stopped. Some even played cards and soccer for a while,
laughing and singing until dawn and then into the day.

Finally, the officers prevailed, summoning their men back to
their own side of the trenches, threatening them with court-
martial or worse. They obeyed and before Christmas Day was

over, the war was on again. The Prince of Peace prevailed only
one night.

I've heard this story told in other places and have also read accounts of it. People usually marvel at what one night can do, yet
my grandmother wept and cried. She said, "Christmas means nothing. It is not for one night. One night mocks God and the reality
of peace and who this child is. One night condemns Christians who
could sing carols and acknowledge they were brothers and then turn
around and kill on command."

Years later, a friend sent me a Christmas letter and quoted from
Thomas Merton's journal *A Search for Solitude:*

Have we ever yet become Christians?

The duty of the Christian is to see Christ being born into
the whole world and to bring Him to life in all mankind.

But we have sought to bring to birth in the world an image
of ourselves and of our own society and we have killed the
Innocents in doing so, and Christ flees from us into Egypt.

Have we ever yet become Christians? (197)

This might appear rather grim for Christmas night, but the readings themselves are about light breaking into violence and despair,
gloom and darkness. Both are there and both remain, although there
is now a chance for the kingdom of light to prevail. It is up to
"those on whom God's favor rests" to join the chorus of angels and
sing the glory of God, not just in words this night but in praise
and decisions, stances and relationships of nonviolence, universal
communion, and a refusal to follow the commands of the world's
powers. Instead, we must choose to go to Bethlehem where God is
found among the poor and the lowly.

A children's story about animals will help us on our way, reminding us of what is important on this night when God gifts us with
a wondrous presence, a child that is Savior and Lord, a child that
is ours to hold and bend over and worship. The story is by Willi
Hoffsuemmer:

✤  Once upon a time as Joseph and Mary made their way to Bethlehem an angel called a meeting with all the animals of the earth
to choose which of them would attend the birth and be allowed
in the cave with the newborn child. The animals were all excited and wanted to be there, of course. First, the lion roared

and said, "I am the king of all the animals. It is only right that I am allowed to be there. I will defend the child and tear to pieces anyone who tries to harm him."

The angel cringed and said, "Too violent."

Then the fox came forward. "I will stand guard over the child, and I'll make sure the baby has good food every day. In fact, I will steal a chicken every day for the family."

The angel looked hard at the fox and said, "Not a thief."

The peacock strutted forward and said, "Let me. I'll spread my feathers, and I'll decorate the cave in a style fit truly for a king. It will rival Solomon's own temple."

The angel sighed and said, "Too proud."

One by one the animals came forward with their reasons why they should be the ones allowed inside. Birds swooped about, darting in and out, making a loud noise. The angel said, "Too loud and disruptive."

The poor angel was getting frustrated and thought, "Why are these animals so much like humans?" The angel looked to see if anyone had been missed and noticed some animals in the field. They were rather old and slow moving, and they had said nothing and were not even in the group. The ox and the donkey were summoned to the meeting, and the angel asked what they would do for the child and his mother on that night.

They looked at each other and neither said anything. They both looked down at the ground and at last the ox said, "We learned a long time ago not to do anything out of line; to be humble and patient and long suffering. Anything else we ever did got us less food and more whippings." They hung their heads and swished their tails. Then the donkey said quietly, "Well, we could keep the flies away by swinging our tails and keep the air moving in the cave."

The angel smiled delightedly, "Exactly! You'll both do perfectly. Come, we must move quickly. Tonight is the night."

This is the night the Christ is born, poor, humble, and lowly, to a world weary and battle-worn. The Christmas carol sings quietly of what is really happening this night: "O little town of Bethlehem, how still we see thee lie, / above your deep and dreamless sleep the silent stars go by. / But in your dark streets shineth the everlasting light, / the hopes and fears of all the years are born in thee tonight." Tonight God announces by the presence of this child that justice will be established on the earth and peace will reign. It will be a peace that disturbs the powerful and mighty. It will shake their hearts and the thrones and kingdoms like those of Augustus Caesar and Domitian; all tyrants and unjust governments will know that this child in a manger proclaims true good news, a new political, social, and economic order that is for all those favored by God because of their long-enduring faithfulness and hope.

This night is about light. In northern New Mexico and in many places in the Southwest and Latin America, it's customary on this night to place small lanterns, *luminarias,* along the side streets, roads, and entrances to light the way for Mary and Joseph as they make their way to Bethlehem. They are just brown, lunch-size bags filled with sand with a small candle in them. Lit at dark, they burn throughout the night, leaving trails of glory and soft radiant light all along the way. It is an announcement for all, believers and unbelievers alike, that our hearts are open and our homes ready to welcome the child and Mary and Joseph within. There is room in our inns for all who are longing for God.

I found a Christmas sermon in a bookshop in Liverpool. It's by Theodotus, bishop of Ancyra, and dates from 455.

✦ The Lord of all comes in the form of a servant; and he comes as a poor man, so that he will not frighten away those souls he seeks to capture like a huntsman. He is born in an obscure town, deliberately choosing a humble dwelling-place. His mother is a simple maiden, not a great lady. And the reason for all this lowly state is so that he may gently ensnare mankind and bring us to salvation. If he had been born amid the splendor of a rich family, unbelievers would surely have said that the face of the world had been changed by the power of wealth. If he had chosen to be born in Rome, the greatest of cities, they would have ascribed the same change to the power of her citizens.

Suppose our Lord had been the son of an emperor; they would have pointed to the advantage of authority. Imagine his father a legislator; their cry would have been, "See what can be brought about by the law." But, in fact, what did he do? He chose nothing but poverty and mean surroundings, everything that was plain and ordinary, and in the eyes of most people, obscure. And this so that it could be clearly seen that the Godhead alone transformed the world. That was why he chose his mother from among the poor of a very poor country, and became poor himself.

This is the lesson of the crib. Since there was no bed, our Lord was laid in a manger. This lack of the necessities of life was the best way of proclaiming the will of God. He was laid in a manger to show that he was to be the food even of simple folk. We know, in fact, how the divine Word, the Son of God, drew to himself both rich and poor, the eloquent and the inarticulate, as he lay in the manger surrounded by poverty.

See then how poverty acted as a prophecy — how his poverty showed that he who became poor for our sake was thereby made accessible to everyone. Christ made no ostentatious display of riches, which would have made people frightened to approach him; he assumed no royal state, which would have driven men away from his presence. No, he came among ordinary men as one of themselves, offering himself freely for the salvation of all.

We are made in the image and likeness of our God, and so tonight we pray with Gerard Manley Hopkins:

Make me pure, Lord; thou art holy;
Make me meek, Lord; thou wert lowly;
Now beginning, and always;
Now begin, on Christmas Day.

Alleluia! Alleluia! Alleluia! O Holy Night. Today is born our Savior, Christ the Lord.

# The Birth of the Lord
## *Christmas Mass at Dawn*

*Isaiah 62:11–12*
*Psalm 97:1, 6, 11–12*
*Titus 3:4–7*
*Luke 2:15–20*

The choice of the readings for this Mass at dawn is based on the assumption that we have already worshiped at night. The readings are breathless and short. It has already been accomplished! It has already been said! Awe seeps in deeper and deeper. God has entered time, become small enough to be enclosed in a child's body and limited to one space and place, mortal and divine. As St. Irenaeus said in the first century: "Because of His boundless love, He became what we are in order that He might make us what He is." This, too, is Isaiah's pronouncement: "See, your Savior comes!" He comes to the ends of the earth, to us, and we "shall be called the holy people, the redeemed of the Lord." We will have new names, such as "Frequented" and "A City That Is Not Forsaken." God is visiting us and staying with us!

A new dawn begins in us with this child's appearance. The light has broken through the darkness of evil, into flesh and blood, into the world, into us. Today is the beginning of endless day and endless light. Everything starts coming true, just not as we expected. After all, God is God and is always expressing himself in clearer, more startling ways, always moving in on us, seeking entrance into our hearts and lives. But we are reminded, even today, that this child, this coming of God among us, happens in destitution, in a cave outside the city. Only strangers, shepherds, the poor, and angels attend his birth. This is a mixing of misery and glory, prophet and broken man who will be crucified and rejected, yet rise. This is Son of God and Son of Man and son of Mary. This is the Savior. Today brings a strange commingling of transcendence and familiarity, with God drawing close, sometimes so close it is not comfortable.

Yet the only response today is joy. The psalm refrain sings out: "A light will shine on us this day: the Lord is born for us." This birth is for us — for all nations and lands, for heaven and earth, for justice and glory. And this birth is especially for the just, the faithful, those who live in opposition to sin, evil, and oppression. The last verse is very direct, describing "those upon whom the favor of the Lord rests":

> Light dawns for the just;
> and gladness, for the upright of heart.
> Be glad in the Lord, you just,
> and give thanks to his holy name.

All the readings, even the psalm, are short, direct, and to the point. They are wild with delight. Light shines on us today! The Lord is born for us! God comes to live with us, for us; die with us, for us; rise with us, for us. No other reasons are given. Light dawns upon us, the just, the upright of heart. Paul's letter to Titus lays out the theological reasons. This day is all about "the kindness and love of God appearing in this child who is our Savior." We are saved by mercy, by the power of the Holy Spirit. We are "lavished" with this gift so that we can be transformed by grace and become heirs of God, in hope.

These first three readings are mini "glorias," paeans of praise to the Trinity, keeping this Child-human-God in the larger context of Father, Son, and Spirit. They remind us of what is to come, the suffering, death, and resurrection that begin in the flesh of this child born today. This is a mystery that one must be silently in awe of and worship wordlessly or lavish with words seeking to express this amazing thing that God has done for us.

Two short poems by Rumi, an Islamic mystic, give us some sense of this day's glories. Each speaks to something of this day's mysteries. The first poem is this:

> Come, Come whoever you are! Wanderer,
> Worshiper, lover of learning.
> Come, Come this is not a caravan of despair.
> It doesn't matter if you've broken your vow
> A thousand times, still and yet again
> Come!

And the second poem:

> I have no more words.
> Let the soul speak with the silent
> Articulation of a Face.

It is a day for poetry, carols, hymns, silence, ancient words, and wonder. Luke's gospel picks up last night's story. It begins by pulling us down to earth again. "When the angels had returned to heaven, the shepherds said to one another: 'Let us go over to Bethlehem and see this event which the Lord has made known to us.'" And so there is another journey, down from the fields and into the town, as the shepherds pull their heads out of the starry night and turn resolutely to reality, this event that is revealed to them by the Holy One. They go "in haste," just as Mary went "in haste" to the hill country when she learned she was pregnant. This also echoes the ragged bands of Israelites who leave "in haste" one night and set off for freedom on a journey out of Egypt and slavery into the desert where they will become a people, God's chosen and beloved people. Good news results in haste! We who hear must go in haste to see, to "find Mary

and Joseph and the baby lying in the manger." Mary obeyed in haste
and now the shepherds obey in haste, setting out on a journey to see
the glory of God in a person, a child born to us.

They see, and "once they saw, they understood what had been
told them concerning this child. All who heard of it were astonished at the report given them by the shepherds." So much ground
is covered in this last sentence! The Word that was proclaimed to
them by the chorus of angels in the heavens at night has come true.
They see and understand! They go and give a report. They preach!
What a sermon they had to tell that morning. Their story elicits "astonishment." This is the same word used toward the end of Luke's
gospel when the two disciples on the Emmaus road tell the story of
the women at the tomb who see angels and hear the announcement
of resurrection. They are astonished at this tale of life over death!
These are the first preachers, singers, storytellers of the good news,
and their listeners hear the report with gladness and joy. They are believed! This is revelation and epiphany showing forth. Revelation is
beginning, slipping out in talk, in reports, in stories that spread like
wildfire, because they are about hope. The shepherds give glory to
God by their words and witness. They see the reality of God among
us, a Savior that is born to us, a poor child swaddled and sleeping
in a food trough for animals. They practice seeing things for what
they really are, from God's-eye view.

The reading tells us that Mary "treasured all these things and reflected on them in her heart." The story is simple, really. Angels sing
it. Shepherds listen and obey. The reality is Jesus, Mary, and Joseph
in a cave, the birth of a child who belongs to the people and who
will save them from their sins. Then the shepherds go off and start
telling the story round about of what they have seen and heard.

Now it is time for all of us to start telling the story in our lives, in
words, songs, relationships, in care for the poor, in the words of angels and the Scriptures. Like the shepherds, we are to tell it around,
to the poor, children, outcasts, those on the fringe of society, the
homeless and migrants, those being counted in the census for pur-
poses of control. The story is astonishing! And astonishment will be
the reaction of most people to Jesus as Luke tells the story. It reeks
of the presence of prophets, of the Word of God — that is justice
and compassion — let loose in the world with people unexpectedly
breaking rules and expectations.

Perhaps Mary is the person who shows us what we should be
doing this day, reflecting, treasuring, glorifying in this Word from

the angelic chorus and the shepherds in the hills. This is the woman who first heard the Word of God and took it into her heart to keep it growing in her. Even though she did not yet fully understand it, she obeyed it. Slowly it dawned on her, as it dawns on all of us, growing in brightness through seeing, pondering, singing, and acting upon it. Our journey through this coming year accompanying this child must be steeped in the Scriptures, the old words of the prophets, the familiar words of the gospels, and the silent gestation of reflection. The event must be shared and told about so that others can rejoice and be astonished as well. It cannot be kept inside, but must be put into practice, piece by piece, day by day, insight by insight, obeying, surrendering, risking more. Today we are asked what we are listening for, whom we are listening to, if we are giving our hearts time to listen, if *we* are worth listening to, if we are astonishing others who need to hear this story. Like the shepherds aloud and Mary in silence, are we "praising and glorifying God for all we have heard and seen, in accord with what we have been told"?

In a Christmas circular in 1939 Dietrich Bonhoeffer wrote: "It is the task of theology only to preserve God's wonder as wonder, to understand, to defend, to glorify God's mystery as mystery" (*A Testament of Freedom*, 472). In the early church a number of theologians sought to express the stunning force and mystery of this birth and this day with eloquence and poetry. One of these writers, John Chrysostom, whose nickname was "Golden Mouth," delivered a remarkable Christmas sermon in a time of religious pluralism and furious theological debate about the identity of Jesus Christ. Segments of it are worth quoting and reflecting upon more than fifteen hundred years later. These selections are taken from an adaptation and condensation from M. F. Toal, *The Sunday Sermons of the Great Fathers: Patristic Homilies on the Gospels*, vol. 1 (Chicago: Henry Regnery, 1957).

> I behold a new and wondrous mystery. My ears resound to the Shepherd's song, piping no soft melody, but chanting full forth a heavenly hymn. The Angels sing. The Archangels blend their voice in harmony. The Cherubim hymn their joyful praise. The Seraphim exalt His glory. All join to praise this holy feast, beholding the Godhead here on earth, and man in heaven. He Who is above, now for our redemption dwells here below; and he that was lowly is by divine mercy raised.

Bethlehem this day resembles heaven; hearing from the stars the singing of angelic voices; and in place of the sun, enfolds within itself on every side, the Sun of Justice. And ask not how: for where God wills, the order of nature yields. For He willed, He had the power, He descended, He redeemed; all things move in obedience to God. This day He Who is, is Born; and He Who is, becomes what He was not.

What shall I say! And how shall I describe this Birth to you? For this wonder fills me with astonishment. The Ancient of days has become an infant. He Who sits upon the sublime and heavenly Throne, now lies in a manger. And He Who cannot be touched, Who is simple, without complexity, and incorporeal, now lies subject to the hands of men. He Who has broken the bond of sinners, is now bound by an infant's bands. But He has decreed that ignominy shall become honour, infamy be clothed with glory, and total humiliation the measure of His Goodness. For this He assumed my body, that I may become capable of His Word; taking my flesh, He gives me His spirit; and so he bestowing and I receiving, He prepares for me the treasure of Life. He takes my flesh, to sanctify me; He gives me His Spirit, that He may save me.

Come, then, let us observe the Feast. Truly wondrous is the whole chronicle of the Nativity. For this day the ancient slavery is ended, the devil confounded, the demons take to flight, the power of death is broken, paradise is unlocked, the curse is taken away, sin is removed from us, error driven out, truth has been brought back, the speech of kindliness diffused, and spreads on every side, a heavenly way of life has been implanted on the earth, angels communicate with men without fear, and men now hold speech with angels.

To Him, then, Who out of confusion has wrought a clear path, to Christ, to the Father, and to the Holy Ghost, we offer all praise, now and for ever. Amen.

No matter what sermons we read from the early history of the church or from contemporary writers, there is a core of mystery that reduces us, after all the words are said, to silence. This birth alters meaning radically — the meaning of being human, of life and death, of suffering and freedom, of hope and the future. Without this child's existence, what would our lives be like? Yet there are many places in the world where this child's birth is ignored, deliberately misconstrued, or insulted. For the past two years I have been invited to Japan around the Advent, Christmas, and Epiphany seasons and have experienced these days of awe and mystery in a land, a language, and a culture alien and foreign to my own beliefs. On my first visit in late fall there was a flurry of decorations. I was taken to visit the "mother of all department stores," Takashimaya, and was greeted with the words, "A hale and hearty Christmas," with tinsel, glitter, lights, Christmas songs, but no carols. This is a land where Christians of all denominations are less than 1 percent of the population, where Judeo-Christian history, values, and traditions are irrelevant and easily subordinated to other values. Externally, Christmas is loudly proclaimed and exploited for all its worth, celebrated for weeks before December 25. But this Christmas is shallow and false and incredibly sad, because there is no birth, no child, no Christ. With no Christ, there is no foundation for hope, no symbols and history of salvation, nothing to stand on and stake your life on when remembering this day. If you ask about the meaning of Christmas, you may be told that it is the birthday of Santa Claus.

Shrines are crowded with people praying and paying to have their fortunes told. They receive them on small, white pieces of paper, and if they don't like what they read, they tie them on the bare branches of trees and leave them behind. This season of Advent and Christmas and Epiphany is about the future, uncertain at best and unpredictable in a world where real religion is often irrelevant or at odds with society's other agendas and values. We're bombarded with messages that tell us Advent and preparation for Christmas are about lights and Christmas carols, bustle and spending, family and gift-giving, decorations, food and celebration, all in expectation of one day, Christmas. This day can be a day of frenzied gift-giving, overgiving, shredded paper and sometimes shredded relationships, frayed nerves, exhaustion and a hollow sense of something essential missing from our lives. In the middle of all of this, there is little room for the Word made flesh, for peace on earth and the praise of God who is the giver of the only gift that matters.

But this is not what the season and this day especially are about, not even the gift-giving and getting. Every reading, each Sunday, proclaims something radically different. This season is about opening a door, a door to the cold blast of wind and air outside, to the lament of evil, selfishness, nations at war, and the politics of profit and greed. It is a season rank with prophets in opposition to all of this, including Isaiah, Micah, Jeremiah, John the Baptizer, and Mary the woman of Nazareth.

In her book *The Violent Bear It Away*, Flannery O'Connor writes of this opening of a door:

God told the world he was going to send it a king and the world waited. The world thought, a golden fleece will do for His bed. Silver and gold and peacock tails, a thousands suns in a peacock's tail will do for his crib. His mother will ride on a four-horned white beast and use the sunset for a cape. She'll trail it behind her over the ground and let the world pull it to pieces, a new one every evening.

Jesus came on cold straw, Jesus was warmed by the breath of an ox. "Who is this?" the world said. "Who is this blue-cold child and this woman, plain as the winter? Is this the Word of God, this blue-cold child? Is this His will, this plain winter-woman?" The world said, "Love cuts like the cold wind and the will of God is plain as the winter. Where is the summer will of God?"

This season is also about peering into the dark, searching and looking for light that at best is far distant, untouchable like the stars. We are encouraged to remember that darkness is a reality all too close and intimate, internal and external. Although the person in this season who knows this sound of the dark best of all is probably the prophet John the Baptizer, Mary and Joseph know it too as do all the parents of the children murdered in Bethlehem. In a Christmas letter in 1942 Dietrich Bonhoeffer wrote of this mystery and its seed within us in this season:

There remains an experience of incomparable value. We have for once learnt to see the great events of world history from below, from the perspective of the outcast, the suspects, the maltreated, the powerless, the oppressed, the reviled — in short, from the perspective of those who suffer. ... We have to learn that personal suffering is a more effective key, a more rewarding principle for exploring the world in thought and action than personal good fortune.

The season is also about a rude awakening, a kick in the stomach, the onset of labor pains that announce that, come what may, something, someone, is coming who will be born in blood and guts, sweat and labor. But we must pray every day for God to "tear the heavens, to rend them and come again" to liberate his people as he once did in the Exodus, creating havoc in the land of Egypt and upsetting all the familiar routines. Now our God is intent on interrupting the whole world, on surprising and jolting all the nations out of their ways of war and into peace and justice. It is as rude as tearing open a womb or rending our hearts.

And the season is about silence, quiet. It is watching in utter stillness and awe a very pregnant woman sleeping, listening to her breathing, and hearing the breath, the spirit, of the child who sleeps deep within her, so close, so near. It's the time to learn the art of hearing God breathing in our midst, near to our own flesh and heart, and of listening to others' hearts. Again, Dietrich Bonhoeffer says it clearly: "Those who cannot hear another person are also no longer able to hear God's Word...or to pray! Our love for another consists first of all in listening" (189). We practice throughout the four weeks of Advent so that on this day we can sit in wonder and watch this baby asleep on Mary's lap, watch with Joseph and Mary as they listen to his breathing, his gurgling, and watch his eyes flutter in his sleep. It is a watching tenderness where we forget all else and attend to God in flesh and in all flesh everywhere, now.

There is a marvelous story I picked up in Japan, one of a master poet, a wanderer and beggar who played with children, lived simply with the people, and sat and contemplated the world. Father Rudy Fernandez, who has lived in Japan for more than forty years, told me this story on a night of a full moon in Hiroshima.

✣ Once upon a time the Buddhist monk Ryokan stood at his kitchen window wondering what he would eat for dinner that night. This was an important thought because he hadn't eaten all day or the night before. He stood in his sparsely furnished room and looked out the window, his stomach growling away. And the moon rose, full and white and perfect through the trees and high above the mountains. He sighed in awe at its beauty. In a moment he was out the door, into the cold winter air, and running under the moon's sweet light.

He raced across the frozen fields, his head thrown back, reveling in the moon, singing to it, admiring its roundness and how it fell upon all things and illumined them with loveliness. The icy bare branches of the trees, the crack of the hard snow under his nearly bare feet, the streams of silver glistening and fast running under the hard crust of ice, the shadows across the hills and valleys. He ran and ran, singing its praises, ecstatic and alive, up one hill and down into the next valley. The moon rose high above him and the sky darkened and suddenly he realized how cold it was outside. He knew he must get back to his little hut or freeze to death, and he turned for home. The way back was longer and colder than the way out, though the moon remained above him, accompanying him every step of the way. Finally, he topped a ridge and saw his little hut on the next ridge, shining brightly before him like a beacon in the dark.

He stopped, frozen in his tracks. Why was there a light in his little hut? He didn't remember lighting his lamp. No! He had watched the moon rise at dusk and left in a hurry. Someone must be in his house! He ran the rest of the way, and then crept up on his house and peered in one of his tiny windows. There was a thief in his house! And the thief was frantically racing about the small hut, pulling out drawers, looking under the bed and in cabinets, trying to find something to steal and having no luck at all.

Ryokan burst into the house, flinging wide the door. He confronted the thief boldly, saying with sympathy, "I know how hard it is to work and come to naught. Here, you mustn't go without anything for all your hard labors. Take my clothes." In a moment he stripped down, gathering all his clothes and putting them into the arms of the very startled thief! The thief hesitated for a moment and tore out the door with Ryokan's clothes.

After the thief left, Ryokan stood in the middle of his bare room, with the front door wide open to the frigid night air and the moonlight streaming. He went and stood at the door of his hut and looked up at the moon once again. "Ah," he sighed, looking up at its radiant face, "what I really wanted to give him was the moon!"

Ah, what our God has really wanted to give us is the moon. In fact, he already has, and the stars and the sun and the Sun of Justice and life and earth and all we possess or hold in trust. Now, this day he has given his child, his beloved, his servant, the Prince of Peace, the looming presence of the Holy One in our flesh, the hope of the ages. We have sung with the angels this past night, "O holy night, O night divine." We have fallen on our knees and heard the angels' voices, this night when Christ was born. What a marvelous night! What a wondrous day! Hope has struck a chord deep within us.

Though our hearts may shiver in the cold this day or other days, we now breathe easier because of this child's birth. In fact, all our small lives are part of a worldwide conspiracy, a breathing together of God, of us, seeking to surprise the world with truth and justice and with, finally, the peace that is the Christ — God's gift to us in the presence of his own beloved Son.

Our Christmas is not "hale and hearty." It is not empty or false or sad like Takashimaya's tinsel decorations and blaring music, ringing sales registers, profits, and business as usual. For we have been given the moon and more: hope, liberation, deep abiding joy, and God's own peace in a person who now dwells with us for all time, the Christ of God.

Asian religions and beliefs are deep and traditional, rich and absorbing, yet have little contact with Christian beliefs and the Christian practice of the justice and peace that are Christ's gift to us born this day. These religions have much to share with us as we have much to offer them in dialogue and in hope for the future. While in Japan, I heard a Chinese story about painting dragons. This story by Yan Fei Tzu is in the same vein as much of what I have tried to say in these reflections for this day of Christ's birth.

✤ Once upon a time there was a very famous painter. He lived at court part of the year and alone in his hermitage the other part. He loved to paint, everything and anything. He painted for nobles and samurai, for peasants and children and princes, usually whatever they wanted or desired. He had an uncanny ability to depict things so realistically that they took your breath away.

One day someone asked him, "What are the hardest things to draw and paint?"

Unhesitatingly, he answered, "Horses, dogs, cats, insects, and most especially faces of the old and children."

Those who were listening to the conversation were very surprised. Someone asked, "Well, what is the easiest?"

His answer was, "Ghosts, monsters, and especially dragons."

They were all dumbfounded. A voice piped up, "But why?"

The painter was serious and responded, "Think about it. What do you see all the time? Common animals, birds, plants and people. We're used to them. They are as familiar as our own hands, and any defect in the drawing is glaring. We see it right away. Because no one really knows what ghosts and monsters and dragons really look like, I can paint them wildly, fantastically, grotesquely, even amusingly, and everyone is pleased. They have no definite shape. They are loose in our minds. But people — they are so hard to paint truthfully."

On this day, all the rules change. All of us have thought we knew what God looked like, oftentimes as fantastical, whimsical, or without definite shape, as myriad forms as there are minds to imagine divinity. Today, though, we are given sight of God, and God looks like every mother's child, every woman and every man ever born. The great mystery now is that because God is so familiar, because he looks like every one of us, it is hard to tell who God is. But this is incarnation. This is God's justice and peace. This is God's presence among us now. No wonder Mary "treasured all these things and reflected on them in her heart!" This is worship, contemplation, and true devotion. It is all we can really do today, for "the Lord is born for us. Alleluia."

# The Birth of the Lord
## *Christmas Mass during the Day*

*Isaiah 52:7–10*
*Psalm 98:1–6*
*Hebrews 1:1–6*
*John 1:1–18 or John 1:1–5, 9–14*

The readings for this Mass shift the focus away from the night and onto the long view of the theological meaning of this birth, this event in history. Three times in twenty-four hours we attempt to celebrate what has happened in the world so long ago and what is happening in our hearts now. We are looking at this moment through a lens of cosmic proportions, of meaning for the universe in relation to God and the creation of the human race. We are backing up in time to before time, to the mind of God and the principles of creation, of order and harmony, to the massive implications of what has transpired in history and is among us now, for all time.

Again, we begin with Isaiah's words of encouragement, of seeing what is to come and what has come to pass. It is a reading that intermingles flesh and divinity, feet and bared arms, seeing directly

and singing with "the salvation of our God." It shifts the focus to
the evangelist, the storyteller, the singer, the teacher, the one who
proclaims glad tidings:

> How beautiful upon the mountains
>     are the feet of him who brings glad tidings,
> Announcing peace, bearing good news,
>     announcing salvation, and saying to Zion,
>     "Your God is King!"
> Hark! Your watchmen raise a cry,
>     together they shout for joy,
> For they see directly, before their eyes,
>     the Lord restoring Zion.

This is a clarion call, a blessing for those who are watchers, those
who raise the cry, for they see directly what God is doing right
before their eyes and announce it to a city in ruins, a people in desperate need of comfort! The call bespeaks a three-way relationship
between those who see, those in need of comfort, and the Lord who
restores and redeems. It is a relationship of storytelling, announcements, and exhortations. The emphasis is on seeing from afar, seeing
directly, and seeing up close and to the end of the earth.

We are commanded in the first reading to "break out together in
song," to follow the watchers in their cry and shout for joy because
of what the Lord is doing for Jerusalem, the city of God. The response to the psalm is just that: "All the ends of the earth have seen
the saving power of God." This is a proclamation of reality; this
is what we believe our God has already accomplished. God's revelation of justice, kindness, and faithfulness is expressed and shown
first toward the house of Israel. The promise is that one day — this
day — it will be shown forth to all the nations, all peoples of earth.
The last verse turns us all into musicians, an orchestra, with harp,
melodious song, trumpets, and horn singing praise to God. It is a
universal hymn, in concert with heaven's song.

This day's readings look at history from God's eye, back beyond
the beginning of time. The introduction to the letter to the Hebrews
begins with the words: "In times past, God spoke in fragmentary
and varied ways to our fathers through the prophets; in this, the
final age, he has spoken to us through his Son, whom he has made
heir of all things and through whom he first created the universe."
It seems that our God has been about communication and speaking aloud since the beginning: in creation and nature, in covenant

and law, in Exodus and land, in king and prophet, in promise and presence. But before the birth, all these were fragments. Think of a broken pot, of trying to put together its bits and pieces without an image of what it originally looked like. The fragments don't provide a real idea of what was originally intended. But now things are becoming clear, crystal clear, in this last word from God's own Son.

What follows is a theological statement of belief that is wide-ranging and inclusive of what God has done and is doing for all of creation in this Son. It includes christology, the Trinity, redemption and incarnation, judgment, the nature of the relationship between God the Father and the Son, and what is true worship. First comes a statement about who this child born today is, in the flesh:

> This Son is the reflection of the Father's glory, the exact representation of the Father's being, and he sustains all things by his powerful Word. When the Son cleansed us from our sins, he took his seat at the right hand of the Majesty in heaven, as far superior to the angels as the name he inherited is superior to theirs. (Hebrews 1:3–4)

This child is God — have no doubt about that fact. He is the exact representation of the Father's being, is in the Father and with the Father from the beginning, is and will be beside him, with him, throughout all of time. And it is God who sustains creation, history, and all that dwells on this earth through this Word spoken so truthfully and intimately, this Word that is presence, power, and person. The Son obeys the will of the Father, which is to save and cleanse, to judge and sit at the right hand of the Majesty in heaven, to preside and reign. There is oneness in this relationship, and domination, even over the angels. The relationship is one of intimacy, freedom, love, communion. The Son is worthy of worship with the Father. This is the Word of God, spoken, breathed out in the original creation, breathed through the prophets and all other levels of revelation for those who can see and hear through nature, history, and goodness. Now spoken in flesh, this Word is God's voice, music, silence, and meaning for all.

The Word involves words, speech patterns, communication, dialogue, between God and us, in history, in fragments and fits and starts, and now in a Son through whom the universe was created. Think of God singing to us in Jesus! This child, this human being, is the reflection of glory and sustains one pure note, drawing all things into harmony again in his name, unspoken, a name far superior to any other. In all the mystical traditions of the world, it is believed that if you truly know the name of God, you refuse to speak it aloud, ever. It words you, speaks you, sings you through and through until you are wordless, a reed, a voice that God passes through.

Today is the birth of the Son of God; the earth, all the creatures on it, and we human beings begin to come back together again. Even the angels gather near to us, sing to us, worship with us this presence of God in the world in a way not even the angels imagined. This is God's design: Father and Son together breathing, knowing, and creating, which is Spirit. Today God speaks a new language: a person, a body, a human being, a baby, mortal flesh that is divine. Until forever we will be learning this language, its music, its cadences, its silences and pauses, its power and expressions. It is at root, at heart, the language of love.

We hear the long form of the gospel (always better, more whole and complete, easier to understand). It takes practice to read. It is poetry. It begins to sing you, not so much from understanding as from being spoken aloud and revealing itself as you speak it publicly. As C. S. Lewis once said: "Some things are far too precise for mere human speech and words." It is the sound as well as the meaning of the words that carry the communication. Images and feelings are evoked and stirred that can transform human life and relationships, knowledge and love. This is the beginning of the new language, the language of Jesus' flesh and spirit, the language of glad tidings.

John is interested in taking us way back, before creation, before time, into God as God is and then leading us forward as God comes toward us and then into us and as one of us. This is John's view, as if from the great eye of a soaring eagle. He gives us a prologue and perspective of all that is to come. It is God's time now seeping through history, rewording all things with the truth. It is about words, about the Word, wisdom, a person, the face and form of God in our faces and forms. This is God's presence among us, sensed, known, unknown. This is God's long-loving look at reality, even the reality that is hard to look at because of what we have refused to see and believe.

This is glory intimately connected to the cross, to suffering and death, to the destruction of God's flesh, to the silencing of the Word. This is new gift, new covenant, new blood, new love that is enduring, revealing. In the Older Testament a person who saw God died. Now we see God and we die, but we are returned to life in God through Jesus. This Word, this sound, this flesh dwells and stays with us, endures faithfully, and is literally and physically in every sense of the term, "God-with-us." We should remember that the Word comes with a warning, a memory of what happened in history and what so often still happens today, that his own did not accept him, did not know him, and refused to speak this language and instead sought to destroy him.

Again, this presence, this glory, is so hard to speak about or to express, and yet it is the source, the wellspring, of our belief, our life, our hope, and our destiny. All the readings of this day are referred to in the Russian Orthodox Church as "a splendid three-day Pascha, a winter Pascha, the Pascha of the coming, the Pascha of the incarnation." Resurrection will begin here in incarnation, but all the shadows and intimations of crucifixion and death are here also. This day is victory over sin and evil and death. This is new birth in the Spirit of God, the Word of God. It is we who are given birth to on this day. It is not nativity that we celebrate, but incarnation, God putting on flesh and pitching his tent among us as dwelling place forever. It is the day God disappears into our flesh, sinking deep inside our human nature and beginning the transformation of each and all of us and all creation by his intimate presence among us.

The Orthodox Church celebrates the incarnation of God with many overtures of the crucifixion and Easter as well as salvation and baptism. Nathan Mitchell, liturgist and poet, once interspersed the verses from the "Royal Hours" for Christmas Eve and Good Friday in one of his articles in *Worship* magazine. Every year since, I have read the two together for a deeper sense of how the church has looked at this day's Scriptures and experience, not primarily as the nativity of Jesus but as the incarnation of God, as transformation of humanity and history. These verses can serve as meditation and points for reflection in the twelve days of Christmas that begin today and end on the feast of Epiphany.

> The One who holds all creation in the hollow of a hand
> is born today of the Virgin.
> The One who hung the earth upon the waters
> is hung today upon the Cross.
> The One whose essence none can touch
> is wrapped in swaddling clothes as a mortal.
> The One who rules the angels
> is crowned today with thorns.

God, who in the beginning created the heavens,
    lies now in a manger.
God, who wraps the heavens in clouds,
    is wrapped in mocking purple.
The One who rained manna down on the people in the
        wilderness
    is fed on milk from a Mother's breast.
The One who set Eve and Adam free in the Jordan
    is slapped in the face.
Today the Church's Spouse calls forth the Magi.
Today the Church's Spouse is nailed to the cross.
The Virgin's Child accepts their gifts.
The Virgin's Child is pierced with a spear.
We worship your nativity, O Christ!
We worship your passion, O Christ!
Show us your glorious Theophany!
Show us, too, your glorious Resurrection!

These interspersed phrases remind us starkly of the three-day feast of Good Friday, Holy Saturday, and Easter Day and let us see more clearly this three-part feast of Advent, Christmas, and Epiphany as one whole piece. And they put in sharp focus the three segments of John's prologue: the first section on the Word of God; the second on John as witness to the light and on the real light that came into the world and was rejected, yet is still offered to all who are willing to accept him; and the final portion that speaks of the one who is "love following upon love," who is the fullness of God, ever at the Father's side.

The prologue of John's gospel contains so much meaning that it is hard to single out individual phrases or sentences as this season's essence. We will, however, look at a few of the more familiar lines and suggest a few ways of looking at what is being expressed. Perhaps the most famous of the lines is this one: "And the Word became flesh and made his dwelling among us, and we saw his glory, the glory as of the Father's only Son, full of grace and truth" (John 1:14). God's dwelling place is among us. This has been the case since the journey through the desert after escaping from Egypt. Originally, the tabernacle of the Lord was the space where God's glory dwelled, the Ark of the Covenant that held the Torah given on Mount Sinai and where the show bread was given to Yahweh as an offering of thanksgiving. The children of Israel carried this ark, this house of God, with them as they traveled to their new homeland.

A more descriptive and closer translation of the Greek is "he pitched his tent" among us, a tent much like those the wandering Israelites "dwelled in" temporarily for forty years while they learned how to become a people in the wilderness and to trust in Yahweh. Once they settled in the promised land they built more substantial dwelling places for Yahweh, culminating in the temple that David began in dream form and his son Solomon finished, a monument of cedar and stone, built to exact specifications. Yet it was destroyed with only a fragment of the western wall, called the Wailing Wall, remaining today.

Now there is a new dwelling place, a new tent for God's presence among us. It is the flesh of a human being, beloved child and son of God, one of us, born of Mary the Virgin, conceived in her womb and given birth to in a cave near Bethlehem. God has entered the world and stays in a body like ours! Now the Word, the essence of God's soul, has been spoken truly. As at creation's beginning, when the Word and intent of God brought forth all the earth and its creatures, now God's Word becomes human, subject to limitations and weakness, and finally subject to death itself. Now we see this "glory of God" that the angels sang about the night of his birth. It looks like us.

The "glory of the Father's only Son is full of grace and truth." In Luke's gospel, Mary is addressed as full of grace, favored by God, but this only Son is full of grace and truth, an image that is bound to the history of Israel and God's covenant (see Exodus 34:6). This grace and truth are about love, about "the way things were meant to be." They concern all of us, individually and together in communion, as God's own people. In this only Son, we will all be born, adopted, made heirs, and become beloved sons and daughters, the children of the Father God. Our humanity is blessed beyond words in the body of this human being, Jesus, "the glory as of the Father's only Son." God has come home, entered into us as closely and as surely as a child dwells in its mother's womb and then enters the world at large to live, breathe, love, and die.

There is a fascinating Chinese children's story called "Youchao and the First Dwellings" that can perhaps add to the meaning of the phrase "pitched his tent and made his dwelling among us." The story also illustrates why this day is so extraordinary and so transformative for the human race and its future.

✤ It was long, long ago when the earth was very old already, but human beings were still young. Since the beginning people had loved the sunlight and being on the earth. They loved hunting and gathering, singing as the birds did early in the morning and gathering together as the birds did at night. But when the sky became shadowy and dusk came, there was fear. They could not look for food. They could not see what was out there, if there was danger. They were afraid to sleep, afraid to be alone, afraid of anyone who traveled and moved at night, afraid of animals and creatures of the night. They longed for light to come, and they posted watchers who would cry at the first sound of danger, but also at the first trace of light returning. They sometimes hid in caves and under ledges, but it was so cold, and though they were out of the rain and wind and snow, it was a hard, hard way to live.

But God used to visit earth whenever he had the chance and see how things were going down below. God would watch and see the people's fear and suffering. This God couldn't bear; it was not meant to be so hard to dwell on the earth. So God sat under a tree and wondered what could be done to help the people in their distress. God dozed and was awakened by the chitter and songs of the birds nested in the tree above. Fascinated with the birds, God watched as they flew back and forth with bits of down, grasses and twigs, leaves and seeds, building a nest for the protection and safety of their young. That was it! The pattern would follow that of the birds. Instead of twigs, there would be bent branches of long willow trees. Instead of dry grass, there would be hay and straw. The first dwelling was constructed, and God rested inside to see if it was adequate. Since it was satisfactory, God thought to build another and another and another, with variations and new ideas, enjoying making nests for the people.

The people found them and entered and slept secure and the word spread like wild-fire. Almost overnight, shelters, houses, and other dwelling places were built on earth. They were comfortable, warm, dry, and good for storing food and other necessities as well as for gathering together in peace. They were the people's nests. And so in honor of the God who visited them and gave them rest and dwelling places, they called their God "Youchao," which means "having nest."

Our God has visited us too and has always been concerned for our safety, well-being, and the quality of life on this earth. And God has visited again and again through judges, kings, laws, and sometimes threats, but more often with gifts of freedom and promises of a land, a secure dwelling place, a way of belonging. Today, history is opened up and God slips in, through the body of a young woman who faithfully and obediently staked her flesh and her life on the Word of God so that the human race might learn a new level of truth. Mary's womb was God's nesting place among us for nine months, but now the body of a human child is God's new nesting place among us. All our bodies, all human beings, are God's preferred dwelling place on earth. God's glory is encompassed by flesh and blood, bones and nerves, tissue and senses. As God was in the beginning, is now and will be, God is revealed, expressed in terms that we can see and touch, understand, even though we can never really understand how this can come to be. This is for believing, for staking our lives upon, and for remembering as we look at every human being now in the world.

In the past, seeing the face of God so utterly destroyed or transformed human flesh that one could only die of the experience. In Exodus, Yahweh speaks to Moses, his most beloved servant: "I will make all my beauty pass before you, and in your presence I will pronounce my name. . . . But my face you cannot see, for no man sees me and still lives" (Exodus 33:19–20). When Moses turns his face toward the stone and lets God pass by, Moses lives. Yet when he returns to the camp of the Israelites, they cannot bear to look at his face because it so reflects the glory and beauty of Yahweh's presence. Moses, unaware of this, is surprised at the people's reaction. So Moses puts on a veil to conceal God's mirrored glory on his skin. "He did not know that the skin of his face had become radiant while he conversed with the Lord" (Exodus 34:29).

But now, in the incarnation, we see the face of God, the radiant glory of God in the eyes of a child. This is the Word made flesh that dwells among us. This is Emmanuel, who is God-with-us. This is, as Old Irish translates the phrase, the Word made meat, food for those who hunger for God, for sustenance, for the bread of life.

And this is "God the only Son, ever at the Father's side, who has revealed him." Patrick Ryan, in *America* magazine (December 12, 1992), writes of a truer translation for this phrase "ever at the Father's side":

Jesus, then, fully God and fully one with us, manifests the unseeable Father in our midst. "It is God the only-begotten, ever at the Father's side, who has revealed him." The phrase from the *New American Bible* translation, "ever at the Father's side," makes Jesus sound a little too much like a press secretary for God or a director of protocol. The image suggested by the Greek proves more intimate: "in the bosom of the Father."

The picture derives from banqueting practice in the ancient Middle East. Lazarus, after a life of destitution spent at the doorstep of the uncaring rich man, spends his time in the world to come in the bosom of Abraham (Luke 16:23). The Beloved Disciple, witness of the fourth gospel, has the same position at the Last Supper. "One of them, the disciple Jesus loved, reclined close to Him as they ate." The most honored guest at a banquet would recline on a couch facing the host and thus be "in his bosom." The next most honored guest would recline at the host's back and have to signal to the Beloved Disciple to find out who would betray Jesus. "He leaned towards the chest of Jesus and said to Him, 'Lord, who is he?'" (John 13:23, 25).

Although there may be no real difference in meaning, Lazarus and the Beloved Disciple are described as being merely "in" or "on" the bosom of their hosts. But the prologue to John's gospel may hint at something even more intimate in the relationship between Jesus and the Father. "It is God the only-begotten, the one who is *into* the Father's bosom, who has revealed Him." (487)

And this beloved Son has expressed God fully, transparently, completely. In a sense there will be nothing more to say. It has been said in Jesus in simple, unadorned terms that are as engaging as each child newly born and asleep at its mother's breast. But it is said with nuance and intonation, shadow and image of the harsh reality — of suffering, rejection, fear, torture, crucifixion, and the tearing to shreds of this child, in betrayal and loss. What we do to one another now, we do to God. Today is for thinking of God not as a child but as flesh, the flesh of the poor, our enemy, our friend, the homeless in the street, the unwanted runaway teenager, the old and sick, the tortured, and even those who do evil. For in being born human God has seized hold of all flesh to salvage us and redeem us and set us free so that we might know how to be truly human, like God.

St. Bernard has a prayer that brings us into this awareness of the glory of God expressed in terms that are physical and divine:

In what blaze of Glory do you rise, O Sun of Righteousness, from the heart of the earth, after your setting! In what resplendent Vesture, O King of Glory, do you enter again the highest heavens! At the sight of these marvels, how can I do otherwise than cry: "All my bones shall say, 'Lord, who is like unto thee?'"

This man Jesus is God's only begotten Son, the glory of the Father, the "real light which gives light to everyone" — this is who has come into the world. This is the "light that shines on in darkness, and a darkness did not overcome it."
A story I have heard told both as a Jewish story and a Muslim tale situates us in relation to this human being who is God's own flesh and ours. It is called "Ahaz the Slave."

✤ Once upon a time there was a poor man who believed in God. This was hard because when he thought about his life, he knew that he was born poor and would, at best, die poor and struggle until his last breath. He was a slave who, covered with mud and bent double, worked in the mines and was near blind from being underground so much. But one day things changed without warning. An officer of the king arrived to find a new attendant for the king. The last attendant had died mysteriously. Ten of the more fit slaves were singled out and taken to the palace. They were fed, clothed, given rest, and cared for, and within a few weeks were presented to the king.

They were lined up in a row and each was given an exquisite glass and told to break it. All obeyed immediately. Then the king went to each in turn and asked him, "Why did you break it?"

The response was simple, "Because you told me to." One after another, they responded in the same way.

Now, the poor man who believed in God, the man whose name was Ahaz, thought quickly, "I can't answer the same thing. What can I say?" He was the last of the slaves to be questioned, and when the king got to him, he stammered, "Forgive me, please. I am so sorry," and bowed before the king. It was exactly what he was thinking and feeling, and that was what came out. The king looked at him, smiled, and chose him as his new attendant.

Ahaz remembered what he had learned — to say and do exactly what he thought and felt, the truth and nothing else, no matter what the consequences. And the king found that he grew quickly to trust this man from the mines, because there were so few people who ever told him the truth or what they truly were thinking. They always coated it or covered it in what they thought the king wanted to hear, or bent it to serve their own advantage. Ahaz took over more and more duties until within a number of years he was counselor to the king in all matters that pertained to the kingdom, and he was also in charge of the king's finances. Because he was trusted explicitly, more and more power and authority was delegated to Ahaz.

Now, when someone rises in power that quickly, others become envious, jealous, and bitter. Ahaz had many enemies and many more who distrusted him and wondered what he did to so enchant the king. They speculated on how he had lodged himself so securely in the king's affections so quickly, for now Ahaz was the king's friend as well. And so the rumors started. When they came to the king's ears, he ignored them. He knew his friend, his servant well.

But they were persistent, and soon his closest advisers and counselors were warning him almost daily. It was always the same: Ahaz was stealing from him, robbing him blind. Couldn't he see it? Why, every day the man waited until everyone had left and then let himself into the king's storeroom. He had a key to the huge inner safe, and he would go in and stay for over an hour and then come out as though nothing was remiss. But that was where the jewels, the land deeds and contracts, the gifts from other rulers were kept. It would be so easy to take a contract, a deed for land, currency, or jewels and put them in his voluminous sleeves. The talk and dire warnings never stopped, and so the king decided to check and see for himself what Ahaz was up to in his daily visits to his storeroom.

Secretly he had two holes drilled at eye level in the wall of the storeroom so that someone could watch what transpired inside. The king took up his position one day after everyone had left for the day. Sure enough, Ahaz arrived and entered the storeroom alone and then entered the great safe with his keys. What the king saw then surprised him immensely. Ahaz went into the safe where the treasures of the kingdom were kept and came out with a carefully folded pile of clothes. They were rags, filthy, smelly, caked with mud and sweat. He placed them on a table along with a candle and a book and some incense. He solemnly took off his robes of state and put on the rags that he had worn the day that he had been removed from the mines and taken to the king's palace so many years ago. Then he lit the candle and incense and began to pray aloud. "Lord God, Master of the Universe, I stand before you as you have made me. Do not let me forget who I am and that I belong to you alone. Help me to remember that all I do is not for the king, but for you alone, for it is you who have blessed me and given me all that I now enjoy. It is you who have entrusted to me the power of this kingdom and the friendship of the king. Do not let me forget who I am and that I am yours, O Holy One, and that I live by your mercy and will." He prayed in this manner, devoutly and intensely, for over an hour. Then he took off the rags of the slave and carefully folded them up again and put them back into the safe. The candle and incense had burned out, and he dressed again in the robes that were the gift of the king and left the storeroom, locking it behind him.

The king met him in the hallway when he left. Ahaz bowed low to the king. The king grasped him by the shoulders and lifted him up, speaking to him, not as friend, but as king. "Ahaz," he began, "you never cease to surprise and amaze me, and you have done it again. All of my counselors have warned me that you are a common thief and that you have been stealing from me behind my back. But you have managed to do something for me that no one else ever has — you have made me remember who I am. I am a king here on earth, but even I, or especially I, must stand before the Holy One and give an account of what I have done and who I am. You have made me remember that before God I am his servant and belong to him alone, and that I have no power here on earth that has not been entrusted to me by God. Do not ever let me forget who I truly am."

The story asks us: Do you remember who you are and whom you belong to? Or have you forgotten? Who makes you remember? And whom do you help to remember who they truly are?

As Christians, we believe that we are the beloved children, the sons and daughters, of God who sent his only begotten beloved Son into our world as one of us to remind us of our dignity, our delight, and our freedom as human beings made in the image and likeness of God. This is our glory. This is what we celebrate this day. We must remember who we are and who God is and that in the Word made flesh God is one of us, human and divine. We are called to be divine and to live up to the dreams our God has had for us since the beginning of time. They are coming true now in Jesus who is "love following upon love." We are to follow in love's footsteps, drawing God close to our hearts and drawing close to one another, as God has drawn so close to us.

We are confronted this day with the hope of salvation. John says it this way: "He was in the world, and through him the world was made, yet the world did not know who he was. To his own he came, yet his own did not accept him. Any who did accept him he empowered to become children of God. These are they who believe in his name." Do we believe in his name? Today our response to the gospel proclamation, "Praise to you, Lord Jesus Christ," is the only response, other than silent wonder, that we can truly give. This is the only gift that reveals our belief, our acceptance, and our surrender to this "love following upon love." It is all that our God has ever wanted of us. This is the length God has gone to in attempting to get close to us. This is God's incarnation today.

# The Holy Family
## *Sunday in the Octave of Christmas*

*Sirach 3:2–6, 12–14*
*Psalm 128:1–5*
*Colossians 3:12–21*
*Cycle A—Matthew 2:13–15, 19–23*
*Cycle B—Luke 2:22–40*
*Cycle C—Luke 2:41–52*

The readings for this Sunday, in between the birth of Jesus Christ and the celebration of Mary the Mother of God, are dedicated to the concept of the holy family. Many of us have all-too-familiar and sometimes tacky images of Jesus, Mary, and Joseph in a carpenter shop in Nazareth, nicely dressed and happy with their small nuclear family. The doting mother Mary is spinning, spindle in hand, and watching her young son, and Joseph is planing a piece of wood, with sweet-smelling wood shavings littering the floor. In reality, their family life was nothing like that at all.

The readings from Sirach and Colossians and the psalm for this Sunday remain the same for all three cycles while the gospels change. The readings from Sirach and Colossians are a jolting contrast to the gospel stories. As the story is told in Matthew (Cycle A), Mary, Joseph, and Jesus are running for their lives as refugees from violence, living always in the shadow of the Herods.

Luke, in Cycle B, tells a different story. On the eighth day, when Mary and Joseph take Jesus to the temple, they meet Simeon and Anna, two prophetic figures of ancient wisdom who situate the child and his mother in the long tradition of Israel's history. Again, the issue of politics and power looms over the couple and their newborn child, in the form of prophecy and what the future holds for them.

In Cycle C, we read Luke's story of Mary and Joseph losing Jesus in the temple in Jerusalem when he is twelve and Jesus' reprimand to them for their lack of understanding of who he is and what he is to do. These three gospel readings contain the remaining texts about Jesus' infancy. Chosen for this day of the holy family, they provide a lens to examine the concept of family, as the Christian community has experienced it since Jesus' preaching, death, and resurrection.

In his books on the infancy narratives, well-known scholar Raymond Brown presents two elements that are core to the formation of these stories and their use in this season: (1) all the texts present Jesus' identity; and (2) all the texts answer the questions of who Jesus is and what the connections are between his existence and the history of the people of Israel. Matthew tells the stories from the perspective of Joseph, descended from the house of David; the child is a son of David, king, shepherd, psalm singer, and beloved chosen of God. Luke tells the story from Mary's experience, especially her encounter with Gabriel and the Word of God. This text makes it clear that the child born of Mary is human flesh, though born of the power of the Spirit, and that he is the divine Son of God. This dual identity is firmly based in all the stories of conception, nativity, and early years of Jesus. It points to what Jesus will teach and proclaim with his words and life in the rest of the gospels. Brown goes on to note that the undercurrent or foundation of all the stories is belief in the experience of resurrection. This one moment highlights and undergirds the infancy accounts, because they were all written in retrospect, after the fact, as the church experienced life in the power of the Spirit and the presence of the Risen Lord. These are not primarily historical narratives, but faith statements of the church in the first fifty years after the death and resurrection of Jesus.

The gospels identify three defining moments in the life of Jesus: conception, baptism, and resurrection. These are revelatory moments that shed light on all the other events in his life and community. The infancy accounts all share the same thrust of announcing the good news that is preached and shared so that the proclamation of who this child is for Israel and the world extends to all the world. The angels, the stars, dreams, shepherds, the magi, and Simeon and Anna are all preachers and missionaries, intent on spreading the good news of salvation so others can hear and respond with their lives. There are also stories of rejection, especially in Matthew's gospel. Herod and Herod's lineage that ruled in Jerusalem and the chief priests and scribes were in league with the political and economic oppression of the Romans and institutional Judaism. Raymond Brown says it this way in a column entitled "The Christmas Stories: Exploring the Gospel Infancy Narratives" (in *Scripture from Scratch* [Cincinnati: St. Anthony Messenger Press, 1994]):

Although the cast of characters differs, each evangelist in his own way is teaching us that Christ's identity is never received to be kept as a private possession. In God's providence there are other people eager to believe in Christ's identity, even if they are not the ones we might have expected. Alas, there are also others who reject Christ: Herod, all the chief priests and the scribes in Matthew; in Luke (in Simeon's prophecy) many in Israel who will fall. Thus the Christmas crib lies under the shadow of the cross, and its joy has an element of sadness. In a very real way, then, the infancy narratives of Matthew and Luke are like mini-gospels. They contain the basic revelation of the full identity of Jesus, and the way in which this revelation was shared, evangelizing some, but causing rejection and hatred among others.

Both sets of stories are interested in making a bridge from the Older Testament and covenant to the newer covenant that God makes with all people — not just Israel — in this person Jesus, who is Son of God and Savior. This is seen most clearly in the prelude to Jesus' birth. Matthew's genealogy goes back to the earliest ancestors of Joseph, son of David, but with significant interruptions of women's names, strategically placed to throw us off our usual reading of history. Matthew begins, "A genealogy of Jesus Christ, son of David, son of Abraham who was the father of Isaac . . ." (Matthew 1:1), and ends with "and Jacob was the father of Joseph the husband of Mary; of her was born Jesus who is called Christ" (Matthew 1:16). This identifies Joseph as the husband of Mary and not as the father of Jesus. Jesus is Jewish through his mother's lineage, and adopted in this world by Joseph.

This Joseph is a namesake of Joseph the dreamer, Joseph of the rainbow coat who so angered his brothers with his dreams that they sought to kill him and then decided to sell him into slavery in Egypt. Eventually, his skill with the art of dreaming places him high on the rungs of power in Pharaoh's court. In time, his brothers come to him and he reveals himself, forgiving them and saving his family from hunger and death. The descendants of Joseph sojourn in Egypt for hundreds of years as oppressed slaves. It is the infant Moses, saved by his sister, Miriam, and his mother, Jocebel, and his adopted Egyptian mother, Bithia, who becomes the liberator and savior of his people by leading them out of Egypt with the power of God's bared arm and presence on their journey.

Joseph, Mary's husband, has many similar experiences. He dreams dreams and obeys the knowledge that he is given in these nightly visits. In the Older Testament, dreams are often considered the forgotten language of God, given to individuals, such as kings and prophets, at a crucial moment in Israel's history. This information is critical for survival and for the development of God's secret design in history. It is only in retrospect that the wisdom of the dream is seen to be marvelously true, leading always to the saving of the people and their growth in awareness of the God who always accompanies them. In accord with his dreams, Joseph takes Mary into his house and adopts her child as his own. The holy family begins with adoption and love, not with just blood ties, in obedience to God's will.

Joseph dreams whenever the child is in danger, when it is time to flee into Egypt and sojourn there, as the child grows in maturity, and then when it is safe to return. Even the choice of where they are to live is decided by a dream. Joseph conceals their identity so the child can grow up in a place and time of peace, although with the always lingering shadow of political repression and the memory of the slaughter of the innocents. These stories parallel Israel's history as the chosen people of God. This child will be the new Moses who will come out of Egypt to save his people, to give them a new law, and to bring a new kingdom into the world.

Luke's story is somewhat different, but he is saying much the same. He seems to use Abraham and Sarah as models for Zechariah

and Elizabeth, but with some role reversal as Zechariah doubts and
Elizabeth rejoices in what God has done for her, a barren woman,
the aged wife of a priest. Again, Raymond Brown summarizes some
of the points that Luke incorporates in this account of Jesus' infancy
and Israel's history:

> He too begins the infancy story with Abraham and Sarah,
> though not by name. Instead he portrays them in the persons
> of Zechariah and Elizabeth — a technique similar to a photo-
> graph that has undergone double exposure, so that one set of
> figures is seen through another. With both Abraham/Sarah and
> Zechariah/Elizabeth, the situation involves the aged and bar-
> ren, an angel announces the forthcoming conception to the
> father who asks, "How am I to know this?" and the sequence
> concludes with the mother rejoicing. Luke's narrative of Mary
> echoes the mother of Samuel presenting her son at the sanc-
> tuary in the presence of the aged Eli and singing a canticle
> magnifying God. Five times Luke notes how, in the incidents
> of Jesus' infancy, his parents are faithful to the demands of the
> Jewish Law. We see from this that Luke's coverage of the Old
> Testament is as comprehensive as Matthew's. (*Scripture from
> Scratch*)

Mary is an unusual mother, betrothed to Joseph, yet obedient to
the Word of God. This child belongs not so much to her as to all
the people of Israel who have lived on promises and hope during
all those years of oppression and occupation. This child is entrusted
to her for safe-keeping, for he will grow up to save his people from
their sins and will fulfill the promises of God to his chosen people.

In this context we look at the folk wisdom from Sirach, which is
the first reading for today. The word "honor" is repeated four times,
once in each of the descriptions of behavior, reminding the Israelites
of the commandment "to honor thy father and mother." The family
unity of father/mother and children (specifically sons) is set in place
by God, who has designed this arrangement. This refers back to the
stories of Adam and Eve and the order of creation in Genesis.

In many ways, the text from Sirach is a commentary on the commandment to honor mother and father. The rewards for obeying
this commandment are numerous and substantial. Honoring one's
parents atones for sin; one stores up riches of grace, virtue, and
integrity; one is gladdened in one's own offspring; one is granted
a long life and brings comfort to loved ones. These are old and

true reminders of the obvious, that compassion and justice begin at home with those who gave us birth, life, and nurturance, and that we live always with an unpayable debt of gratitude for the care given to us as children. This compassion and nurturing are to be returned graciously when our parents become old, senile, or weak. The reminders of courtesy, human kindness, and gratitude for life are as basic as they can be. One generation teaches them to the next, so they can be passed on and practiced in the generations to come.

Many cultures have stories that reveal the same wisdom as Sirach. This version, called "The Broken Bowl," is from Thailand and India.

✠ Once upon a time there was a family of mother, father, three sons, three daughters, and the aged grandfather [or grandmother in some accounts]. One of the youngest boys doted on his father and imitated him in absolutely everything. He followed him around, mimicking his walk, gestures, talk, and way of eating; he picked up small details in the father's behavior that the father didn't notice but everyone else did, recognizing them instantaneously as belonging to the father. They smiled and knew the child would grow out of it, but retain much of what he had acquired by such imitations. It was a part of growing up.

One evening at the dinner table the boy noticed that after his father and all the children and their mother were served their food, the leftovers were put into a broken bowl and brought over to the grandfather and left by his place. He did not sit at the table with the others, and he received his food only when everyone else had finished eating. Some nights he got a lot from what they did not want, and other times, more often, there was little or nothing in the bowl. The young child watched and absorbed it all.

A few days later the father, sweaty and tired, came in from working in the fields and found his young son working on a piece of wood, carving it. When he saw his father he brightened immediately and showed his handiwork to his father, who pretended to admire it, complete with gouges and nicks and splinters of wood still sticking out of it. "What is it?" he asked his young son.

"Why, it's your bowl," the boy answered. The father had a blank look on his face, not understanding what the boy was saying to him.

"What do you mean, my bowl?" he asked.

"You know," the boy said, "for when you get old and sit in the corner and get fed the leftovers in your broken bowl."

In an instant the father saw what he had been doing and how his young son had concluded that this was how to treat an aged and infirm father. He felt remorse, regret, and guilt, along with rueful acceptance of what his son intended for him — exactly what he was giving his own father.

That night, another place was set at the table, a place of honor, and the old grandfather was treated with lovingkindness and served the first and the best of the food at the meal. And this was the custom from that day forward.

The story is told in northern European countries as well. In Norway, a sled, not a bowl, is the main prop. In the Philippines, a mat and a palm leaf are used. The characters may be a daughter and granddaughter and grandmother, but the story always reveals that the treatment of elderly parents indicates the treatment to be received in the future from one's own children. It is passed on either consciously or unconsciously. This transmission of values speaks to family life, but also of compassion and justice for all others, including those who serve us.

The feast of the Holy Family is fairly new, about seventy-five years old. It is included in the midst of this hectic season of Christmas to offset the deterioration of family, relationships, and human decency by modern culture and materialism, which work to erode moral values and faithfulness, even common courtesy to one another. The reading from Sirach speaks of the duties and responsibilities of grown children toward their parents. They include the virtues of compassion, mercy, tenderness, and kindness, virtues that must be practiced as children grow up. The reading is also about one's relationship to God. When we honor our parents, we honor God. Jesus himself will honor Joseph and Mary, obeying them and being subject to them, and obeying God his Father even unto death.

As a Jew, Jesus would honor his commitment to his mother; as a firstborn son, he would care for her needs for thirty years after Joseph's death, as stipulated by the law. While dying on the cross, he passed that responsibility on to the Beloved Disciple, according to John's gospel. The spirit of the law is found in how one protects, comforts, and cares for another in honoring them. Respect, reverence, bending toward, serving, being faithful without fail, with gratitude and gladness — all these will be characteristics of Jesus himself, who is later described in the gospel "as a mother hen seeking to gather all her chicks under her wing," mothering the city of Jerusalem and all of Israel, weeping over them as a mother weeps over her straying and errant children. Our reverence toward our parents reflects our reverence toward God and others.

The psalm response is a beatitude: "Happy are those who fear the Lord and walk in his ways." Psalm 128 speaks of families, of generations of children as a blessing and reward in a life of prosperity and health. The second part of the psalm extends this to the city of Jerusalem, that it may see peace and prosperity. The blessing is bound to nation, to religious affiliation, and to family life. It is Jewish and traditional to the core.

The reading from Colossians describes the proper behavior of God's chosen people and adds a strong admonition to wives and husbands, children and parents. These family relationships are to be understood in light of the first part of the reading:

> Because you are God's chosen ones, holy and beloved, clothe yourselves with heartfelt mercy, with kindness, humility, meekness, and patience. Bear with one another; forgive whatever grievances you have against one another. Forgive as the Lord has forgiven you. Over all these virtues put on love, which binds the rest together and makes them perfect. Christ's peace must reign in your hearts, since as members of the one body you have been called to that peace. Dedicate yourselves to thankfulness. Let the word of Christ, rich as it is, dwell in you. In wisdom made perfect, instruct and admonish one another. Sing gratefully to God from your hearts in psalms, hymns and inspired songs. Whatever you do, whether in speech or in action, do it in the name of the Lord Jesus. Give thanks to God the Father through him.

This is a new set of commandments, couched in positive language, to practice virtue. They are listed: heartfelt mercy, kindness, humility, meekness, and patience. We are to practice forgiveness and love; make peace and be at peace; be thankful and worship with emphasis on the Word of God dwelling in us; admonish one another and sing the goodness of God in words and in our lives. Whatever we do, we should do it in the name of Jesus, living out the Eucharist by giving thanks to God for what he has done and con-

tinues to do for us in Jesus Christ. This primer on Christian life is
for everyone, whatever their vocation, lifestyle, or relationship. How
our lives would change if we took just one of these commands a
year and worked on it all year long! What a difference there would
be among us. And we are to practice this kind of behavior because
we are God's chosen, holy, and beloved ones, the people of the new
covenant. This will be our baptismal garment, our shining raiment,
our swaddling clothes that declare publicly that we are children of
God's family.

The last four verses of the reading list specific practices for wives,
children, husbands, mothers, and fathers. The duty of wives to be
submissive rankles, but when seen in the context of "Let the word
of Christ, rich as it is, dwell in you," it becomes more understand-
able. It is submission to the Lord and to another in love, whenever
that person asks or demands within a relationship what is good and
just, what is true, and what is born of the Word of God. It has the
same meaning as the next admonition, that husbands are called to
love and hold no bitterness toward their wives. The other exhortation that follows is directed to children and parents. There is to be
obedience, no nagging, and no behavior that makes someone in the
family lose heart.

In all these admonitions, we may assume the reality of a nuclear
family of mother, father, and children. But the configuration of the
family is not always so easily described, and the spirit of the gospel
suggests these guidelines are intended also for the family of God,
religious communities, and all those who, in Jesus' words, are family. In each of the gospels of Matthew, Mark, and Luke, Jesus asks,
"Who is my mother and brother and sister? Anyone who hears the
Word of God and obeys the will of my Father, is mother, brother
and sister to me."

This line has staggering implications for believers. It is the basis
of family with Jesus. God is his Father, and intimacy is defined by
obedience to the Word of God. In Luke's gospel, it is the obedience
of his mother, and in Matthew's account, it is Joseph, the dreamer,
who obeys. Mary and Joseph are mother, brother, and sister to him
because of their obedience to the Word and will of his Father, God.
Obedience is the source of our familial roots and of our place in the
family of God as chosen ones, holy and beloved. The three different
gospel selections should be read in light of this commentary and
insight.

## Cycle A: Matthew 2:13–15, 19–23

Who is this child, and what shall he grow up to be? What will he do? We are told that those in power had designs on his life. The child of peace brings forth rage from those like Herod, whose lives are based on evil and violence. As a result, the child and his mother and father must run for their lives. This time the dreams are a warning. The holy family goes into exile, hiding for long years from those who would kill the child, along with all hope, dreams, and possibilities of salvation and freedom. The Savior of the world begins life as a political refugee in a family that must slip out of a country in peril of murder. Others, we know, will not escape the wrath. A simple, casual association with this presence of peace is cause enough for the slaughter of the innocent living in the neighborhood of Bethlehem. There is so much destruction so close to Christmas. It is the shadow of the cross, the intimation of the struggle that lies ahead.

The parallel between this Herod and the Pharaoh of old is striking. The birth of Moses as told in the first two chapters of Exodus is the backdrop for the birth of the child Jesus. In an article entitled "Baby Jesus, Refugee: Matthew's Advent Story" (*Catholic Agitator* [December 1987]), Ched Myers writes:

> The parallels between Pharaoh and Herod are uncanny. The challenge of an infant unleashes a policy of infanticide — naturally justified by "national security" (cf. Ex 1:16–20). Their attempts to work through accomplices, however (Pharaoh with Hebrew midwives, Herod with the astrologers), fails because these accomplices choose life and are prepared to deceive their superiors to protect the innocent. We never again hear of these midwives and astrologers; they have only bit parts in the biblical drama. Yet can two more consequential acts of conscience be found anywhere in history? (5)

Mary and Joseph eventually return to their home in Nazareth to raise the child, but they will carry with them the memory of the horror that accompanied the birth of their child. Again, the Lord appears in a dream to Joseph and commands him to take a journey from Egypt to the land of Israel. Again, Joseph obeys. Joseph's dreams and "revelations signal divine intervention, showing that Yahweh is intimately involved on the side of the weak and disenfranchised in a struggle with the Powers (represented by Herod) for true sovereignty" (ibid.).

Christmas may stop horror momentarily in this world, but oftentimes the death and suffering caused by others and sin can seem worse in relation to the respite of peace and the fleeting experience of harmony and hope. We are told that the family settles down and the child grows and matures. It is a silent and hidden growing, in an out-of-the-way place. Although the Word is quiet, it is sure and ever stronger and truer.

A few folks know. Earth knows. Something has been set in motion. T. S. Eliot says it this way:

> With the drawing of this Love and the voice of this calling
> We shall not cease from exploration
> And the end of all of our exploring
> Will be to arrive where we started
> And know the place for the first time.

We start here, quietly saving what we can from violence and suffering, believing in mercy, in the presence of God, in salvation and redemption at work silently among us. The holy family shows us how to bend toward each other in reverence and service and love, in the face of inner and outer turmoil and history's violence and evil. Jesus, Mary, and Joseph are together in spite of, or because of, the pain, suffering, trials, and loneliness that they experience. This is how God works through history. Jesus' existence and survival were realities because of choices made by others. Much of the story is unknown, with just hints or intimations, and there are huge gaps. We are told: "Instead, because of a warning received in a dream, Joseph went to the region of Galilee. There he settled in a town called Nazareth." Life is a blend of concrete facts and the Word of the Lord. Herod dies, but his son Archelaus succeeds his father as king of Judea. Joseph is still afraid to go back, and so he relies on the presence of God in his dreams.

It is God who is calling the shots, calling out to Joseph in dreams, calling his son out of Egypt, and leading them to Nazareth. Matthew situates the history of Jesus in the context of the history of Moses and liberation. Matthew's Christmas story and its aftermath are quite unlike Luke's quiet and joyous account.

> It [Matthew] speaks only of ambiguity, political violence, displacement and danger. Which is to say it speaks of real life as it is for the poor. It is a story for our world today: teeming with refugees, filled with the chorus of Ramah as mothers

weep for their children; cursed with the murderous designs of the powerful. But this is the world in which God is with us, into which the Lord has come and yet will come with the promise of liberation. God slips into our world among the innocent, the cast off, the oppressed, trusting that people of conscience will recognize the Presence, and act accordingly. (Myers, "Baby Jesus," 5)

Gustavo Gutiérrez presents another perspective on the reading from Matthew:

At Christmas time it is often said that Jesus is born anew in each family, in each heart. But these "births" cannot ignore the first empirical fact: Jesus was born of Mary in the bosom of a people who at the time were dominated by the greatest power of that period. That was Jesus' "here and now." If we forget this, the birth of Jesus becomes an abstraction, a symbol, a figure. Without its historical coordinates, the event loses its significance. For the Christian, Christmas is recognized as a "bursting in" of God into human history: the birth of smallness and service in the face of the power and arrogance of the great of this world. An arrival accompanied by the smell of the manger.

The Christian faith is a historical faith. God is revealed in Jesus Christ and, though him, in human history. Only by starting from this point is it possible to believe in God. Believers cannot place themselves above history and watch life pass. We must learn to believe out of the concrete conditions of our life: in the midst of oppression and repression, but also in the midst of the struggles and hopes that exist in Latin America today. Under dictatorships that sow death among the poor as well as in the "democracies" that barter away their needs; in the civil war raging in El Salvador; in the harassment experienced by the heroic, long-suffering people of Nicaragua.... No, ever since the first Christmas, it has been impossible to separate Christian faith and human history. We discover Christ in our own "here and now." Christmas celebrates the very historical fact that is the basis on which Jesus can say, if you gave food to the poorest, "you gave it to me," and if you failed to do so, "you failed to give it to me" (Matt 25:31–46). The judgment of history will permit no equivocation. (*El Diario Marka* [Lima, Peru], December 26, 1982)

Matthew's ending of the Christmas pageant pulls us out of the personal or family sphere of celebration and "places it squarely at the fork in the road of history, where it becomes a call and a challenge to men and women who journey along it" (ibid.). This family knows many of our present realities: rumors of too-early pregnancies, adoption, stepfathers, births in solitude and poverty; fleeing violence, destruction, and destitution; fear, absence of relatives or support from others, living in a foreign country, living in the worst neighborhoods. The story also tells of covenants of friendship and love, faithfulness, reliance on God's providence and presence in history, and belief in the ultimate triumph of justice with peace. The family of three is aided by strangers both high (astrologers) and low (shepherds and innkeepers who share caves). They encounter the law, the temple, prophets (Anna and Simeon), personal prayer (dreams and angels and stars), and the beliefs and experience of God in other lives. This is a bracing and truthful model for family life.

## Cycle B: Luke 2:22–40

Luke's telling of the infancy narratives includes a story unique to his gospel, the story of Jesus' presentation in the temple and the offering of a sacrifice of "a pair of turtledoves or two young pigeons," in accordance with the law of Moses and the law of Israel. Mary and Joseph, who are described as "fulfilling all the prescriptions of the law of the Lord," are among the faithful of Israel, waiting in hope for the coming of the Messiah.

It is within this context that they meet Simeon, who is also a faithful man, "just and pious and await[ing] the consolation of Israel, and the Holy Spirit was upon him." This is a remarkable description. Simeon shares the virtues and characteristics of Joseph, for Joseph is also "just," pious, devout, reverent, and attentive to the honor of God. Simeon waits for God's consolation and mercy to be extended again to Israel. He is a prophet — whether anointed or not — because the Holy Spirit "is upon him." This is not a chance encounter; it is a graced meeting, as portentous as any visit of an angel or the appearance of a star in the night sky. Simeon lives looking for the Anointed of the Lord, knowing that he will not die before he sees him. This is his personal spirituality. He comes now, prompted by the Spirit, to the temple to meet Mary and Joseph as they consecrate their firstborn to the Lord. Obedience to the law draws them, and obedience to the Spirit draws Simeon. When they meet in the temple, the old man takes the eight-day-old child in his arms and blesses God! The time has come! God is moving among his people. Simeon rejoices and proclaims the effect this child will have on the world.

His prayer is part of the Night Office, and it is also used to prepare for death. Its real significance, its deepest meaning, though, is that it marks the end of one era and the dawning of a new age in history:

> Now, Master, you can dismiss your servant in peace;
>     you have fulfilled your word.
> For my eyes have witnessed your saving deed
>     displayed for all the people to see:
> A revealing light to the Gentiles,
>     the glory of your people Israel.

The first few lines of the prayer sound vaguely like the Magnificat of Mary. Simeon is a servant of God, and he has also witnessed the marvelous deeds of God shown forth for all to see. God's presence is now a light that will bring salvation to the Gentiles and reveal Israel's glory. This is one reason why Luke's gospel is often called the missionary gospel, the story of bringing the good news to the Gentiles. In this way, Luke's story parallels the magi in Matthew. The light is out, free to shine. Its source is this child's body and presence in the world for those who have the eyes to see. What Simeon has waited for has been given and received.

Jesus' parents marvel at what is being said about their son. The old wise one blesses them as a family and then addresses Mary, who, in Luke's gospel, often represents the believer. Simeon foretells how the child will affect Mary's life in the years ahead. His utterance is sharp and political. It draws in the destinies of nations and personal choices, life and death issues that swirl around the child's very being. The words are so familiar, yet they are layered in meaning and need to be pondered and treasured. The message is directed to all believers. From the moment of our baptisms, when we were presented to God in the church and given our baptismal candle and blessed with oil in the sign of the cross and exhorted to listen to the Word of the Lord, this message was given to each of us: "This child is destined to be the downfall and the rise of many in Israel, a sign that will be opposed — and you yourself shall be pierced with a sword — so that the thoughts of many hearts may be laid bare."

The one sentence is devastating. It begins with the child who will cause the demise or the ascension of many in his own nation and who will be opposed by individuals, institutions, and governments. It is a prophecy for all time. It also carries the jubilant announcement of Mary's song of delight in what God is doing for his people in her child to be born. She sings:

> He has shown the power of his arm,
> he has routed the proud of heart.
> He has pulled down the princes from their thrones and
> exalted the lowly.
> The hungry he has filled with good things, the rich sent
> empty away.
> He has come to the help of Israel his servant, mindful of
> his mercy. (Luke 1:51–54; Jerusalem Bible)

Already, others know what this child will do. This is Simeon's gift to Mary, confirmation of her "yes" and of the role she will play in the future life of her child. She will stand by him and be "pierced by a sword." In the traditions of the Jewish community and in our own writings, the Scriptures are a "double-edged sword." In Hebrews we read:

> The word of God is something alive and active: it cuts like any double-edged sword but more finely: it can slip through the place where the soul is divided from the spirit, or joints from marrow; it can judge the secret emotions and thoughts. No created thing can hide from him; everything is uncovered and open to the eyes of the one to whom we must give account of ourselves. (Hebrews 4:12–13)

Mary's child is the Word of God, the double-edged sword that has pierced her heart and will do so countless times in the future. It will cut and lay bare; it will empty her of tears and rend her with sorrow. She will struggle with the growing awareness of who this child is, and she will have to deal with the effect the Word of God has on others — from his disciples to crowds and strangers and those who will kill him.

There is another witness, the prophetess Anna, who is described by tribe, age, and vocation. Married and widowed, she is now a contemplative in the temple who fasts and prays for Israel. She enters the scene "at this moment," driven by the Spirit that pervades her whole life. Anna blesses God and talks about the child to "all who looked forward to the deliverance of Jerusalem." Both Simeon and Anna are faithful children of the covenant, watchers at the gates. Their faith heartens and deepens the faith of Mary and Joseph as they begin their life with this child as a family of God. In Luke, the holy family includes the old and widowed servants of God and the poor, for Joseph and Mary give two pigeons, the offering of the poor in the temple. Luke's holy family includes all of Israel's children who bless God in this child and all who will come to believe in this light that has entered the world. This child is the star that illumines the Spirit of God. His presence and power are recognizable to those who pray and watch, obeying the will of God and hoping on behalf of the people. The holy family includes all those who are consoled by the presence of this child of peace who has come into the world.

The last lines of the reading mention the rules for a holy family. They must fulfill all the prescriptions of the law; they must be devout, religious, just, and pious, as were Simeon and Anna. And the ending is simple: "The child grew in size and strength, filled with wisdom, and the grace of God was upon him." John F. Kavanaugh sums it up:

It is fitting that the holiness of the family also be celebrated at this time. For it is only by the ordinariness of being born, nurtured and taught, so frail and dependent upon those who have welcomed us into their lives, that we ever grow in strength and grace.

God enters these intimacies, too, just as surely as God wants entry into all of human history. And so the wisdom of the father and the authority of the mother and reverence of the child reveal the splendor. Sometimes the wise old ones in our midst, like Simeon, help us name the glory. Other times, it is the prophetic ancient, like Anna, who sees the truth of our ordinary radiance.

Paul reminds us that the virtues of daily life — kindnesses, thankfulness, patience and forbearance — embody our good and gracious God, who has willed to dwell in us. Our submission to each other, our love, our care lest the frail among us lose heart, is the making, once again, of the word into our flesh. ("The Word," *America,* December 18, 1993)

In the Orthodox Jewish community it is believed that the Shekinah, the holy presence of God in exile, descends to earth every Sabbath and remains to embrace those who live faithfully. When the Shekinah descends, the tabernacle of peace envelops all those who welcome her, and their lives "are rocked as if in a cradle of peace."

There are many stories of how to keep this tabernacle of peace here on earth. Some say that the tabernacle is bound to earth by four thin golden threads, sometimes tied to the fringe of the *tallis,* the prayer shawl of the holy ones in the community. Another way to keep the tabernacle close to earth is the study of the Torah, the law given to Moses on Mount Sinai. As long as there are discussion of the Torah and reverence for it, the tabernacle remains close by. Two other ways to hold this peacefulness around the family and the community are to tell stories of God and to sing the praises of the Holy One. Then even the Angel of Death cannot break through the threads that hold this peace on earth. On this feast of the Holy Family, we have these four threads to make use of, not just on the Sabbath but every day. Prayerful study of the Torah (which is often theological discussion or religious education), the telling of the stories of God (of faith; of Mary and the saints like Joseph, Simeon, and Anna; and of one's own ancestors in faith), and the praise of God in hymns, songs, psalms, and holiness of life. No matter what trials and opposition we face, we will grow in strength and wisdom in the gospel.

## Cycle C: Luke 2:41–52

This is the last of the infancy narratives, the bridge between Jesus' childhood and his coming of age as a Jew. We are told that Joseph and Mary went up to Jerusalem each year for the feast of the Passover, and in the year when Jesus is twelve they go again, "as was their custom." It was the time to celebrate Jesus' bar mitzvah, his rite of passage into the larger community of believers as an adult. The rituals are attended to, the law and the story told and celebrated in the Passover meal, and then they return home. They would have traveled in the company of others, friends, relatives, neighbors from their village of Nazareth and surrounding towns. A large group offered protection from bandits, soldiers, and wild animals on the ninety-mile trip. The journey was as much a part of the festival as the entrance into Jerusalem and the rituals in the temple. Those in the procession would have prayed and told stories of their history as they traveled. Their hopes and hearts would have been centered on the coming of the Messiah, even more than usual at this time of the remembrance of God's past deeds on behalf of the Israelite nation and of the promise of liberation and freedom. It was a mini-Exodus. It is not surprising that Jesus was not missed the first day out. Each of his parents assumed he was with the other or with friends and neighbors.

At some point, they began to search for him, looking "among their relatives and acquaintances," but they did not find him. They retraced their steps and still did not see him. Finally, "on the third day they came upon him in the temple sitting in the midst of the teachers, listening to them and asking them questions. All who heard him were amazed at his intelligence and his answers." Jesus has grown up, as the previous lines suggested, "in size, and strength, filled with wisdom, and the grace of God was upon him."

Once again his parents are astonished. This is a favorite word of Luke in describing people's reactions to Jesus' words and deeds. But Luke usually seems to be describing consternation, confusion, and doubt rather than belief. Here, Mary's reaction is quite motherly, revealing that she does not understand his behavior. She takes personally what he has done: "Son, why have you done this to us? You see that your father and I have been searching for you in sorrow." And his response is sure: he has done nothing to them. He has turned from his primary relationship of nuclear family to assume his duties as Son of his Father God. While Jesus is Mary's son, that is not his essence. He is Son of God, Savior. The Spirit of God is upon him, and he has been born of the Most High. This is what Mary was told at the Annunciation. But now Jesus' actions are unexpected, out of the ordinary, and she reacts as a worried parent with a wayward child. Jesus, however, is not only her child, but God's, and Jesus sees himself already in the larger family of Israel. The covenant and the law tell him that he must be in the temple, "in his Father's house."

Family life is foundational, but it is not the primary reason for existence or the primary focus of all relationships. In Jesus' life of dedication to the will of his Father, there is room for many, and inclusion is not based on marriage or blood ties or physical birth. It is based on surrendering to the Father's will and honoring God's design and bringing his kingdom to earth. This account in Luke echoes the story of the resurrection. Then, also, at the end on the third day, there will be a new temple. Christ's risen body will be his Father's house, instead of the temple in Jerusalem. His new family will be the Body of Christ, the dwelling place of the Spirit in the world. His disciples will search for him and, surprisingly, find him alive in the world and in their lives.

The twelve-year-old Jesus returns with his parents to Nazareth, and he is obedient to them. While he obeys his parents, his first and primary concern will be the will of his Father and the work of salvation, the preaching of good news to the poor and the bringing of God's kingdom into the world. Jesus will "progress steadily in wisdom and age and grace before God and men." This is the bulk of life, for Jesus and for each of us, living day-to-day in the shadow of the Spirit, slowly growing in grace and understanding. It is the way Jesus spends three decades of his life. All of us are to learn wisdom and practice the virtues listed in Paul's letter to the Colossians (3:12–21). It is a lifestyle, whether it is begun and experienced in our biological families or in our chosen families of parish, community, discipleship, or singleness. Our vocation is to grow in wisdom and age and grace. Being family — however we experience it — is intimately involved with the Divine, and it calls us to obedience.

Again, Mary returns to the attitude that characterized her at her child's birth: "She meanwhile kept all these things in memory." These few words describe much of her life. Jesus was born of her, but he is not hers; he belongs to his Father God. That is his primary vocation and identity. For now, though, as a twelve-year-old boy, he is still subject to Joseph and Mary. The hidden grace and power grows within him, unknown even to those closest to him.

God's intimacies with each of us are singular, and not necessarily shared even among family members. We are, to paraphrase Paul, to bear with one another, forgive one another, put on love, let peace reign in our hearts, dedicate ourselves to thankfulness, and instruct and admonish one another. All of that is worship of God, submission to the Word of Christ. It is our life's task and glory to live in this manner.

A marvelous story from the Turkish tradition called "Hide and Seek" will help us take all this to heart and hold it in our memory.

✤ Once upon a time there was a man who sought wisdom and studied with the wise ones of many countries and faiths. And one day a wise child was brought to him, with the explanation that this child was profound in his understandings and ability to speak. When the man asked whom the child had studied with, he was informed that the child was naturally wise, that his spirit was unsullied, and that no one had taught him. And so the man questioned him. The child answered in utterly simple and direct responses. The man was stunned and overcome with emotion. What child was this? The man was full of questions that he had carried all his life. He poured them out in a stream of never-ending proportions, one building upon the next.

But the child grew restless and decided he wanted to play a game, a game of hide and seek. He told the man, "You hide and I'll find you."

But the man insisted, "No, you hide and I'll find you. After all, I have great knowledge, and I can find anything, and you are just a child."

But the child refused. "No, you go first. Hide and let me find you."

So the man snapped his fingers and disappeared. The child was delighted and searched for the man. But soon the child was disappointed and almost in tears, because he realized the man had disappeared into another world.

Out loud, he said, "That's not fair. You're not supposed to hide in another world. This is a game for here."

The man came back, marveling at the boy's insight and perceptions. And, in that instance, the boy disappeared. It was a game of hide and seek, and now it was his turn. The man looked everywhere, but couldn't find the child. The child had leapt into the man's heart, a place the man rarely ventured, alone or with anyone else. Finally, desperate to continue questioning the child, he pleaded, "Where are you?"

The boy answered, "Right here."

The man listened, but the sound, though near, so close, was also far away, indistinct, barely discernible. "Where?" he called again.

The child laughed, "In your heart, of course."

But the man was lost. He did not know how to get into his heart. The child reappeared before him, stern and sad, and looked at him for a long time. And then he spoke, "You know, if you do not look in your own heart you will never know what wisdom and truth are or their power to reveal and transform. Deep, deep down there are rooms and caves that are full of riches and treasures, memories and hopes." After a while, he spoke again, "And if you don't look into others' hearts you will never find faith or love."

With that the boy turned to leave and the man grabbed for him. "No," the child said, "I have to go. There are many people I want to play my game with. But someday I will come back to play with you again. I hope you've practiced a lot and explored a lot more by then. Goodbye, until we meet again." And the child vanished.

And the child vanished, as Jesus vanished into a small town on the border of an oppressed country, living simply and learning wisdom. Our God's game of hide and seek is in full swing. Only those who spend time "remembering all these things in their hearts" and those who surrender in love to others' hearts will ever find the child and recognize him when he comes again, grown now into the way, the truth, and the life. The wisdom of God incarnate, Jesus the Christ, born of Mary, adopted by Joseph, hides in out-of-the-way places, in the countryside, on borders, in the dwelling places of the poor, and especially among those who watch and wait for the glory of God to be revealed. These are the chosen ones of God, his holy and beloved family.

We end with a prayer from the Syrian Clementine liturgy:

O God, you are the unsearchable abyss of peace, the ineffable sea of love, the fountain of blessings, and the bestower of affection, who sends peace to those who receive it. Open to us the sea of your love and water us with the plenteous streams from the riches of your grace. Make us children of quietness and heirs of peace. Enkindle in us the fire of your love and sow in us your fear; strengthen our weakness by your power; and bind us closely to you and to each other in one firm bond of unity. We ask this in the name of Jesus Christ the Lord, in the power of his Holy Spirit to the glory of your name, O God the Father. Amen.

# Mary, Mother of God
## *January 1*

*Numbers 6:22–27*
*Psalm 67:2–3, 5–6, 8*
*Galatians 4:4–7*
*Luke 2:16–21*

This is the first day of the New Year, according to the world's calculations, though we as Christians began the year of the Lord, the year of grace, over a month ago on the first Sunday of Advent. Time in this season is God's time, not history's time. It is the time of grace and truth, of growing in the Spirit and understanding God's intent at creation, when all was set in motion. On this first day of the year, we celebrate Mary, the woman who slips in and out silently, unobtrusively, meekly, yet with strength. This season is about comings and goings, ends and beginnings, dreams and the daunting courage it takes to make the dreams of God come true in a world that has turned away from such hopes for the human community.

This day has known a number of names in the past fifty years: Mary the Mother of the World, Mary the Mother of Peace, and now Mary, Mother of God. Even now, we are encouraged to celebrate the World Day of Peace on this feast with these readings. The church is trying to say more about this woman of courage, of truthfulness, of obedience and trust in the Word of God. The readings begin with an ancient blessing that comes from the mouth of God to Moses.

> The Lord said to Moses: "Speak to Aaron and his sons and tell them: This is how you shall bless the Israelites. Say to them:
>
> > The Lord bless you and keep you!
> > The Lord let his face shine upon you, and be gracious
> >     to you!
> > The Lord look upon you kindly and give you peace!
>
> So shall they invoke my name upon the Israelites, and I will bless them."

This blessing is a welcome assertion that we dwell always in the presence of the Holy One, that we are attended to by God, and

that all that transpires on earth is meant to lead to peace, graciousness, and kindness. We are meant to be a blessing to one another
as God has blessed us. It is a blessing to use at the end of liturgy,
as we set out into the world after celebrating God's gift of incarnation and God's gift of a mother in heart and Spirit. As we have
been given, so we are to give, generously and graciously, so that we
are like mother, like son, like mother, like daughter, like Father, like
children, like God!

In the psalm, in the response to the praise of God, we plead
that God, who once blessed the Israelites in the desert, will bless
us again. Mary's song of the Magnificat (when she blesses God for
"his mercy on all those who fear him in every generation" and his
promises and his faithfulness to his people) echoes this psalm's plea
that God "bless us in his mercy." Again, we ask for pity and for the
"light of God's face to shine upon us." This line, of course, takes on
more significant and personal meaning in the face of Jesus Christ,
God's spoken blessing upon us in flesh and spirit. We pray for this
blessing upon ourselves so that others may know in our lives "the
way of God upon the earth, and among all nations, the salvation
of God."

Again, our prayer is connected to the presence of God. We pray
that one day all the nations and ends of the earth will come to know
and fear our God. In this instance, it is holy fear, reverence, and submission to God. As Jesus describes his own relation to his Father, "I
revere God" (John 5). God blesses us, and our response must be to
become a blessing upon the earth, magnifying the name and presence of God among us, as Mary blessed God in her obedience and
trust in the Word of God that was spoken to her. God has blessed
Mary's relatives and ancestors and continues to bless the children of
her heart and soul in the person of her firstborn son, Jesus who is
Christ the Lord, a Savior born to us this day.

The reading from Paul's letter to the Galatians centers on Mary's
child, the heart and meaning of her life, and what this child of hers
has done for the world and for her: "When the designated time
had come, God sent forth his Son born of a woman, born under
the law, to deliver from the law those who were subjected to it, so
that we might receive our status as adopted sons." This is theological language. It focuses on relationship, on designating and altering
biological patterns so that understandings of the Spirit prevail.

Just as Mary's son is born of a woman and of the Most High,
we are born of the Spirit first of all. In this reading, grace must

prevail to deepen our understanding of who we are and what our relationship to God is. Otherwise, it is impossible to express our limited and often flawed understanding of what Paul is trying to tell his community of believers. What is at stake here is how we are bound to God and how God has chosen to bind himself to us in grace, in Spirit, and in our humanity. Paul is trying to describe the blessing that is the person of Jesus Christ, Son of God and son of Mary, and how that blessing draws us all into a privileged relation with God the Father, with Jesus the Son, with the Spirit of God, and with Mary. It is a blessing that grows, that permeates and saturates all of existence, affecting bodies, hearts, and souls in history and eternally.

First, we are reminded that God "sent forth" his Son born of a woman, with no mention of her name. The one who is sent goes forth from God. This is about Jesus' mission to rescue us from the condition of slavery, from sin and evil, and from our own weaknesses and selfishness. God never designed or intended that we be slaves to anyone, let alone to sin and our own idolatry. We were all born under the law, which is a way of describing the covenant that Yahweh made with the people of Israel for all time. It is not a particular or personal relationship with individuals, but with a people. We, who are so obsessed with self-realization and so independent of one another — although we talk a lot about community — do not often think of ourselves in terms of being bound together and responsible for one another before God. But this is the law, the kindness and blessing of God upon the people of Israel.

God has always wanted us close. God has always wanted us to know and be known intimately. We were invited to life and to knowledge and love of God through obedience, but we declined. Each of us — all of us — has declined, has sinned. It is a mark of our humanity, and we all are responsible together for the state of the world, for the state of the human race, even for the state of the earth's resources. We have failed miserably as a people, if we are honest about where humanity stands today.

In the Jewish tradition, the language of fathering, the use of the word "son," has been reserved for the nation, the people of God as a whole throughout time (Exodus 4:22; Hosea 11:1). It is not based on blood ties, but on God's choice. God singles out the children of Israel as belonging to him, and their responsibility is to become a light to the nations that will lead others to glorify and bless God's name because of Israel's justice and peace. In Exodus,

Moses is instructed how to approach Pharaoh, to work miracles, and to do marvelous things. This is what Yahweh tells Moses to say to explain why God wants this particular people out of Egypt:

> Then you will say to Pharaoh, "This is what Yahweh says: Israel is my first-born son. I ordered you to let my son go to offer me worship. You refuse to let him go. So be it! I shall put your first-born to death." (Exodus 4:22–23)

God intends to liberate the children of Israel and teach them to cling to the covenant and honor of God as their base of power and identity in the world. Yahweh will continue to bless this "son" even when the people refuse to acknowledge their relationship with God and disobey the covenant of the law. Israel's history is the story of God chasing after his "son" and trying to impress upon him the great love that he has for him. The prophets' refrain of lament is about the "son's" errant ways and reckless disregard of God's presence and choice and his refusal to obey and to be faithful. Hosea speaks tenderly of God's feelings for this "son":

> When Israel was a child I loved him,
> and I called my son out of Egypt.
> But the more I called to them, the further they went from me;
> they have offered sacrifice to the Baals
> and set their offerings smoking before the idols.
> I myself taught Ephraim to walk,
> I took them in my arms;
> yet they have not understood that I was the one looking after them.
> I led them with reins of kindness,
> with leading strings of love.
> I was like someone who lifts an infant close against his cheek;
> stooping down to him I gave him his food.
> (Hosea 11:1–4; Jerusalem Bible)

Over and over again the image of son is used for the people, for "them," the chosen ones of God's own heart, who are like children, wayward, selfish, unthinking and petulant, stubborn and even vicious on occasion. God's lament continues just a few lines further on:

My people are diseased through their disloyalty;
they call on Baal,
but he does not cure them.
Ephraim, how could I part with you?
Israel, how could I give you up?
How could I treat you like Admah,
or deal with you like Zeboiim?
My heart recoils from it,
my whole being trembles at the thought.
I will not give rein to my fierce anger,
I will not destroy Ephraim again,
for I am God, not man:
I am the Holy One in your midst
And have no wish to destroy.

(Hosea 11:7–9; Jerusalem Bible)

God is disturbed by Israel's infidelity. Israel refuses to acknowledge God's choice, God's favor, and God's kindness. The children of Israel will be entrapped by their stubbornness and reliance on other nations. When God tries to reveal the relationship that he desires with this wayward "son," God uses the language of a parent, who tenderly tries to hold a wiggling small child intent on its own wishes and struggling to escape even if headed into danger. But God is clear about his intentions and responses to this "son." God is not human and has no wish to destroy. God, the Holy One, is in our midst, and the will of God has been and is for peace, for life, and for holiness always.

Now, with the birth of the son Jesus Christ, this favor, this grace-filled selection, is being extended to all who will accept it. We are told in Galatians that it is again by the favor of God that "this Spirit has been sent forth into our hearts, and it is this Spirit in us that cries out 'Abba, Father!'" We are no longer slaves but a son! And we are an heir, by God's design. This means all of us, the people upon whom God's glory shines, all of us "upon whom God's favor rests," as the angels announce to the shepherds keeping watch over their flocks the night of the birth of Jesus. In this Jesus, as Paul continues in his letter to the Galatians, we share in sonship, this privileged relationship that Jesus shares with God the Father. Paul writes:

Before faith came, we were allowed no freedom by the Law;
we were being looked after till faith was revealed. The Law

was to be our guardian until the Christ came and we could be justified by faith. Now that that time has come we are no longer under that guardian, and you are, all of you, sons of God through faith in Christ Jesus. All baptized in Christ, you have all clothed yourselves in Christ, and there are no more distinctions between Jew and Greek, slave and free, male and female, but all of you are one in Christ Jesus. . . . Let me put this another way: an heir, even if he has actually inherited everything, is no different from a slave for as long as he remains a child. He is under the control of guardians and administrators until he reaches the age fixed by his father. Now before we came of age we were as good as slaves to the elemental principles of this world, but when the appointed time came, God sent his Son, born of a woman, born a subject to the Law, to redeem the subjects of the Law and to enable us to be adopted as sons. (Galatians 3:23–28; 4:1–5)

These lines, which precede today's reading, are crucial to understanding Paul's image of adoption and sonship. Sonship is not about gender, but about a shift from slavery and the law to the intimacy of children and freedom, from an ego focused on self to communion, being one body in Christ. The sign of this shift, this radically altering of existence, is simple: it is the name we use to address God. The term that fits this new intimacy of being chosen and saved is "Abba" (Father), a term of endearment that expresses faithfulness, obedience, and surrender to God's will. This relationship is God's design, God's hope, and God's fervent will, and it is possible only by God's mercy and grace. God's gift of the Spirit in Jesus Christ is not so much about nativity or gender or biology, but about faith, freedom, baptism, and belonging to God in a closeness that was unthinkable before. Especially in this season of Christmas and Epiphany, we need to reflect on this mystery, this gift, and this blessing that God offers to us in Jesus Christ.

This relationship shifts all the other relationships of human beings for all time. It offers an alternative to violence, war, discrimination, nationalism, greed, selfishness, and the callousness of human beings one to another. Stanley Hauerwas, who writes of ethics, morality, and virtue, states that the fact of incarnation and our invitation to be adopted by God stipulate that we begin with basics, such as the serious intent to never kill another human being because we are *all* adopted by God and taken close to God's heart.

No one who kills another can turn and say they worship the God of Jesus or call God "Father."

This brings us to the feast of Mary, the Mother of God. It is easily accepted that Mary is the mother of Jesus, but it requires a leap of faith to say that Mary is the Mother of God. It is a statement of belief in who Jesus is, who Jesus' Father is — God. Mary is the Mother of God by God's gracious favor and blessing and by Mary's obedience to the will of God. How this is possible is another matter altogether. It is a matter of faith, perhaps learned only by believing, praying, and "pondering all these things in our hearts."

The gospel reading is the same as that for the Christmas Mass at dawn, when the angels depart back to the heavens, having delivered their message to the shepherds. And the shepherds rush to Bethlehem to find Mary and Joseph and the baby lying in the manger. It is interesting to note that the shepherds found Joseph with Mary and the baby. This is the first time really that Joseph is found with Mary. Joseph has been witness to the waiting, to the birth, and now to the story of the watchers in the field. While Joseph figures strongly in Matthew's gospel, he is barely discernible as a person in Luke's gospel, with its emphasis on Mary, the mother of the baby in the manger. Here, Joseph, the dreamer who found it in his heart to take Mary as his wife and take her into his house, is found with his family as the shepherds come in from the fields to the city. Somehow Joseph has understood what the shepherds now see and understand about this child.

The shepherds return to their life and astonish anyone who will listen with the report of the night's happenings, of God's great deeds on behalf of his people upon whom his Spirit now rests. They return, glorifying God for all they have seen and heard, in accord with what had been told them. It is a description of believers who see with the eyes of faith, hear the good news, and obey it in haste, relying on the Word that has been told to them, witnessing to it publicly to all who will listen and come to belief. The shepherds are becoming a light to the nations.

On Mary's feast day, we find her "treasuring all these things and reflecting on them in her heart," seemingly one of Luke's favorite descriptions of her. She is blessed by the God of her people, the Israelites, the remnant of believers who hope in the promises of God. Like the angels, she has heard the Word of God and acted in haste to make it come true in reality. She can withstand the presence of danger, running from the law, from relatives and religious sentiment that could kill her unborn child or see her stoned to death for apparently breaking the law and transgressing the covenant. One of the ancient titles for Mary is the Lady of the Book, the Woman of the Word, because her whole life is based on the Word of God and her surrender to it: "Behold, I am the handmaid, the servant of the Lord. Let it be done unto me according to your Word" (Luke 1:38).

Mary the woman has much to reflect upon, much to treasure, and much to ponder. She must come to understand what she has heard concerning this child from the shepherds. And she must come to understand what she hears from Anna and Simeon in the temple when the child is taken to be circumcised and named — an event commemorated today, on her day, January 1. This feast of Mary, the Mother of God, was first decreed in the Council of Ephesus in 431 C.E., when the church called her Theotokis, the God-bearer. In a sense, in honoring the mother we obey the Son, as she did, bending before her own child and coming to believe that he is not just her son, her child, but God's own. Mary is mother of the child, daughter of the Father, beloved of the Spirit.

Jesus is the Word of God, made flesh of her flesh, and born of the Spirit of God that quickened in her and overshadowed her. She brought forth a child both God and human. The church says that anything we say of Mary, we also say of ourselves. We are to listen to the Word of God and let the Spirit overshadow us and let God's Word take flesh in us. We are "to bear God to the world," as she did, to become sons and daughters of God. We can all call God "Abba" with intimate freedom. We have inherited Jesus' relationship to God, and the Spirit of God dwells in each of us, all of us, by baptism. We too are born of God.

Mary treasures what God has done and is doing in her life. Like her, we must hold God in our hearts, let the child be born there and grow to maturity there and take over our lives. We must learn from her how to mother God. In a piece titled "Christmas Message" (*America,* December 14, 1996), George W. Hunt wrote:

> Ever since the decrees of the Second Vatican Council, Mary has preeminently been the image of the church. This role fits her best of all, for even her name in Arabic translates as "a woman who loves human company and conversation" (in Hebrew it is "the beloved"). This insight dates back to the earliest Fathers of the Church, who saw her as the mother of Christ giving birth to "the members of the body of Christ"

and as the "mother of all recreated things" in the new creation wrought by the incarnation. The great Jesuit poet Gerard Manley Hopkins, in more allusive language, captures well this happy circumstance in his poem, "The Blessed Virgin Compared to the Air We Breathe":

> Of her who not only
> Gave God's infinity
> Dwindled to infancy
> Welcome in womb and breast,
> Birth, milk, and all the rest
> But mothers each new grace
> That does now reach our race
> . . . . . . . . . . . . . . . . . . . . . .
> Of her flesh he took flesh:
> He does take fresh and fresh,
> Though much the mystery how,
> Not flesh but spirit now
> And makes, O marvellous!
> New Nazareths in us,
> Where she shall yet conceive
> Him, morning, noon and eve;
> New Bethlehems, and he born
> There, evening, noon and morn...

Because of Mary, Christ now Nazareths in us and Bethlehems, too. This is but a figurative way to describe Christian identity, for to call oneself a Christian means that one has appropriated afresh the biblical narrative as a dynamic and revelatory part of one's own life. (3)

God has been interested in only one thing for us since the beginning, in making us the children of mercy and blessing. We all become that anew in Mary's heart-filled yes to God. Her virgin heart was wide open to God's word. Thomas Merton writes about this *point vierge,* the virgin heart, in his letters to Louis Massignon, saying: "The inmost desire in the heart of Christ makes itself somehow present in us in the form of that little point of nothingness and poverty in us which is the *point* or virgin eye by which we know Him!" (in *Letters,* ed. N. B. Stone, J. Lauglin, and Brother P. Hart [New York: New Directions, 1968], 160).

In a wild, poetic piece of reflection on this *point* he also writes:

> The first chirps of the waking day birds mark the *point vierge* of the dawn under a sky as yet without real light, a moment of awe and inexpressible innocence, when the Father in perfect silence opens their eyes. They begin to speak to Him, not with fluent song, but with an awakening question that is their dawn state, their state at the *point vierge*. Their condition asks if it is time for them to "be." He answers "yes." Then, they one by one wake up, and become birds, beginning to sing. Presently they will be fully themselves, and will even fly.... All wisdom seeks to collect and manifest itself at that blind sweet point.... For the birds there is not a time that they tell, but the virgin point between darkness and light, between non-being and being. (131–32)

Like Mary, Merton's life was centered on contemplation, on reflecting on and treasuring all these things in his heart. It is the vocation of a monk to do this single-heartedly and single-mindedly, but it is everyone's calling as a Christian, as a disciple and child of God. As children of Mary, we are all called to know and experience the Word of God in the depths of our soul and to be constantly open to conversion and transformation, to God's need of us in the world. We are called to respond by magnifying the Lord in our hearts and by singing out the gladness that God gives to us in the gift of his Spirit in our souls. We must learn to live only for the glory of God and let God be born again and again in the depths of our hearts.

The gospel passage for January 1 contains a brief text that is not included at the Mass at dawn on Christmas Day. It is particular to this day's commemoration: "When the eighth day arrived for his circumcision, the name Jesus was given the child, the name the angel had given him before he was conceived." The law decreed that on the eighth day a child was to be brought to the temple and offered as a sacrifice, given over to the service of God and circumcised according to the covenant. Then, the child was named. This child, though, had been named by God, through the angel Gabriel, at his conception. It is God who in truth names each of us; each of us by our water- and Spirit-birth belongs to God in sacrifice, as offering. God has a prior hold on each of us because Jesus has saved all of us by his birth, life, death as a human being, and resurrection.

It is important to note that after this incident Mary stays silent until twelve years later when she and Joseph lose Jesus and then find him in the temple in Jerusalem. Then she falls silent again, throughout all of Jesus' mission and work on earth. She appears again in Luke's gospel at Pentecost with the coming of the Spirit upon the Jesus community. The intimacy between Jesus and this new family of God is based on obedience to the Word and taking this Word into one's heart.

All of this is worth treasuring and pondering in this season and daily in our lives. The readings begin with a blessing from God on Mary. By her obedience she extended that blessing to all of us. Now, we have the Mother of God as our mother, the Father of Jesus as our Father, Jesus as our brother and friend, and we have the Spirit to work in us. On this first day of the year, we are invited into the practice of contemplation, of treasuring God's Word and presence in our lives. We are encouraged to learn devotion and faithfulness from Mary, who finds great favor with God and gives birth to such hope and love.

The monk, Thomas Merton, tells us:

> Fickleness and indecision are signs of self-love. If you can never make up your mind what God wills for you, but are always veering from one opinion to another, ... from one method to another, it may be an indication that you are trying to get around God's will and do your own with a quiet conscience. So keep still, and let God do some work.

This is good advice for the first day of a year. The opening prayer for today's liturgy puts it in more traditional language:

> God our Father, the first thing we do in this new year is to come together to thank you. With Mary we marvel at your Son's birth and with the shepherds we adore him and express our love. With the help of the prayers of the Mother of God, fill us with your blessings and grant peace to our world, today and the whole year long. We ask this in the name of Jesus the Lord. Amen.

## Mass for Peace in the World
*Isaiah 2:1–5*
*Sirach 36:15*
*James 3:13–18*
*Matthew 5:38–48*

Today's worship is also focused on peace, with the Mass for Peace in the World. The theme of peace is threaded through the readings. Mary is a woman of peace, of God's peace, born of obedience to justice and truth. Isaiah's dream of peace (Isaiah 2:1–5, from the first Sunday of Advent, Cycle A) brings home to us God's hope of a world without war, without weapons and stockpiling of arms. There is also an emphasis on growing food and sustaining life, as this child of Mary was so intent on doing in his own life, by feeding crowds both food and hope and by becoming bread for the world, the bread of peace and justice. This is walking in the way of the Lord, the path of God. This is the beginning of peace that can become abiding, deep, a virgin point of our lives.

The responsorial psalm is from Sirach 36:15: "Give peace, O Lord, to those who wait for you." Simple, direct, an arrow straight from our hearts to God's and back again.

The second reading is from the letter of James 3:13–18, with pragmatic suggestions for peacemaking, peacekeeping, and nonviolence as practices that characterize this family of God, this community whose mother is Mary, who knew the devastation of murder and violence from the very beginning of her child's life. The last line is perhaps the most important: "The harvest of justice is sown in peace." Again, there is this commingling of food and peace, of justice and this child in a manger asleep among the poor and animals. We are the family that cultivates peace as one tends a garden.

The gospel reading is from Matthew 5:38–48, the last portion of the Sermon on the Mount, the blueprint for believers who are the children of God, especially those who work for and craft peace in a divided, unforgiving, ruthless, and murderous world. It is a demand for and a call to nonviolence, service, resisting evil with goodness, and turning aside from the Older Testament's "eye for an eye" (which makes everyone blind) to the indiscriminate practice of love for all, even our enemies and those who are unjust and mean-spirited (like us, perhaps). It is a call to conversion, to start acting like God, our Father, with Jesus, in the power of the Spirit, remembering that we all have the same mother and that she chooses that we act with love and compassion toward all our brothers and sisters on this earth.

Now, I want to tell a story, because stories can help us see in profound and deep ways that elude our rational thought or logical precision. Entitled "The One Hundredth Name of God," it is a Muslim story, told often to children. There is a tradition in the Islamic community that God has one hundred names and that those that are holy know all but one. That one name is the most holy, the most descriptive of God, and the most powerful for intercession and transformation, for becoming holy. God's usual name in the Islamic community is Allah, the Most Compassionate One. (Shulamith Oppenheim has written a version of this story, with the same title, for children.)

✣ Once upon a time there was a young boy who lived in Egypt. He was often sad, though he lived with his mother and sisters, his father and his beloved camel, named Qadim, the Ancient One. It was a strange name for his camel because he was only as old as the boy, Salah, who was almost eight. They were inseparable friends, and Salah would often sleep outside under the stars of the desert with Qadim and talk to him. Salah was sad because Qadim was sad. He was wrinkled and looked old. Salah knew that all camels looked this way, sad, so sad, even on the day that they were born. And they hung their heads all the time. Salah loved his camel dearly, maybe even more than his family, and couldn't bear to see his friend so unhappy. He knew, too, that the camels worked hard and that none of the people would be able to exist without them. They needed the camels desperately to survive in the harsh desert. But the people all made fun of the camels, looking so old and wretched, sad and forlorn. No wonder they hung their heads so ashamed. Salah would talk to Qadim and question him on his sadness, and he would explain to him that he knew and understood his sadness. Qadim, the Ancient One, would lower his eyelids whenever he understood what Salah was saying, and his eyelids were lowered now.

Salah's father would tease him saying, "You're moping around so much, you're beginning to look like that camel of yours." But he knew his son's heart and understood his love for the camel and his concern. It revealed the great heart of his son, so young and yet so open to compassion. It boded well for him, and the father was proud of his son.

Every day at noon Salah and his father would stop working and before having a lunch of dates, figs, bread, and water, Salah's father would take out his prayer rug, roll it out on the sand in the shade, and begin to pray, first standing facing the east and then kneeling with his head lowered to the ground in submission before Allah. Then he would rise and pray. Salah watched, for soon he too would be required to pray during the day, acknowledging the power of God. After the prayer, when they were eating, Salah spoke with his father about his concern for his camel, Qadim. Salah's father look at him and told him, "I pray because Allah wants all of us to be happy, to know peace, and to live decently. So Allah does not wish any of us to be sad, not even your camel, Qadim." Salah explained to his father that his camel was sad because he looked so old, even though he was only seven, nearly eight like him, and that people were always making fun of the camels. If only he had something to be proud of, then he would walk proudly with his head high.

Salah's father looked at his son and said, "There is no reason for your camel to be so sad. After all, look at how he lives. He has plenty of fresh water, rest, care, and food. He has dates and figs and cakes of hay, and he even has you as his best friend who loves him so dearly. You can't have everything you want. Why, look at us. We work hard to eat and make a living. We try to keep from quarreling and stay away from stealing and making war, to live in peace and raise our children in love. We pray and honor Allah, but we don't even know all the names of God. In fact, we don't know the most important name of God, that one hundredth name, and yet we don't walk around moping and looking sad, our heads hanging in shame. That is the way it is — there is suffering and hardship, but there is joy and peace too. We pray knowing that Allah wants us to be happy. Come, let us go back to work." And they did, all three of them, Salah, his father, and his camel, Qadim.

But that night Salah had an idea. He slept outside with Qadim, which he loved to do, and in the middle of the night, at the darkest time, he got up quietly, went to his father's possessions and took his prayer rug. He stepped quietly over Qadim, who looked to be sleeping, and slipped out into the desert air. Away from the camp, he rolled out the rug and prayed as he had seen his father do: first standing facing the east, then kneeling with his head on the ground in submission to Allah's will. He prayed as fervently as he could, as long as he could, asking Allah, the Most Compassionate One, to have mercy on his dear friend, Qadim, and to do something for him so that he wouldn't be so sad. Salah believed what his father had said about prayer having great power, and he firmly trusted that Allah would do something to make his friend hold his head up high. And he remembered that all human beings pray and yet they die without ever knowing that one hundredth name of God.

Next morning he was up early, looking for Qadim, who was up before him. He ran into his father, who was laughing at him. His father motioned to the camel and asked, "What in the world got into that camel of yours last night? Look at him, with his head held high and walking so proudly. Only Allah knows what happened to him!"

Salah was overjoyed. He ran to Qadim, wrapped his arms around his neck and spoke to him. "It's true isn't it? You know, don't you? Allah, the Most Compassionate One, heard my prayer and told you, didn't he?" He looked at his camel and he was sure, because now Qadim was no longer sad. In fact, now he looked wise, not old but wise. Salah whispered into Qadim's ear, "You know the hundredth name of God. He told you!"

In response, Qadim lowered his eyelids and opened them and lowered them again, three times. Yes, it was true! And Salah went on, "But you can't tell, can you? Only the other camels know! It will be your secret forever!" And Qadim stood tall and proud.

Salah's father urged him on, "It's time to go to work, you and that proud, wise-looking camel of yours. Let's go." And they did, off into the desert, Salah dancing alongside his beloved friend, Qadim, the Ancient One, who was wise and happy, with his head held up proudly, regally. And that's why camels walk and look the way they do, even today. We may know the ninety-nine names of God, but they are the only ones who know the one hundredth, and they have never told! Some say, they never will. God is great. God is good. *Allahu akbar.*

Today is the first day of the year, and we turn to the woman of compassion who loves all her children as she loved her first born, Jesus, the servant of God. She cares especially for those who are sad, for those caught in the traps of violence and rage, hate and horror, that killed her child and continue to kill her children. Her heart aches as she watches the violence of her children toward one another, praying in her heart that we will learn peace, compassion, and love for one another, we who call her mother and claim to belong to God and to be followers of her son Jesus. She treasures all these things in her heart, opening always ever more deeply to the wisdom and secret mystery of God in her life, in the life of his people, his children, and her own beloved children. She prays with us: "Our Father who art in heaven, hallowed be thy name. Thy kingdom come, thy will be done on earth in my children now as it is in heaven. Give us daily bread, enough to share, and forgive them only when they forgive and heed one another's pain, and lead them by the Spirit home to you. Protect them from evil and teach them in wisdom to hold fast to one another and to be one in heart, in spirit, and in love. Our Father, they are my children too. Let them grow up to be like your first born and mine, Jesus the Lord. Amen. Let us pray that it may be so. Amen."

# Epiphany
## *A, B, and C Cycles*

*Isaiah 60:1–6*
*Psalm 72:1–2, 7–8, 10–13*
*Ephesians 3:2–3, 5–6*
*Matthew 2:1–12*

The light has come to us. Although it is still dark in the world, although evil and death still have their time, the light cannot be contained. It will burst forth like the sun breaking over the mountains and glory will stream across the earth. It is the time of the manifestation, the showing forth of the glory of God. It is time for us to stand and lift our faces to the light, to the Sun of Justice, and to let the face of God make our faces radiant and set our hearts throbbing with life and hope.

Advent, Christmastide, and Epiphany form the season of light, light that is afar off, light that interrupts and explodes into night's darkest hour, and light that is loose in the world. The light is seeping into the world, making its presence felt, softly, gently at first, in the face of a mother and child and those who come to worship, to kneel in awe at the glory of God among us. Divinity has made itself small enough for us to hold it in our arms and bend our heads tenderly over it. But the season is full of shadows, too, of hatred, evil, ignorance, and resistance to the light.

Originally, the early church had two pivotal seasons of the year, Easter and Epiphany — the poles of light at the beginning and end of the life of Christ, the light of the world. These were the times for baptism, for extending the light to new believers. Over the centuries, especially in this past century, the focus shifted from Epiphany to Christmas. This is unfortunate for it blurs the power of the symbolism of light and its confrontation with those who are intent on shutting it out, ignoring it, or covering it up. It is crucial to see and understand how the light is taken from its place of beginning and dispersed into the world — it is the strangers, outsiders, and wise ones from the east who see the signs and catch sight of a star, a portent of another power come to earth. They come searching, wanting to offer their gifts and homage, and to align themselves with what is being born on the earth. They stumble into Herod's palace, the domain of those who care only for their own place in the world, and they announce a new presence, a new king on the earth.

As soon as the wise ones leave Herod's palace, a place of intrigue and plots, the star finds them again and leads them home. It is as if the star was waiting for them to pass through the glaring lights of evil and violence so that they can see more clearly what they are following. The star rests over the place where the child sleeps with Mary, its mother. They enter, prostrate themselves in worship, and give over their hearts. Then they, too, begin to have dreams and to recognize evil and know wisdom. They are given gifts, and they learn how to go home by another way. Another way — that is what Advent and Christmas are all about — another way to live, another way to love, another way to belong, another way to show forth the glory of God.

Another "way" was described in a poem written by a twelve-year-old girl from Beersheva. It was later set to music and performed at the Nobel Peace Prize ceremony honoring Yitzhak Rabin, Shimon Peres, and Yasir Arafat. It is called "I Had a Box of Paints."

I had a box of paints
Each color glowing with delight:

I had a box of paints with colors
Warm and cool and bright.
I had no red for wounds and blood.
I had no black for an orphaned child.
I had no white for the face of the dead.
I had no yellow for burning sand.
I had orange for joy and life.
I had greens for buds and blooms.
I had blue for clear bright skies.
I had pink for dreams and rest.
I sat down
And painted
Peace.

For the rest of the year we are summoned to honor this child, Peace, who will grow up to bring mercy and save us all. Peace dwells among us, hidden now but growing stronger. We are encouraged to keep our eyes open so we will catch a glimpse of the glory of God.

But the feast of Epiphany, the revelation of the light of the world, is also set against the darkness that will rise and challenge its very existence and fight furiously to destroy its promise and hope. Epiphany sets a demarcation line and demands that we choose on which side we will stand, if we will resist evil or practice it. The manifestation, the glory, of the Lord always exposes and reveals us — individuals and nations alike — for what we truly are in the sight of God.

Isaiah proclaimed this light. He sang it out, cried in joy and with unbelievable passion:

Rise up in splendor, Jerusalem! Your light has come,
the glory of the Lord shines upon you.
See, darkness covers the earth,
and thick clouds cover the peoples.
But upon you the Lord shines,
and over you appears his glory.
Nations shall walk by your light,
and kings by your shining radiance.
Raise your eyes and look about;
they all gather and come to you:
Your sons come from afar,
and daughters in the arms of their nurses.

Then you shall be radiant at what you see,
your heart shall throb and overflow. (Isaiah 60:1–5a)

The focus is all on the light, our light, the light of Jerusalem, the city of God, the city of peace. God is present in the city, shining upon it, even though the earth is still covered by darkness and thick clouds hang over the people. Isaiah presents an image of a burst of light, illuminating for a moment this one place, but the light shines — it is sustained and strong. This appearance of God's glory is accompanied by another promise: "Nations shall walk by your light and kings by your shining radiance." This light heralds a change of focus and direction for all the world's peoples and governments. It is a beacon that draws all people home.

The promise is directed first to those who have been faithful, the remnant of sons and daughters that finally returns. Their return is a homecoming of glory that makes hearts beat faster in excitement and wonder. The vision Isaiah proclaims is of a people burdened with sin and oppression, exile, and loss of their homeland and temple, a people who have disobeyed and yet still belong to God. And the sight described by Isaiah is hard for the people to believe. It is a sight to behold! Nations and foreign lands, Midian, Ephah, Sheba, will come in procession with all the riches of earth and sea, with homage, tribute, and gifts, specifically gold and frankincense. Most important, they will come "proclaiming the praises of the Lord." This religious pilgrimage will come seeking authority to worship and to do homage, to experience the light.

We who are called Christians, the bearers of the light of Christ, believe that this light is a reality in the world. We are convinced that the child born in Bethlehem and heralded by hosts of angels who sing the glory of God to the shepherds in the fields is such a shining radiance. We believe that the vision has come true in the face of the child Jesus, Emmanuel, God who is with us always. The document of Vatican II that describes the meaning and power of the church in the world is called the Dogmatic Constitution on the Church, also known as *Lumen Gentium* (meaning the "light of the peoples," the "light of the nations"). We are that lighthouse that beckons and gives light to steer home by, especially for those in distress, those searching, and those who plot their course by the hope of resurrection.

Psalm 72 states a conviction, a belief: "Lord, every nation on earth will adore you." Addressed to the Lord, it affirms our hope,

but it convicts us too. As always, it is a fervent hope for justice that
is the hallmark of this light, this child, our God. This child is a king's
son, and his kingdom is characterized by a government with justice
for all and, especially, a judgment in favor of those who are afflicted
in the land. The second stanza of the psalm is a mantra worth inter-
nalizing and repeating until it becomes as much a part of our minds
and hearts as the blood that courses through our veins: "Justice shall
flower in his days and profound peace, till the moon be no more. /
May he rule from sea to sea and from the river to the ends of the
earth." This is the rule of God extending out, flowing out like a
radiance, healing, flowing over broken hearts and torn treaties and
severed hopes and limbs of those caught in the rage of governments
and evildoers. As at the beginning of Advent, we are encouraged,
even more so now, because of the birth of this child among us.

Homage and tribute, gifts and service from all nations and kings
and their peoples are due to this child of God because of what this
child does on the earth. In four lines we are told four times what
is the heart of this king's agenda and whose faces are made radiant
because of his presence in the world.

> For he shall rescue the poor man when he cries out,
>     and the afflicted when he has no one to help him.
> He shall have pity for the lowly and the poor;
>     the lives of the poor he shall save. (Psalm 72:12–13)

One word reveals the glory of this God: the "poor." This child
born of Mary and of God will bring radiance to the poor and the
afflicted, those without justice, who cling to the lifelines of promises
as their only hope. This is the first shining revelation of Epiphany!

This deeper and more hidden meaning of the feast day is closely
bound to the second shining revelation of Paul's letter to the Ephesians. Paul himself describes it in terms of "God's secret plan" that
was known to the holy apostles and prophets, but now this plan is
broadcast to all the world of believers: "It is no less than this: in
Christ Jesus the Gentiles are now co-heirs with the Jews, members
of the same body and sharers of the promise through the preaching
of the gospel" (Ephesians 3:6).

This is it. Now, no one is excluded from the hope of salvation, of
glory and enlightenment, the revelation of God. All are included; all
are welcomed; all are invited to the light, to freedom and liberation,
to fullness of life and resurrection in Christ Jesus. Emmanuel, our
God, is with us, all of us. We are all the same body. We are all chil-

dren of God. We are all bound together in heart and mind. We all share in God's generosity of forgiveness, of the Spirit, and of grace. All are favored and embraced.

There is a story told — in India, I think — that has all sorts of connections to today's readings about light, stars, gifts, announcements of good news, and dreams. It is said that stars, angels, and dreams are pieces of the same reality, that they all are messages from God, shreds of glory loose on earth, invitations to closeness to divinity. Why these messages, these interruptions, are needed by human beings at specific junctures in God's plan is described in the story "The Hidden Star."

✤ Once upon a time there was a gathering of the stars, a shining convergence of light. They came together to boast of their service to humanity and what they had done in obedience to God's command to shine forth and bring light in the heavens. They knew that their glory lay in obeying God and in serving those he had put upon the earth. They didn't gather very often, but when they did it was a sight to behold.

They shimmered and shone, pulsed and throbbed with every color of white; they let off tiny specks of light and brilliant showers, bursts and long-lingering trails. One star spoke amid the music of their coming together. "I am the pole star," she sang out. "If it weren't for me, humans would be lost. They would have no sense of direction, no feel for distances. Their journeys would be nightmares that never ended. Because of me they know where they are on the earth and so can go from one place to the next. They are not always lost."

Another star spoke and said, "Well, I don't have a name, but what I have done is really spectacular, for I am the star that proved Einstein's theory of relativity correct! Yes! that was me. I darted behind the sun at just the right moment during an eclipse and forever changed the shape of earth's science."

The others beamed and glowed in recognition. Others spoke up and cited their contributions to science, to art, to music, to the beauty of earth's dome. The music and sound spilled over and over and wove in and out of the light. Then, everyone heard a small cough and stopped for a moment. It was the Sun, who politely but firmly pointed out that he, too, was a star, probably the most potent and necessary for the service he rendered daily to the creatures and dwellers on the earth. The stars all deferred to the Sun's obvious power.

Then someone noticed one star who hadn't said a thing. It was quiet and remote, and it looked like it was trying not to be noticed or seen. It was singled out and asked what it had done for humankind. It was silent a moment and then confessed honestly that it hadn't done a thing. In fact, it hadn't even been discovered; its existence was totally unknown.

After a moment of silence, some of the stars exploded with laughter and derision, commenting, "Of what use is a star if it isn't even known to exist?" After all they were told to be lights in the firmament and to shine forth to the glory of God and to encourage humankind.

The star listened and pondered these things, wondering how to reply. Then it had a flash of insight. It smiled and spoke up in its defense: "Wait, maybe I have done something for human beings after all. It's true, as I said, that they don't know me. But they are not fools. They study the heavens and plot the trajectories of the planets and other clusters of stars, bits of dust, meteorites, and black holes, even quasars and quarks, and they know that something is missing! They have noticed deviations in orbits and gravitational attractions, and they know that there is something else out there that will explain what they can see.

"So, my contribution is really very crucial, for I keep them awake! I remind them of mystery, of the unknown, and what has yet to be discovered. In fact, I think my being so hidden lures them further into the skies and to the awe and grandeur of God who is maker and keeper of all things in the heavens and on the earth. I'm glad that you challenged me on my existence and presence in the heavens, for now I know that I want to stay hidden for a long time. I want them to know they have much yet to discover and that there is so much mystery out there. Perhaps they will remember that the heavens reflect much below and that the mystery within them is just as deep and far flung among themselves."

The stars were silent as they listened. All returned to their places in the sky, humbler and more in awe of God's hidden plans and secrets. For now even they wondered what they didn't yet know about themselves and about the Creator who is light itself. (A version of the story is in *Tales of the City of God,* by Carlos Vallejo [Prakash, India: Gujarat Sahitya, 1992])

Hidden stars, secret plans, quiet mysteries, humble origins, and momentous, auspicious meetings. This is Epiphany!

And so we come to the gospel of Matthew and the "star of wonder, star of light, star of endless beauty bright." It is the story of wise ones, astrologers who studied the heavens and saw a star that appeared in their part of the sky. These seekers from afar looked for portents and wisdom in the night, enlightenment, and someone to worship with their lives. It is a story about outsiders who see and insiders who are blind. It includes the fear and agitation of a city and its ruler Herod, a petty, mean king who uses scribes and priests and institutional religion for his own violent ends. So it is also about deception, lies, hypocrisy, and how power is used without wisdom or light.

It begins with a star and a house where a child and its mother dwell. The outsiders journey to bring homage and gifts. This peaceful beginning is interrupted by dreams and changes in routes. The light begins to seep into the world, breaking boundaries and gathering in all who can see, all who are open and humble, all who will worship and give their hearts to God. Whether the proud, the arrogant, the cunning, and the violent know it or not, their power is being overcome by the poor, strangers, and children.

The radiance is in the world, hidden in unlikely faces and places, but for those who honestly watch for the signs, it is there and the journey begins. In the seeing of the star and the child, in the giving of homage and gifts, there is another sight given. The gift of wisdom, recognition of what is truly good and what is genuinely evil, is the gift given by God to those who seek. Epiphany proclaims that there is a hidden glory shining here on earth, a radiance beneath even horror, disdain, or evil.

This light is the foretaste of resurrection, of power and life. The time of light continues now, brighter and fiercer. It cannot be contained, as the Word of the Lord cannot be bound, as God cannot be grasped, as mystery cannot be fathomed. There is always more to know and understand. The light slips in everywhere there is an opening and slips away from anyone who would try to grasp it and use it for their own ends. In the end, this story is about power: Herod's, the world's, a nation's. Institutional religion can use its power in collusion with governments and economic policies, but God's power is revealed in the poor, in strangers from afar, in stars and gifts and dreams. The story also brings together majesty and misery, a life-giving power and slaughter, the peaceful mother and child and the treachery of kings. There are choices to be made. Much is revealed in this child, so dangerous and so hopeful.

Jesus' birth is a line drawn across human souls and political destinies, even religious affiliations. We start in a place of power, Jerusalem. Into this city with its people, king, scribes, and priests come strangers, astrologers with their heads in the stars and their hearts on their sleeves. They are naive in the face of brutal power and so intent on their own spiritual search that they do not see how evil uses them for its own deadly ends. They will see, but the damage will already have been done. Their very announcement of good news — the rising star of another king — is met with disturbance, dismay, and turmoil. The reading declares allegiances. "We observed *his* star at its rising and have come to pay *him* homage." The appearance of an unknown star and the birth of an unknown child pose a threat.

The reaction of power, entrenched in self-interest and lack of care for the people, is quick and sure. Herod summons the chief priests and scribes, those who tend the knowledge of religion and should have the best interests of the people at heart. He inquires of them where the Messiah is to be born. Herod is given threatening news: "From [Bethlehem] shall come a ruler who is to shepherd my people Israel." It has all the vibrant echoes of the shepherd-king David, the greatest of the kings in Israel, beloved of God, mighty in battle, psalm-singer and sinner, yet devoted to God's kingdom. This is enough to set Herod's steel-trap mind in motion. He has already killed a number of his own relatives to secure his position in power. What is another child?

Next Herod approaches the sincere seekers, the astrologers whose knowledge obviously has not taught them to discern the presence of cold-calculated evil when they are being used by it. They give him the exact time of the star's appearance. Destruction is set in motion. They are instructed to go, to find more detailed information, and to report back, to feed hatred more of what it needs to destroy the possibility of life, of another's power and presence. Herod compounds his order with deceit: "Bring me word, so that I may go and offer him homage too."

The story began with the words "After Jesus' birth," and now it continues with the words "After their audience with the king they set out." The star reappears and leads them to the place of the child's resting. Their reaction now is overwhelming joy, perhaps even stronger because of their encounter with evil in Jerusalem.

Entering the house, they find the child with Mary his mother. They prostrate themselves and do him homage; they open their coffers and present him with gifts; they receive a message in a dream, and they go home to their own country by another way. These simple descriptions of the astrologers' behavior are really directions for all those who seek the light and wisdom and a way to worship. Matthew's gospel has been called "the house of disciples" gospel by theologian and exegete Michael Crosby. He believes that whenever a house is mentioned it refers to the church, the house of disciples. When the strangers enter and find the king, a poor child with its mother, they prostrate themselves in worship. Like the shepherds, they understand and recognize the glory of God in the presence of a child with its mother. They worship and give gifts to the child and mother, opening their hearts and hand with the best of what they have — gold, frankincense, and myrrh. They hand over their lives and their treasures, and in return they are given wisdom, the knowledge of discerning good and evil, life and death. That is what they take home, a way of light and truth and life. It is a way that is revealed in depth only to those who worship and whose gift-giving reveals the dedication of their lives and the intent of their hearts. This is a blueprint for life for those who enter and come to believe.

What do we bring to this child? There is a story told in India.

✤  In one very poor district, there are no lights in the streets and very few in the houses because of the expense of oil. But, as in all areas of India, there is a temple, frequented by the poor. The structure is primitive, with a huge brass chandelier that hangs from the roof and has spaces for one hundred small lamps. These spaces are empty until those who come to pray and worship arrive.

Each worshiper comes from home carrying a lamp through the darkened streets and then places the lamp in the chandelier. Slowly the darkened temple begins to glow with light that builds and grows stronger. The empty places are noted, and those who are missing are sought out after the service, questioned, given care or words of comfort, or challenged. Their light is necessary for all to worship.

Each of us must bring our light through the darkened areas of our world and add it to the communion of those entrusted with the light of Christ at baptism. The radiance and splendor of our worship depend on the universal coming together of those who believe in the light.

Like the astrologers who came to worship the child, others still come from the East to contribute to the light of the world, to add their lamps to the light of peace that is meant to shine on all. Bede Griffiths, a monk who dedicated his life to the experience of Eastern and Western religions and to bringing those religions into dialogue, wrote in his Christmas message in 1986:

> At Christmas we celebrate the coming of the Magi, or wise men, who came to offer their gifts to the infant Jesus. Some believe that these men came from Persia; Fr. Heras made out a case for their coming from India; but it does not really matter where they came from. They represent the "Gentiles," the "pagans," in other words the other religions of the world. May we not see in these wise men the representatives of the other religions who bring their gifts to Christ and which the church today is called to receive in his name?
>
> Could we not say that the Hindus offer the gift of gold, of interior religion, of the pure heart in which is found the presence of God? The Muslim can be seen to offer the gift of frankincense, the incense of the prayer of adoration, of worship which the Muslims offer five times daily to the one supreme God. The Buddhist can be seen to offer the gift of myrrh, the symbol of suffering and death, the sign that this world is passing away and that our destiny lies beyond the grave with the risen Christ. ("The Gifts of the Magi," *Tablet* [1986])

Our God, the God of all nations, wants all our gifts, whatever anyone wants to give, even if we don't have gold or frankincense or myrrh. Years ago I read on the back of a *Maryknoll* magazine: "The frankincense offered to the Christ Child by the Magi of old continues to rise heavenward in the prayers and suffering of the poor." The gifts traditionally acknowledged who the child was — gold for kingship, frankincense for divinity, myrrh for humanity. The gifts also represent the many nations that will adore this child as Lord. A short article entitled "New Gifts of the Magi" suggested gifts that countries of Africa, Latin America, and Asia might offer, symbolizing the best of those cultures' resources and gifts. In asking what gifts

Americans might give, the authors suggested three: an Indian head-dress of eagle feathers on behalf of the Native Americans, showing the leadership of this child and respect for the earth; a plowshare made from spare parts of an atomic submarine in response to Isaiah's call to peace; and a replica of the Statue of Liberty in memory of our freedom from sin and death and our commitment to welcoming the stranger and serving one another (Akio Johnson Mutek and Joseph Healey, M.M., "New Gifts of the Magi," *Maryknoll* [June 1995]: 55–56).

What would each of us give? What could your family give? What would your parish offer? As a nation of believers at the end of this century, what do we offer this child of justice and peace? As a universal church, what gifts do we need to give as we prostrate ourselves before this child and his mother Mary? Guidance for us should come from knowing that they are poor and in danger of death from a violent government fearful of hope; they are a family without resources who will soon be exiles, aliens, immigrants unwanted and living in the shadow of death for the rest of their lives. Our gift-giving reveals the nature of our worship and whom we kneel before and serve. It reveals that true worship is expressed by going another route, in conversion and repentance, and that way is revealed by the child: the way of the cross, life for all, justice shared.

If and when we meet the Savior in this season, we must be changed. We must seek a different route as we go back to our homes. We go home in the peace of Christ, empty-handed, open-hearted, clearer and wiser about life and death, more aware of good and evil hiding in our midst. Our new route is the way of the child, the way of peace, the way of the cross, the way of light, the way of resurrection, the path Mary and Joseph went, the way of the poor. The child is glory dwelling in our midst, hiding among us in the innocent, the nonviolent, the truthful, those who worship God alone. This child is the only power on earth we obey and serve and seek to know and prostrate ourselves before, emptying our coffers and hearts. This is God, the Word made flesh who pitches his tent among us. This is the story that is coming true, that is now revealed. This is our meaning and our mystery, and nothing can stop it from coming true.

A closing story may help us to remember and live with such mystery. It is a version of a Sufi story found in the book *Essential Sufism*.

✤ Once upon a time there was a sheikh by the name of Junaid who had many disciples. He was a wise teacher and many sought his wisdom. He taught them music, dancing, poetry, the disciplines of fasting, prayer, begging for their sustenance, wonder at the world, hospitality, and ecstatic awareness of the Holy One in their midst. But it was soon obvious to all his disciples that there was one who was preferred above all the rest. One was singled out, whose company was sought after, whose mistakes and clumsiness were easily excused. This disciple was loved by the master more than the others. The master made no secret of it. He offered him the best portions at the table and always asked him to accompany him and walked with him in the night. The other disciples were jealous and angry. They could not see what the master saw in this one who was slow and simple, no great shining light. They grew bitter and shunned the one so loved.

Then one day the master called them all together and told them he wanted them to do something, to obey his instructions carefully and to come back and report what they had done. It was simple. Each was to go to the marketplace and buy a chicken. They were to take it home and kill it without being seen by anyone and then report back. They would wait to report until all had gathered. Off they all went.

In less than an hour the first was back. He considered himself the real disciple of the master. Then another who was truly dedicated returned, and then another and so on, until all had returned except the one beloved of the master. They laughed and wondered what was taking him so long. After all, all he had to do was kill a chicken without being seen by anyone.

Finally, he arrived, sad and distraught, with a live chicken under his arm. The derision and ridicule were immense. The master arrived and called them all together. The first reported in: "I took my chicken home from the market, entered my house, closed all the curtains and blinds and killed the chicken."

The second spoke, "I did the same, except that after I closed the curtains and blinds, I went inside a closet and killed the chicken."

The next had done the same, adding that once inside the closet he had blindfolded himself and killed the chicken. The ones that had taken longer explained that they had gone outside the city, to the wild reaches of the forest or darkest cave where no one would see them.

Finally, it came to the last, the poor disciple who still had his chicken. He stumbled over his words, with tears in his eyes. "Master," he said, "I tried, really I tried to obey your orders. I bought the chicken, as you can see, and went home. Like the others I pulled the blinds and curtains closed and locked the doors of my house, but I couldn't kill the chicken. There was a Presence there. So I went into the closet and it was closer and stronger still. I blindfolded myself in the closet but the Presence was there full of power and strength. I fled into the hills, into dark caves and the Presence was there, into woods and wild places and the Presence was there. Finally, I realized there was no place that I could go where I could not be seen by the Presence. I came back here, with the chicken. What am I supposed to do?"

The master smiled and ran over to his beloved disciple and wrapped his arms around him. He spoke to the others in the embrace of this one whom he loved, "This is why I love him. He knows the Presence! And I must stay close to him." (James Fadiman and Robert Frager, eds., *Essential Sufism* [San Francisco: Harper San Francisco, 1997], 210–11).

It is Epiphany, and the presence — the light, the peace, the truth — is loose in the world. There is no place any of us can go where the presence does not see. There is no nation that does not know the presence. One day all will worship, do homage, and adore this presence among us. For now, we are called to be the beloved who knows the presence and senses it everywhere no matter what we are doing or where we find ourselves. And the presence certainly cannot abide killing! It is the presence of God, the presence of life itself and liberation, freedom, and hope. The presence is also peace with justice. It is God's own child, and Mary's. It is the child born in our hearts this season who will grow up to be the beloved Son of God, Jesus Christ the Lord, crucified and risen from the dead. The revelation is set in motion. The story is told in flesh. In the babe, divinity wears a human face. The splendor of our God waits for us to come and worship, to empty our hearts and go home with the light within. The presence enters us now and summons us to be the light to the nations, the glory of our God for all to come home to and find welcome. One day all nations will adore. Come, bend low, rejoice, and take God into your heart. It is time for us to be God's epiphanies and light up the world. It is time to let God use our flesh to come into the world this year. May it be so. Amen.

# Second Sunday after Christmas
## A, B, and C Cycles

Sirach 24:1–4, 8–12
Psalm 147:12–15, 19–20
Ephesians 1:3–6, 15–18
John 1:1–18 or John 1:1–5, 9–14

This particular set of readings is for a Sunday remembrance that is not often celebrated. It all depends on the calendar and when Epiphany is celebrated. Epiphany is always the Sunday closest to January 6, and depending on which day of the week Christmas falls, this Sunday often gets lost. And the gospel is the prologue to John, a long reading, the same as that of Christmas Mass during the day.

On this day we begin with Wisdom, who surprisingly "sings her own praises," much like Mary singing of her greatness in the presence of God the Most High. And Wisdom speaks of the Creator who commanded her and formed her and chose the spot for her tent. This passage is chosen to give an allusion to the portion in John's gospel about the Word being present at creation and to the statement in John that "through him all things came into being, and apart from him nothing came to be. Whatever came to be in him, found life, life for the light of men." And so we know that the Word had a hand in making and forming Wisdom and sending her to earth to dwell among his people in Israel. In fact she is described as "coming forth from the mouth of the Most High, like breath," or as it says so poetically: "and mistlike covered the earth."

God chooses where Wisdom will pitch her tent, and she obeys: "In the holy tent I ministered before him and in Zion I fixed my abode." Her roots are in Jerusalem, which is her domain, and she belongs with the "glorious people, in the portion of the Lord, his heritage." She has aligned herself with Israel, with the chosen people of God, and that is where her residence is. And in John's words, "The Word became flesh and made his dwelling among us, and we have seen his glory: the glory of an only Son coming from the Father, filled with enduring love." The Word pitches his tent among us, accompanying us in our sojourn on earth as Wisdom dwells in the city God chose for her and where God has given her rest. And the

glory of the only Son comes from the Father as Wisdom has come
forth from the mouth of God. The images are many and overlaid.
Wisdom is sometimes understood to be a personification of God,
part of the Trinity, but the poetry of the book of Sirach stops short
of saying this. Wisdom speaks and reveals that "before all ages, in
the beginning, he created me, and through all ages I shall not cease
to be." The Word is not created. The very first line of John reads:
"In the beginning was the Word; the Word was in God's presence,
and the Word was God. He was present to God in the beginning."
Wisdom is perhaps more an attribute or an expression of God's presence, a gift to God's "portion, his glorious people, his heritage." The
whole thrust of the reading is on the relationship between God,
Wisdom, and the people of God, and that mirrors the thrust of
John's prologue with its revelation of God, the Word, and those he
was sent to: we who either find life in him or do not accept him.
We either become the children of God in believing in this light or
we prefer the darkness.

We need God's Wisdom to understand the mystery of this season,
of God's coming into the world to pitch his tent among us and
to make his dwelling among us, as one of us. This is incarnation,
and it is best described as "love following upon love." There is a
true story that can show us clearly what wisdom does for us in the
realm of seeing and believing. The story is about an obscure Dutch
spectacle-maker named Hans Lippershy, who lived around 1600.

✜ One day when he was working in his shop and intently bent
   over lenses to repair them some children came in curious about
   the glasses and lenses and began to play with some of the lenses.
   He did not even look up so intent was he on his work. The children however were delighted with their new toys. By chance they
   picked up two lenses and looked through both of them out the
   window of the shop at a weathervane on the church that was
   some distance away and lo and behold! it was close and mag-
   nified in their seeing. They were so excited and loud in their
   discovery that Lippershy came over to see what the commotion
   was about and discovered for himself the depth of magnification
   that was possible. And with the discovery of the children he set
   to work making telescopes. (Daniel Boorstin)

In many ways Wisdom allows us to magnify and draw closer to
the mysteries of God present in our universe and in our everyday

lives and especially in anything that is bound to God's will. Wisdom ministers to us, revealing and illuminating events, suffering, the wonder of creation, the clash of history, and God's constant presence in the world, whether it is welcomed, rudely ignored, or opposed.

The response to the psalm's praise is a statement of belief that changes the context of reality and highlights every detail of existence now: "The Word of God became man and lived among us." And it declares that what God has done for Israel, his chosen portion of the nations, he has not done for any others. He has gifted them with his law, statutes, and ordinances which bring a portion of wisdom and meaning to their lives, with peace and the best of the wheat, providing for his people. He has given them strength and security, has blessed the children who dwell within his city, and has given his Word to them. This Word is prelude to the Word that will be spoken in the flesh and that will be a human being that is God from the beginning.

The opening of Paul's letter to the Ephesians is a prayer of thanksgiving and praise of God the Father for the mystery and gift of Jesus Christ that brings with it every spiritual gift imaginable. We are given something of far more value than even wisdom: the divine favor of being adopted as the sons of God. And this has been God's intent from the beginning: "God chose us in him before the world began to be holy and blameless in his sight, to be full of love. . . . This is the will and good pleasure of our God for us. This is hidden in and bestowed upon us in his beloved." This is marvelous, wondrous, mysterious, and needs to be given thanks for and lived and known in light of God's wisdom and the long history of God's gifting of his people. Being chosen from the beginning to be holy, to be God's, to belong in Jesus Christ, to live blamelessly, to be destined to be adopted and taken into the family of God in the person of Jesus Christ — these are mysteries that we must steep our minds and souls in; they are rich sources that we must tap into like springs of water that run deep and true, fresh and free flowing. They are the source of life, of wisdom, and of our relationship to God and with one another.

The second part of the reading reveals Paul's love for his community and that he prays for them constantly with gratitude. His prayer is one that we can pray for ourselves certainly, but we can also pray it for our communities, for the church, and for the world:

May the God of our Lord Jesus Christ, the Father of glory, grant you a spirit of wisdom and insight to know him clearly.

May he enlighten your innermost vision that you may know
the great hope to which he has called you, the wealth of his
glorious heritage to be distributed among the members of the
church.

God wants us to know him. This has been his desire and hope for
all of us since the beginning. And the depth of what God wants to
share with us, give us, and how he wishes to express his abiding love
for us deepens as our capacity to understand, accept, and respond
to it grows. In Christ our capacity to receive, to understand, and
to love is beyond human possibilities. We are invited into dwelling
with God in his tent among us. We are invited into the body of
Jesus, his presence and Word, his body the Eucharist, his body the
church, and his relationship with God the Father, in the Trinity. This
blessing is like a horizon. As we approach it, it keeps moving, and
we move deeper and deeper into the mystery that God designed for
creation since the beginning.

And this brings us to the beginning of John's gospel. St. John of
the Cross in his *Spiritual Canticle* 37 (4) wrote: "[Christ] is like an
abundant mine so that, however deep men go, they never reach the
bottom, but rather in every recess find new views with new riches
everywhere." And the Scriptures, the Word of God, especially John's
gospel, are like this: an inexhaustible resource and dwelling place.
The text at hand alternates between soaring poetry and interruptions
of prose that operate like commentary or asides on the text itself,
first remarking on John that he was sent by God to testify to the
light as a witness but then stating that he was not the light. Next
there is a comment on those who believe in this light and in this
name (which is never written or mentioned precisely) and on the
nature of believers' birth, which rests solely in God's willing it to be
so. Then again, John is brought back in to testify that this one is
the one he serves and precedes and is below in rank. And lastly there
is a comment on the gift of God that was given through Moses:
the law and the ever-greater enduring gift of love that has come
through Jesus Christ to us. And a fact is registered: "No one has
ever seen God. It is God the only Son, ever at the Father's side, who
has revealed him."

And the nature of this revelation is "seeing the face of God in
human flesh!" How? Thomas Aquinas said, "The greatness of God
was not cast off, but the slightness of human nature was 'put on.'"
This is the mystery of incarnation, and that is our faith as Christians,

the followers of the light that shines in the darkness and that no darkness can overcome. This is the light of the Isaiah readings that is proclaimed so strongly at midnight on Christmas and is referred to over and over again as light for all the nations as well as hope for those who are faithful to the covenant and promises of God. Let us look at one small piece of the text for a moment:

> He was in the world,
> and through him the world was made,
> yet the world did not know who he was.
> To his own he came,
> yet his own did not accept him.
> Any who did accept him
> he empowered to become children of God.
>
> (John 1:10–12)

We more often quote the first few lines of the text (John 1:1–4), which refer to the Word that is life, that creates and brings life to all and sustains all that exists. The two texts together (that is, John 1:1–4, 10–12) thus seem to speak of a secret design of God that has slowly been revealed over time and has become reality now and will transform and make holy all of creation at the fullness of time. Jesus did not come, however, as a total secret, without warning: the intervening text (1:6–9) says that John the Baptist went before Jesus to prepare the people for him, calling for repentance that would lead to the forgiveness of sins. And the response was mixed. Crowds that listened, heard. Soldiers and tax collectors asked what they should do, yet others, sent by the authorities in Jerusalem, wanted a straight answer on whether he was the Messiah or not. You have the sense that many hoped he wasn't the Messiah, because that would mean life could proceed as usual. There are always many of us who do not want this light to come crashing into our darkness and reveal us for what we are: hypocritical, shallow, without faith or commitment, following the whim of the culture, the crowd, or whoever is in power. Or worse we resist and oppose any real possibility of hope, of transformation, and of true work for justice and peace. They simply aren't that important to us, and we have made our lives to resemble the world around us. We give a nod to Christian celebration and ritual, but inwardly we serve other gods.

At the beginning John makes it clear that Jesus Christ, the only Son of God, is a dividing line between those who become children of God and can stand in that light of glory and those who serve sin and evil and resist the light or, at least, ignore it. Knowing the light, knowing the Christ, is not automatically a result of being baptized or superficially attending services. It is a gift of faith, given graciously, but it must be accepted, practiced, and attended to diligently.

A story from Alaska can cast some light on this choice and reality. After I had given a talk in Fairbanks on John's gospel, a young Eskimo woman came up to me and handed me the story, very shyly. It was handwritten on two small pieces of paper and had the name John Dostobek written on the back of it. This was what was written on the paper.

✝ Once upon a time there was a poor young Eskimo girl. She didn't have enough to eat or clothes warm enough to keep the arctic cold away. One day a newspaper reporter came into the village where the little girl lived. He saw the girl's poverty and decided to ask her a few questions. He asked her, "Do you believe in God?"

"Yes, I do," said the little girl.

"Do you believe God loves you?" asked the reporter.

Again, the girl said, "Yes, I do."

"If you believe in God and believe that he loves you, then why do you think you don't have enough food or enough warm clothes to wear?"

She answered: "I think God asked someone to bring me these things. But someone said NO!"

That is about as clear a commentary on this passage of Scripture as one can find. Because of the Word made flesh, we believe that God who made the world has provided for all and entrusted us with the abundance of his creation for us to use in trust and share among ourselves. The nonviolent prophet Mahatma (Great Souled) Gandhi admired the Christian faith but found Christians severely lacking in their practice and belief. In fact, after visiting a Catholic church for liturgy in South Africa and being asked to move to the back of the church with the blacks, Gandhi decided not to become a Catholic and returned to India to practice Hinduism. His words have become standard fare for anyone struggling to bring the light of justice and peace into the world and to resist the darkness: "Earth provides enough to satisfy every man's need, but not enough for every man's greed." The wealth of the few and the poverty of the many are darkness and resistance to the light in concrete form. This resistance is practiced by those who "do not know who he was and did not accept him" and still refuse to be seen in the light "which gives light to every man who comes into the world." We are reminded in the last lines of today's gospel proclamation that

of his fullness
we have all had a share —
love following upon love.

In a commentary for the feast of Mary the Mother of God, J. J. Greehy writes of what this fullness, of which we have all had a share, looks like in reality:

The beautiful Jewish greeting, Shalom, wishes you the fullness of divine promise. It prays that you may possess all the qualities that fulfill the human condition, rather than any circumstance that may wreck it: a spiritual tranquillity rather than inner disquiet, a mental stability over against deep anxiety, an emotional security rather than a lack of loving-kindness, a physical capability in place of ill health, and a material possibility in any danger of real poverty. No son or daughter of Israel, of course, would neglect that last ingredient of Shalom — enough of this world's goods to be content. We remember the prayer of the book of Proverbs: "Give me neither poverty nor riches, feed me with the food I need, or I shall be full and deny you and say 'Who is the Lord' or I shall be poor and steal, and profane the name of my God" (Prov 30:8–9). The post-exilic prophet of the book of Isaiah repeats the divine promise of peace for his afflicted people: "I saw their ways, but I will heal them and lead them; I will give full comfort to them and to those who mourn for them, I, the Creator who gave them life. Peace, peace, to the far and the near, says the Lord, and I will heal them" (Is 57:18–19). We pray that the Holy Spirit of our healing God will guide the peace process among our divided peoples toward the fullness of his promise. (*Scripture in Church* 109 [January 1 to March 31, 1998]: 37)

We, like John the Baptist, or Isaiah, or Mary of the Magnificat, testify to the light that has come into our world by showing forth, proclaiming, and sharing our portion of the fullness we have all received from God.

When I teach I often use this definition of justice: it is love expressed in terms of sheer human need. God's love endures in Jesus Christ. Our love endures in sharing of the fullness we have received from Jesus Christ, especially with those who have known and been crushed by the darkness of the world and sin. This is the way we reveal and give glory to our God. This is the season of Epiphany, the time of showing forth and spreading the glory of God to the far ends of the earth so that all nations will come to believe. This is the work of justice, the work of peacemaking, and the work of filling in the gaps between rich and poor and drawing divided peoples back together again, reconciling as God has reconciled with us in the flesh of Jesus Christ.

This is expressed in liturgical terms by Ita Ford, one of the Maryknoll Sisters who was killed in El Salvador. She wrote the text during her reflection year home at Maryknoll, in New York, when she was between stints in Chile and El Salvador. She writes:

> One day at mass here, the words of consecration went booming through me — this is my body given for you. The connection was instantaneous — all those giving their bodies — the possibilities there are for us to give our bodies — it was all so possible and powerful — Jesus' having given his because he loved.

This was years before Ford herself would literally give her body in her work with the poor of El Salvador. Long before she was ambushed on a back road one night, raped, tortured, and murdered, she practiced sharing "of his fullness / we have all had a share [in] — / love following upon love." But she was gifted with wisdom, a glimpse of understanding that began to transform her daily life.

And this light that has come into the world has seeped into every corner and affects the souls and lives of many. Nelson Mandela, of South Africa, has written to his own people who struggled for decades against apartheid:

> You are a child of God. Your playing small doesn't serve the world. There's nothing enlightening about shrinking so that other people won't feel insecure around you. We are born to manifest the glory of God that is within us. It's not just in some of us, it's in everyone. As we let our light shine, we unconsciously give other people permission to do the same. As we are liberated from our fear, our presence automatically liberates others.

The "life for the light of men shines on in darkness, a darkness that did not overcome it." This is the continuing reality of the world that the only Son of God entered nearly two thousand years ago. It is the reality faced by those who believe and generously stake their lives on this light that endures and will overcome the darkness one day. And as Nelson Mandela said: "It's not just in some of us, it's in everyone." That is crucial to remember. There is only one ultimate choice: to liberate people from the darkness or contribute to it.

In Tokyo during the week of Epiphany one year, I became acutely aware that sometimes those who do not know the only Son of God live more in the light than many who call themselves Christians. I was given a book to savor while I was in Tokyo. The book was *Dewdrops on a Lotus Leaf: Zen Poems of Ryokan* (trans. John Stevens [Boston: Shambala Centaur Editions, 1996]). Ryokan was an itinerant Buddhist monk and enlightened poet who played with children and shared his meager meals with prostitutes and strangers on the road. The following untitled poem sheds some light on the "fullness of love following upon love":

> When I think
> About the misery
> Of those in this world
> Their sadness
> Becomes mine.
>
> Oh, that my monk's robe
> Were wide enough
> To gather up all
> The suffering people
> In this floating world.
>
> Nothing makes me
> More happy than
> Amida Buddha's Vow
> To save
> Everyone. (72)

John's prologue is a source of endless inspiration, understanding, and challenge for all those who wish to serve the light and who believe that because the Word became flesh and dwells among us still, we must treat the flesh of others with great care. This glorifies God and testifies to the light. This proclaims to all that we are the children of God.

I would like to end this rather serious reflection on a lighter note. The season of Epiphany is short, twelve days only and sometimes an extra Sunday thrown in for good measure. There is, of course, a Christmas song that fits these days, a song that has been played with by economists and stores who tabulate what it would cost if you gave the gifts described in the carol. It is "The Twelve Days of Christmas." The period begins on Christmas Day and ends on the feast of the Epiphany. In my travels someone approached me and said: "Do you know the background of the song?" I didn't and was given a photocopied sheet that explained that the song was written by some "wily Jesuits who were playing a dangerous game in sixteenth-century England," where anything Catholic was banned and any practice of the Catholic faith was severely punished. Indeed, many believers, many Jesuits among them, were martyred for the public acknowledgment of their faith. But many practiced underground, and in an effort to encourage the faith of Catholics in a time of peril and danger, some Jesuits wrote the song. It's in code and was intended to be sung out loud as an outline of basic beliefs of the faith and as a proclamation during this season of the heart of God's love for all. This is what the sheet of paper said:

"My true love gave to me" is God speaking to the anonymous Catholic. "Twelve drummers drumming" are not, as you might guess, the twelve Apostles, but rather the twelve beliefs outlined in the Apostles Creed. The "eleven pipers piping" are the eleven apostles — Judas having left — who pipe the faith in an unbroken tradition. The "ten lords a-leaping" are the Ten Commandments. The "nine ladies dancing" are the nine choirs of angels. The "eight maids a-milking" are the eight beatitudes. The "seven swans a-swimming" are, of course, the seven sacraments; the "six geese a-laying" are the six precepts of the church; the "five golden rings" are the Pentateuch, the first five books of the Bible; the "four calling birds" are the four gospels that sing the Good News; the "three French hens" are the three gifts the Magi brought; the "two turtle doves" are the Old and the New Testaments; and finally, of course, the "partridge in a pear tree" is the resplendent Christ reigning from the cross.

So, in sixteenth-century England, the children of the light found imaginative and creative, even playful, ways to express their faith. Wisdom prevailed even in dark times, or perhaps it prevails especially well in dark times, growing stronger with opposition, and more dear. And Matthew, Luke, and John did the same with their Spirit-filled and Spirit-inspired narratives of the birth of the Christ, the Son of God, Savior, light, and child of peace. The Word is flesh and dwells among us. We have the rest of the liturgical year and the rest of our lives to let that reality transform our flesh into words of hope, words of justice and peace, words of "love following upon love." Christmas is a marvelous season, but it is only the beginning of God's glory being revealed among us. It is a flickering candle next to the starfire of Easter's glory on the radiant face of Christ, risen from the dead. . . . Ah, but that is another story.